WEST END WOMEN

Maggie Gale's *West End Women* uncovers groundbreaking historical material about women playwrights and the staging of their performances during the period from 1918 to 1962.

West End Women documents a dynamic era of social and theatrical history, analysing the transformations that occurred in the theatre and the lives of British women in relation to specific female-authored plays of the period. Focusing on the work of playwrights such as Clemence Dane, Gordon Daviot, Dodie Smith, Esther McCracken and Bridget Boland, Maggie Gale examines the cultural and political context within which they enjoyed commercial success and great notoriety.

In the first and only survey of its kind, Maggie Gale provides a unique reading of a thriving slice of theatrical London. *West End Women* is an invaluable contribution to its field and a must for students and scholars of this period of theatre history. It will also be of interest to students of cultural studies and women's studies.

Maggie B. Gale is Lecturer in Drama and Theatre Arts at the University of Birmingham. She is co-editor of the *Women and Theatre Occasional Papers* series.

GENDER IN PERFORMANCE
General editors: Susan Bassnett and Tracy C. Davis

The *Gender in Performance* series reflects the dynamic and innovative work by feminists across the disciplines. Exploring both historical and contemporary theatre, the series seeks to understand performance both as a cultural and a political phenomenon.

Also available:

CONTEMPORARY FEMINIST THEATRES
To each her own
Lizbeth Goodman

ACTRESSES AS WORKING WOMEN
Their social identity in Victorian culture
Tracy C. Davis

AS SHE LIKES IT
Shakespeare's unruly women
Penny Gay

GETTING INTO THE ACT
Ellen Donkin

FEMINIST THEATERS IN THE U.S.A.
Staging women's experience
Charlotte Canning

WEST END WOMEN

Women and the London stage 1918–1962

Maggie B. Gale

London and New York

First published 1996
by Routledge
11 New Fetter Lane, London EC4P 4EE

Simultaneously published in the USA and Canada
by Routledge
29 West 35th Street, New York, NY 10001

© 1996 Maggie B. Gale

Typeset in Baskerville by Routledge
Printed and bound in Great Britain by
T J Press (Padstow) Ltd, Padstow, Cornwall

British Library Cataloguing in Publication Data
A catalogue record for this book is available from the
British Library

Library of Congress Cataloguing in Publication Data
Gale, Maggie B. (Maggie Barbara), 1963– West End
women: women and the London stage, 1918–1962/
Maggie B. Gale. (Gender in performance) Includes
bibliographical references and index 1. English drama –
Women authors – History and criticism. 2. Feminism and
literature – England – London – History – 20th century. 3.
Women in the theater – England – London – History –
20th century. 4. Women and literature – England –
London – History – 20th century. 5. English drama – 20th
century – History and criticism. 6. West End (London,
England) – History. 7. Women in literature. I. Title.
II. Series.
PR739.F45G35   1996
822'.91099287–dc20   96–1821   CIP

ISBN 0–415–08495–4 (hbk)
ISBN 0–415–08496–2 (pbk)

For Ben J. Partridge and in memory of the late Blossom Galinski

CONTENTS

ACKNOWLEDGEMENTS

I would like to thank the inter-library loans librarians at the University of Warwick and Melanie Christoudia at the Theatre Museum, London, for all their assistance. This book would never have been written if it had not been for the consistent support of my parents, Liz and Tony Gale, and the financial support of the late Blossom Galinski. Thanks to all my friends and colleagues who encouraged and supported my efforts, Kerry Grady, Joanna Labon, Pauline Urwin, Michael and Siv Robinson, Juliette MacDonald, Alison Altman, David Waring, Conchita Morello and John Deeney. Special thanks for all their kindness and for their good humour and willingness to listen to Clive Barker and Susan Bassnett. Thank you again to Susan Bassnett and to Tracy C. Davis for their careful and useful comments and to Talia Rogers for commissioning the book in the first place. Lastly, I would like to thank Ben for his generous love, good cooking, humour, support and practical help during the last two years of this project.

Extract from *The Matriarch* by G.B. Stern is reproduced by permission of Samuel French Ltd.

Extracts from *Partnership* by Elizabeth Barker are reproduced by permission of Samuel French Ltd.

Extract from *The Man Who Pays the Piper* by G. B. Stern, published by Heinemann Ltd. reproduced by permission of The Peters Fraser Dunlop Group Ltd.

Extract from *Sixteen* by Aimée and Philip Stuart, published by Victor Gollancz, reproduced by permission of The Peters Fraser & Dunlop Group Ltd.

Extract from *Escape Me Never* by Margaret Kennedy reproduced by permission of Curtis Brown, London.

ACKNOWLEDGEMENTS

Extract from *Cousin Muriel* by Clemence Dane reproduced by permission of the Estate of Clemence Dane

Extract from *The Sport of My Mad Mother* by Ann Jellicoe, © Ann Jellicoe 1958, reproduced by permission of Casarotto Ramsay Ltd. All rights whatsoever in this play are strictly reserved and application for performance etc., must be made before rehearsal to Casarotto Ramsay Ltd., National House, 60-66 Wardour Street, London W1V 4ND. No performance may be given unless a licence has been obtained.

Every effort has been made to contact copyright holders for material reproduced in this volume. In some cases this has proved impossible, for which the publisher apologises.

The author wishes to thank Julian Barnes for permission to quote from the literary estate of Dodie Smith also Samuel French for permission to print from Aimée and Philip Stuart's *Her Shop* and *Nine Til Six* and from Gertrude Jennings' *Family Affairs*.

1

INTRODUCTION

West End women,
a force to be reckoned with

Old paint on canvas, as it ages, sometimes becomes transparent. When
that happens it is possible, in some pictures, to see the original lines: a tree
will show through a woman's dress, a child makes way for a dog, a large
boat is no longer on an open sea. That is called pentimento because the
painter 'repented', changed his mind. Perhaps it would be as well to say
that the old conception, replaced by a later choice, is a way of seeing and
then seeing again.

(Hellman 1974: 1)

Women playwrights who wrote for the London stage between 1918 – the
point at which some women were granted the vote – and 1962 – the year
which saw the publication of Lessing's *The Golden Notebook* (Lessing 1962a),
which many feel paved a way for a renewed radicalism within the
women's movement – have made vital, witty and various contributions
to the British theatre which should no longer be ignored. During the
1980s and 1990s there were a number of London revivals of both British
and American plays by women playwrights of the mid-twentieth century.
The Royal National theatre's productions of Sophie Treadwell's *Machinal*
and Lillian Hellman's *The Children's Hour* received great critical acclaim,
and these followed in the wake of other successful British revivals of plays
such as Susan Glaspell's *Alison's House* and Enid Bagnold's *The Chalk Garden*
as well as the star-studded production of Clare Boothe-Luce's *The Women*
at the London Old Vic. These plays represent only the tip of the iceberg in
terms of the number of successful plays by women that were originally
produced on the London stage during the years which span the end of the
First World War to the early 1960s. However, in both feminist and non-
feminist histories of British theatre, the inter-war years and those leading
into the early 1960s are usually presented as being less than fruitful for
women playwrights. Brief acknowledgements of the fact that women were
writing for the theatre are followed by comments on their lack of a feminist

1

perspective or innovative strategy – in other words, there is an assumption that their work does not warrant serious examination. Their work is often dismissed because they were middle class, writing for a commercially oriented theatre.

In a recent anthology of plays written by women and produced on the London stage between 1900 and 1950, the editor frames her choice of included texts with the following statement:

> There were ... scores of women playwrights during this period ... most of them ... fall outside of the mainstream of the theatrical movement. ... I started my search for plays by reading everything that had been put on in London, hoping that I would stumble across a lost masterpiece. It didn't take long to realise that the likelihood of this was slim, and the task would take a lifetime.
>
> (F. Morgan 1994: xv)

Indeed there were 'scores of women' writing for the theatre between 1918 and 1962, most of whose work existed *inside* the mainstream. These mid-twentieth-century women playwrights, who at one time were household names and popular public figures, have largely been allowed to disappear from conscious historical-theatrical memory. It would probably take a lifetime to analyse all of the plays written and performed, but to use the search for a masterpiece as a working criterion is rather short-sighted and in many ways irrelevant; this search depends on such outmoded agendas that it is hardly worthwhile. Morgan falls into a trap of censoring as identified by Davis, whose antidote is that the 'feminist historian's task is to address the censoring impulse, to validate the experience, and to connect the woman with the work and the work with the world at large' (Davis 1989: 66–69). Morgan gives too much credibility to the comments which male historians of the past have made about the women writing for the theatre of the period under discussion, whereby prolific and successful women playwrights like Clemence Dane and Dodie Smith are discussed in the following terms:

> Briefly, in Clemence Dane and Dodie Smith we have the tempest and the teacup-storm. Each, in its way, has been felt in the theatre. Yet I think Aphra Behn, turning the play-bills of nearly three hundred years, would have to shake her head. Women's Hour upon the stage is sparsely filled indeed.
>
> (Trewin 1953: 132)

This book aims to challenge such notions and provide a starting point for

those interested in the work of 'West End women', female playwrights
who wrote for the London stage between 1918 and 1962.

Texts have been selected and examined both in the context of the
theatre of the time and of the changing society in which women lived and
worked. Although there is no immediate common political thread which
binds the plays together, many of the texts shared certain key thematic
preoccupations which shaped the way in which woman and the feminine
were inscribed within narrative. Questions around women and work, the
family, mothering and the 'female condition' in general are dramatically
foregrounded. The playwrights took into conscious and active consideration the discrepancies between the social expectations and the lived
experiences of women. Discussions around women's role in both post-
war economies and in the 'making of Britain', marriage, family life and
women's social status were frequent and, at times, explicit. These were the
same issues which both fuelled public discussions and created debate
within the women's movement and the popular press of the time.

> It's a curious thing that nobody ever has a good word for the
> modern girl. Nevertheless, she is more useful than the weather as a
> subject of conversation. She is always the centre of interest and
> always in disgrace. When she wears long skirts men rail upon her for
> her unsanitary ways: when she shortens them they tell her that she is
> immodest. . . . When she sits at home and takes no interest in public
> life she is told that she is a doll in a doll's house; when she beats the
> Senior Wrangler they exclaim indignantly that a woman's place is
> in the home. . . . It is a fact, I'm afraid, that she is less reverent than
> once she was. . . . She is too busy keeping fit: educating herself:
> playing games: running a business: running a home: flying an
> airplane, or looking after a baby. . . . Seeing her thus healthy, able to
> be wealthy by her own exertions, and much wiser than most of the
> 'modern girls' who have preceded her, the critic has only one
> weapon of offence left: so nowadays he tells her that in becoming
> what she is she is losing her femininity, that she may become a
> female magnate, but that she will never again be a Helen of Troy!
>   (Clemence Dane, 'Modern beauty has nothing to fear',
>   *Evening Standard*, 27 March 1930)

Over the forty or so years covered here, debate and theorising on what it
meant to be a woman was fervent. The debate often presented a woman's
life choices as being polarised – she should choose between a career or a
family, marriage or work and so on. The plays examined in this book are
viewed in the context of this debate.

This book provides a 're-charting of an historical canon of plays by women' which, as Aston has observed, 'does not engage in a more radical re-thinking of what constitutes theatre history' (Aston 1995: 28). However, documentation, description and analysis are combined with questions around how the work was perceived and whether it reflected women's lives and experiences of what it meant to be a woman. The impact and variety of the wealth of plays is only indicated here. This book represents the beginnings of research which needs to be carried out, first, by a number of researchers and, second, from a number of ideological positions. My own position of analysis was influenced by a desire to transgress the boundaries of research on the history of women's playwriting which were already in position. The formation of these boundaries itself reflects the many assumptions which have been made by some feminist theatre historians who have been eager to 'challenge the canon'. The limitation of the male-dominated canon was integral to the research, but the danger of re-marginalising women's playwriting through an attempt to insert it into a purely feminist framework was also a concern. The purpose here has been to examine the way in which women, as a social and cultural 'out-group' – lacking real power in criticism, management, programming and so on – infiltrated and integrated with a dominant form of theatre. Similarly the investigation of 'out-group' contributions to legitimate or dominant forms of theatre is bound to reveal information about less visible, less legitimate theatre activity and possibly invite re-thinking of theatre history itself. Klein suggests that when we look at the role of an 'out-group' within any given society, we learn much about the social structure of that society itself (Klein 1989: 4). Certainly, the results of this research should encourage a questioning of the way in which histories of playwriting for the London stage have thus far been constructed. Re-charting the work of women playwrights is not only a 'useful and necessary part of challenging the male canon', it is also a continuing process, the results of which need constant expansion and analysis (Davis 1989).

PERIODISATION

In general, twentieth-century theatre in Britain has been periodised according to either social or economic events such as the First and Second World Wars, or 'theatre events' such as the now almost mythologised introduction of the 'angry young man' in 1956.[1] Equally, there is a temptation for theatre historians to use the inauguration of the new state-funded theatres as some kind of measuring stick for turning or even starting points and new theatrical eras, carrying with it the assumption that a new era in terms of structure and economics brings with it a new kind of play. The political events of 1968 in Western Europe are pinpointed as the context for the fruition of the Fringe and later the 'alternative' theatre for which the ideological position was that of left or socialist politics and a desire to re-invest theatre with the 'popular' simultaneous to finding new audiences. Although these events have a great significance for theatre history, there has been a tendency to see them as fixed points, each one inspiring a completely new direction in the making of theatre. Thomas Postlewait stresses that this kind of agenda frames the way in which history is re-created and received. As he points out:

> The concept of periodization, in its normative if somewhat misleading usage, delineates one aspect of history, the condition of stability (or identity), in relation to another aspect, the process of change (or difference). . . . The continuous flow of time is organised into heuristic categories, episodes of our creation. As such, periods are interpretative ideas of order that regulate meaning.
> (Postlewait 1988: 299–320)

In truth, the 'well-made play' still dominates the component of mainstream British theatre which produces plays. Equally, Findlater's observation in 1952 that, 'Going to the theatre is still for most Englishmen (sic) . . . a holiday treat. The Englishman, whatever his income, does not visit the play for week-to-week entertainment' (Findlater 1952: 194) would arguably be just as applicable today. Play-going is still, it would seem, a predominantly upper- and middle-class habit.

The years 1918–1962 have hitherto been largely neglected in terms of a re-assessment of women playwrights in particular. Thus taking 1918–1962 as a phase in women's playwriting cuts across traditionally accepted periods of theatre history. Michelène Wandor states:

> During the 1920s and 1930s organised feminism was far less visible; struggles to improve the position of women within society continued less publicly. Organisations continued to argue and work around specific issues, such as contraception and child care, and within working-class organisations . . . feminism still found a presence. But theatre work controlled by women, and linking feminism and aesthetics, ceased to command its own space. There were a number of women who were active within the Unity Theatre Movement . . . and there was the occasional play about the 'women question' – equal rights for women, equal educational

opportunities, abortion. But it was only well after the Second World War that feminism and theatre again came together; this time in a greatly changed social and political situation in which radical post-war changes to the family had produced intense and contradictory pressures on women.

(Wandor 1981: 10)

Wandor is writing about a specific historical period, but in general terms. There was apparently no centralised theatre organisation similar to the Actresses Franchise League during the period under examination here (see Chapter 3). However, there were many women managing small companies or theatres, directing and producing or writing plays. The criterion for the inclusion of plays here is simply that the play was performed, not necessarily professionally, and that it is available in print. The framework within which the plays are examined is the social, historical and theatrical context in which they were performed. Although on one level Wandor's statement about the linking of 'feminism and aesthetics' in theatre can be taken as true, it is based on a simplified notion of what happened to the feminist or women's movement during the period in question. It also negates the existence of many plays written by women that, in effect, centred their narratives on the 'woman question', and the intense and contradictory pressures on women which were felt, developed and grew in intensity continuously between the two world wars, up until the early 1960s and beyond.

THE LONDON STAGE 1918–1962

A history of the London stage during the first half of the twentieth century is characterised by complaint, disorder, difference, indifference, innova-tion, financial crisis, elitism, populism and competition. The plays written by women or male/female teams, moreover, represent approximately one-sixth of the total number of new plays which were previewed and produced during the period. The drama, as exemplified by the 'well-made play', is only a proportion of that which made up the dramatic and theatrical content of the London stage as a whole. This book examines the context, content and reception of plays written by women in the commercially oriented theatre. Here, a distinction must be made between the commercial drama – produced by commercial managements – and the commercial theatre.

During the late nineteenth century the belief that theatre as art could exist for art's sake gained popularity alongside a belief in the educational potential of theatre. That drama could be educational as well as entertaining created an environment in which plays could focus on social and political/moral issues – but these plays would not necessarily draw the large audiences needed for theatre to be profitable. Arguments for a non-profit-oriented theatre plagued the minds of critics and theatre historians of the inter-war and post-Second World War theatre. Similarly, the search for a drama which contained the means to interest and represent an audience beyond the social elite inspired the work of many playwrights and a number of producers. Some, however, were concerned that the drama maintain its interest for the minority, as an art form that should not pander to the needs of the 'masses', lest it be contaminated by the trivial concerns of their lives. The identification of 'trivial' concerns in the drama has had a significant influence on the way in which the work of the women playwrights in question has been historically and critically positioned. Domestic stage spaces are regularly assumed to be the place where the 'trivial' concerns of women's lives, of interest to a 'minority', are played out. Thus many of the plays by women, because they take 'domestic life' as a starting point, have been considered unworthy of critical analysis.

Numerous critics and historians in the 1950s hailed the Royal Court and the writers whose work it promoted as a new departure point for the drama. Through the Royal Court a new generation of writers emerged in London, playwrights whose interest lay in an 'other' class, and an 'other' perception of playwriting and the power of the drama as an art form. In the early days, the Royal Court may have reached out to different audiences, but certainly not larger ones. The plays may have reflected more honestly the lives of the 'masses', but this does not mean that the masses flocked to see them. New playwrights may have borrowed from the popular but it would be difficult to prove that their work re-popularised drama and play-going as a leisure activity.

A history of the drama during the period in question is not only plagued by the frequent questioning of purpose and form, but also by a number of assumptions about the desired effect of theatre, both as a culture-producing and culture-reflective institution. Many critics questioned the idea that drama should entertain, finding it hard to accept that for some the theatre represented a social event more than anything else. In their eyes, entertainment was the job of the entertainment industry, not the serious playwright. That a play should contain a serious and discernible social or moral message was primary, entertainment value was of secondary concern.

Thus that which concerns us here is not an art form with clearly defined lines for critique. The value system applied to defining what constitutes a 'good' play, used by a critic, will differ somewhat from that put into operation by the playwright, the historian or the theatre producer at any point in theatre history. Each has a specific agenda which influences the whole framing process of their evaluative system. This is important when examining women's work in theatre, where gender difference is arguably the primary factor affecting the development of historical documentation and the application of any critical value system.

WHAT'S ON IN THE THEATRE?

Socio-theatrical histories of playwriting in the twentieth century have been shaped by the (usually) aesthetic interests of the authors. There are very few critical works on theatre in London during the first half of the century which inform the reader as to what was actually being produced in the theatres and, in turn, what were the criteria for labelling a production as 'successful'. The lines between what is and what is not considered to be 'successful' are blurred. In terms of the dramatic text, realism was the dominant form during the period under examination here. Yet it would seem that the nature and context of that realism (which reality was being fictionalised and re-constructed on the stage, and to whom did it belong?) has had a significant influence upon the way in which the plays were received by critics, and the ways in which they have, in turn, been placed in history.

From a contemporary standpoint, many of the plays written for the London stage during the years which span 1918–1962 re-affirmed already existing class barriers and re-presented the lives of the middle and upper-middle classes; the dramatic text serviced the dominant classes. Many contemporary feminist critics argue that realism as a dominant genre does nothing to challenge the status quo. If the women playwrights, as a group, chose to utilise a dominant form which was, for them, a relatively new means of expression, this fact should not cause us to negate the importance of their work. Sheila Stowell's observation has relevance here:

> In offering audiences a 'seamless illusion', it is argued, realism precludes interrogation, portraying an arbitrary but self-serving orthodoxy as both neutral and inevitable. . . . This position raises a number of problems, beginning with its assumption of a simple and direct relationship between reproduction and reinforcement. While genres or styles . . . may not be politically neutral, they are

surely capable of presenting a range of ideological positions . . . dramatic forms are not in themselves narrowly partisan. They may be inhabited from within a variety of ideologies.

(Stowell 1992: 100–101)

The vast majority of the plays examined in the following pages were written within the boundaries of realism, and in this they differ little from the majority of plays produced in the mainstream theatres of the time. What fuels the lines of discussion here, however, is that there appears to have been a direct correlation between the authors' choice of subject and theme and their position as women within their culture. During the years in question women gained the vote on an equal basis with men for the first time; and many women remained unmarried and supported themselves through work, or worked to support families made fatherless by the two world wars. Divorce laws were liberalised – although divorce remained stigmatised – and women moved into the professions, becoming journalists, doctors, lawyers, social theorists and generally participating in the public world in far greater numbers than ever before. To be female was a very different proposition from what it had been during the nineteenth century.

THE ACTRESS AS PLAYWRIGHT

The vast majority of the earlier playwrights whose work is examined here began their careers as actresses, either training in the relatively new drama school establishments, or through their connections with already established 'theatre families', that is to say, 'on the road'. Many of them continued to perform as well as write and/or direct or manage productions or theatre companies. So we have a new generation of playwrights, trained as actresses, with significant experience of performance in professional theatre, who used playwriting as a vehicle for expression. Perhaps as a result of this move into the position of woman writer, as opposed to female performer, the majority of plays centre narrative and plot on women's lives, either within the domestic, work or historical context. Thus in a market economy where her position as actress set her in competition with other out-of-work actresses all looking for employment in productions in which male characters predominated, the move from actress to playwright was, it would seem, a wise one.

That many of the women playwrights had begun their professional lives as actresses may also have been a contributing factor to the predominance of female characters in their plays. Kruger has pointed out that:

the theatre institution can absorb individual female successes without any threat to the legitimacy of the masculinist and capitalist definition of that success. Adding 'significant *stage* roles' ... for women, may well reinforce existing relations of production in the theatre and thus participation in the institution, since it neither challenges the traditional roles of women in the theatre (sexually on display as actresses or serviceably out of sight as clerical workers) nor provides the means for women to run the show themselves.

(Kruger 1990: 28–29)

In Kruger's terms, it would appear that women working in theatre have a duty to challenge the whole theatre system itself. This may be so in the context of a contemporary theatre where feminist ideology and practice have been of significant and necessary importance and impact. Yet in mainstream theatre it is less of a reality than it is an ideal. Equally this contemporary political/ideological context was not, however, the one in which the women playwrights in question here were writing. The move from enactor of text to creator of text represents a challenge to existing traditionally acceptable roles for women in the process of making theatre.

Kruger also stresses that plays by women can be turned by theatre as an institution into the 'trademarks of a new commodity' (ibid.). Therefore theatre as an institution, once it accepts a new idea, will turn the idea to its own use. First, this is arguably the way in which all institutions and dominant ideologies work: the majority position is defined in relation to its ideological other which, in turn, defines itself in terms of its difference to the majority position – new commodities become normalised, and so on. Second, the theatre for which these women playwrights wrote was gradually but unquestionably becoming an industry, the continuance of which was based on economics rather than aesthetics. In this context, the actresses turned playwrights found an alternative and, in some cases, a very lucrative means of earning a wage, from a theatre institution largely owned and run by men.

VITAL STATISTICS

Table 1 provides a number of insights into comparative figures of lengths of production runs and numbers of plays written by men, with those written by women or male/female teams. The figures do not include musicals, ballets or revivals of pre-twentieth-century plays, and a revival of a twentieth-century play is tabulated as a new production. Novels written by women but adapted by men are included in the male figures and male/female co-authored plays are included in the female figures.

There are a number of discrepancies with the figures in Wearing's volumes of *The London Stage*, in that they are not always consistent with other publications which also give production figures (Wearing 1982–1993).[2] However, his is the most comprehensive and detailed account of productions of plays in West End London theatres between 1918 and 1959, so I have opted to assume a consistency on his part. Although he provides lists of productions in the non-commercial, club and subscription theatres, they are not as detailed as those in the main text, which mainly document productions in the West End. The figures show that there was an explosive increase in the numbers of plays produced on the London stage during the early decades of the period in question. Over the period as a whole there is a considerable variation, but the maximum (1930–1935) is at least three-and-a-half times the minimum. If the figures for 1930–1935 were removed, the average percentage of plays by women or male/female teams over the whole forty-two-year period would be 16.7 per cent as opposed to 13.8 per cent. Even so, for the average percentage of new plays by women or male/female teams to be as high as nearly 14 per cent over a forty-two-year period is perhaps surprising. More recent season figures of London productions of plays by women run at around 10 per cent (see Donkin 1995: 188 for 1989–1990 figures).

In terms of length of production run, it is difficult to ascertain a figure which marks the boundary between success or non-success. In her study of women playwrights on Broadway, Olauson analyses plays on the 'basis of apparent success with audiences or critics: that is, all the plays (which)... sustained a continuous run of at least thirty performances on Broadway or off-Broadway stages' (Olauson 1981: viii). Here, however, I have taken a run of fifty-one or more performances. This figure is not particularly high, but not all productions had high costs and it is quite feasible that a production would have at least paid for itself by the end of fifty performances, and that, depending on the size of the theatre, the production would have by this point reached a fairly large audience.[3] It should also be pointed out that success with the critics did not necessarily produce long runs, and also that long runs were not a sign of a positive initial reception by the critics, a point which I take up later.

The implications of these figures are many. They suggest that the period under examination was fruitful for the woman playwright, not only in terms of the number of plays, but also in terms of the length of production run. Plays by women do not dominate the London stage but they have a fairly consistent place, and appear on average to have run for

Table 1 Percentages of total productions by male, female and male/ female authors, and percentage totals of production runs. Collated from information in J. P. Wearing's *The London Stage*, in the volumes which cover 1910–1959.

Year	Total	% M	% F M/F	% M 51+	% F 51+	% M 101+	% F 101+
1918	66	81.8	18.2	37	25	22.2	12.5
1919	74	89.2	10.8	50	12.5	33.3	12.5
1920	133	84.2	15.8	32.1	23.9	19.6	23.9
1921	195	85.6	14.4	28.7	25	19.2	10.7
1922	176	81.2	18.8	29.4	27.3	11.9	18.2
1923	125	81.6	18.4	34.3	39.1	17.6	21.7
1924	178	83.2	16.8	20.3	40	10.1	23.3
1925	212	83.9	16.1	18	14.7	10.1	5.9
1926	195	80.5	19.5	27.4	23.7	15.9	10.5
1927	229	78.6	21.4	22.8	8.2	12.8	4.1
1928	257	84.4	15.6	19.8	15	11.1	2.5
1929	261	83.9	16.1	20.5	19	10	9.5
1930	258	89.1	10.9	16.1	28.6	10	17.9
1931	307	87.6	12.4	18.9	18.4	8.9	5.3
1932	277	89.2	10.8	9.2	13.3	8.9	6.6
1933	254	87.4	12.6	15.8	18.7	9	15.6
1934	219	86.3	13.7	17.5	36.7	11.6	20
1935	213	84.5	15.5	24.4	9.1	13.9	6.1
1936	181	79.6	20.4	27.8	35.1	14.6	27
1937	177	81.4	18.6	22.2	9.1	13.9	9.1
1938	146	80.1	19.9	22.2	27.6	12.8	20.7
1939	103	87.4	12.6	27.8	30.8	11.1	23.1
1940	51	86.3	13.7	18.2	57.1	2.3	14.3
1941	44	88.6	11.4	35.9	60	25.6	40
1942	44	84.1	15.9	45.9	71.4	27	71.4
1943	52	81.1	18.9	39.5	55.5	32	44.4
1944	60	85	15	35.3	66.6	29.4	66.6
1945	45	77.7	22.3	45.7	60	28.6	40
1946	84	80.9	19.1	32.3	50	25	25
1947	121	93.4	6.6	34.5	0	24	0
1948	122	83.5	16.5	29.2	31.2	16	12.5
1949	118	84.7	15.3	30	33.3	22	27.8
1950	84	83.3	16.7	37.1	21.4	25.7	21.4
1951	81	84	16	32.3	46.1	13.2	15.4
1952	92	80.4	19.6	29.7	38.9	20.3	22.2
1953	85	82.4	17.6	30	26.7	24.3	20
1954	84	82.1	17.9	42	40	31.9	26.7
1955	64	82.8	17.2	47.2	9.1	37.8	9.1
1956	81	76.5	23.5	45.2	26.3	30.6	21
1957	70	84.3	15.7	33.9	27.3	28.8	18.2
1958	100	87	13	31	30.8	16.1	30.8
1959	91	84.6	15.4	29.8	57.1	25.9	35.7

12

longer and thus been 'safer' investments for managements. Another implication is that, during the Second World War, there were fewer productions of plays by women but they were more popular. If one can assume that there were fewer men around in the years leading up to and including the war, perhaps it is possible to assume that the women left behind who went to the theatre were more inclined to go and see plays by women.

AUDIENCES – 'THE FLAPPER ELEMENT'

Thus, women have understood that an alternative to society-as-it-is can be displayed and experienced through the fantasy world of the theatre.

(Pasquier 1986: 197)

The old saw, about the drama's laws the drama's patrons give, had insistent relevance in the War-time theatre, and the ruler of the roost was the half-baked, over-heated flapper. Damn her... flappers in the stalls wanted to see flappers on the stage. No heroine need apply for the suffrages of the flappers if she looked a day older than twenty-one.

(Vernon 1924: 220–221)

During the years which immediately followed the First World War, a number of critics showed concern that the theatre was being ruined by that which they termed the 'flapper element'. Vernon was troubled by the fact that the 'flapper drama', through which he felt wartime theatre had been 'butchered', still prevailed after the war (ibid.: 119). In Vernon's opinion, the 'flapper' (and here one can assume the term to signify little more than a young, unmarried woman with an income of some sort) had, along with wartime theatre speculators, ruined not only the drama, but the 'shape' of theatre itself. Short, writing in 1942, also saw these 'flapper' audiences as having had an effect on the 'shape' of theatre during the first half of the century:

Among the repercussions due to the flapper element in post-war audiences, were the plays which showed that young women were in no mood to limit their choice of men friends to those whom parents judged as desirable home-makers... this environment provided space for Gentlewomen to shoulder their way into theatrical careers with men... with full assurance and success.

(Short 1942: 191–199)

13

Audiences will invariably influence the reaction of the critic to a production. Levels of influence will obviously vary, but the reactions of first-night audiences will, in most cases, be taken into account by the average critic. In a 1935 interview with Margaret Rowland, James Bulloch stated that, although first-night audiences were still as enthusiastic and critical as ever, as a group they had undergone 'one great change'. Bulloch commented on how the 'masculine element' in theatre had been for some time in decline; there no longer appeared to be a breed of enthusiastic theatre-going men, who would, without fail, scramble for a seat at a first-night performance. In his opinion, the average 'first-nighter' was now either a man taking his fiancée out for the night, or a woman alone or with her female companions:

> the steady increase in the feminine element is altering everything in the theatre: the first-nighter has changed, the play has changed, the acting has changed... the dawn of the feminine influx and influence that's now filling the theatre, with such comfits as 'Sweet Aloes' and 'Our Own Lives'. These things are written to please. To please who? The feminine first-nighters of course.
>
> (*Era*, 11 December 1935)

Critics often alluded to the belief that theatre was somehow being transformed by a visible increase in the number of women in the audience. There appeared to be a fear among critics that the theatre was becoming somehow 'feminised'. Certainly, from the figures shown in Table 1, it is possible to speculate that this may have been the case, during certain periods at least. I would propose that this fear of 'feminisation' was caused by a combination of the fact that, during the years under examination, on average somewhere between one-seventh and one-sixth of new plays in production were by women or male/female teams, and by the visible increase in the numbers of women in the audience. Similarly, John Carey has pointed out that concern about the numbers of women in the audience may have had as much to do with a snobbery about their class origin as it had to do with their gender. These women were seen as originating from the suburbs, a place considered by a number of intellectuals to be the site of 'specifically female triviality'. Carey quotes Louis MacNeice:

> of people – mainly women – who use theatre as an uncritical escape from their daily lives. Suburb-dwellers, spinsters, schoolteachers, women secretaries, proprietresses of teashops, all these, whether bored with jobs or idleness, go to the theatre for their regular

14

dream-hour off. The same instinct leads them which makes many hospital nurses spend all their savings on cosmetics, cigarettes and expensive underclothes.

(Carey 1992: 87)

Whatever the cause of the varied tirades about how theatre was being taken over by women, there was, it would appear, an influx of women and an increase in the level of women's participation in theatre, on both sides of the curtain. This fact arguably calls for a re-evaluative study in itself.

CRITICAL RECEPTION: WOMEN PLAYWRIGHTS AS PART-TIME PROFESSIONALS

Performances of plays by women during the period under examination here were often received by critics in terms of the gender of the author, as much as the quality of the text. References to the authors' private lives or their roles as mothers and housewives, and assertions that playwriting was really a sideline to their acting careers, were common. The proposal that a number of these playwrights were gifted amateurs, rather than professionals working with a craft, was not uncommon.

> She mostly wrote, she told me, sitting on a pouffe with a pad of paper on her knee while family life boiled about her and her attention was constantly called upon for the solution of its problems. To produce work of the quality she achieved in such circumstances was a miracle; but do I malign her by saying that playwrighting was for her a hobby rather than a vocation.
>
> (*Daily Telegraph*, 12 August 1971)[4]

The notion that these playwrights were not professionals, merely dilettantes, provides an undercurrent to the way in which their plays were critiqued. Thus, for example, it was quite common for a critic to talk about the rarity of a woman writing more than one successful play. On occasions the women themselves supported this view. One article on Dodie Smith, written after the opening of her play *Service* in 1932, began with the statement ' "C. L. Anthony" thinks out plays – in her bath.' The article goes on to quote Smith's view on women and playwriting; for Smith it was important to show that a woman could write more than one successful play. In her view, there had never been a 'really successful woman dramatist' (*Evening Standard*, 12 October 1932). This view appears to have been shared by a number of critics. It is interesting that Smith was almost always critically framed as a *woman* dramatist, a fact which she used to her advantage as a means of setting herself apart from other dramatists, both female and male. This could be seen as a manipulation of publicity for at the time of making her statement a number of women playwrights had in fact experienced significant successes with their plays, in London and elsewhere. All this boils down to the way in which success is defined and by whom.

Smith had a series of West End hits in the 1930s, but had fewer London productions of her plays than a number of other female playwrights of the time. Taking into consideration the female and female/male to male ratio of productions, women actually fared proportionately rather well in a theatre system where there was an influx of new plays by new playwrights. Over the period 1918–1959, three or more of the plays by Bridget Boland, Clemence Dane, Rose Franken, Gertrude Jennings, Margaret Kennedy, Esther McCracken, Aimée Stuart, Lesley Storm, Dodie Smith, Fryn Tennyson-Jesse and Joan Temple, ran for fifty-one and, in many cases, more performances. Many of their plays were made into films or, later, television dramas. The critical reception of their work did not always correlate with its success.

One of the methods of critical misrepresentation was, it would appear, to re-affirm the playwrights as a group, even though in many cases there were significant differences in their approach to the dramatic medium. If the critics and historians saw the women playwrights as some kind of 'breed', it was also assumed that they served the interests of a certain type of audience, with a certain type of play:

> The play-going public suddenly... picked on a new type of comedy... characteristically English. Like the tortoise-shell cat, it is also predominantly female. It is completely undramatic... ran interminably.... About? The ditherings of ordinary people seen through the magnifying glass of an observant sentimental humour. It is the vindication of the women playwright, for it is usually written by a woman... the delight of mainly feminine audiences. It is with us still in 1945.
>
> (Hudson 1946: 59)

The woman playwright was critically framed by her penchant for sentimentality, the domestic nature of her plots, the humour with which she treated the machinations of middle-class life and the seeming lack of social critique and wealth of romance in her plays. O'Casey, in the process of critiquing the critics themselves, complained that the realism of which critics were so fond had taken 'all the life out of the drama' (O'Casey 1971: 123). Here – and O'Casey is not talking in particular about women playwrights (although Dodie Smith comes in for some fairly vitriolic commentary) – O'Casey outlined one side of the critical argument between which the many women playwrights were caught. On the one hand they were grouped largely as creators of the domestic comedy, a supposedly frivolous form of drama, which put on stage the lives of 'ordinary' people, usually women, going about their everyday business. On the other hand, a number of the women playwrights were criticised for being too experimental, like the American expressionist Susan Glaspell, or for pandering to an intellectual, but 'feminine', need for discussion, such as G. B. Stern and, at times, Clemence Dane – both actresses and novelists turned playwrights.

O'Casey highlighted the discrepancies between theatre as an art form and theatre as an industry. The fact that women's plays could fall into either camp was largely ignored. When looking at the way in which women playwrights' work has been received it is possible to argue that the domestic comedy, rarely defined in any critical detail, has been denigrated both by critics and historians then and now – first, because it affirmed fears about the growing fact of theatre becoming an industry based on profit, and second, because it was seen as a form utilised mainly by women. Traces of this form can be seen in modern day 'soap opera', which again is commercially produced and presents idealised and fantasy versions of 'real life'. Women playwrights, who showed perhaps more consciously 'artistic' leanings in their plays, were identified as a whole, and therefore marginalised, because the social and ideological basis of their artistic expression was derived from their experience and position as women.

Thus women playwrights of the period 1918–1962 have, to a great extent, been manoeuvred out of history. In terms of the construction of history, it is interesting that Ernest Short's respectable 1942 volume on British theatre had a chapter entitled 'Women in the British theatre: the women dramatists', which closed with his praise for the fact that a 'second sex' was taking the theatre with 'due seriousness and contributing its special experiences in order that British drama may fully represent British life' (Short 1942: 204). Yet when he published a re-worked and larger volume, the same chapter was integrated into a chapter headed 'Theatre women, jazz and the dance craze'. This chapter begins and ends with statements about the domination of theatre by 'feminine audiences', and the peculiar suggestion that men usually now go to the theatre because 'women tend to dictate the entertainment' (Short 1951: 325–336).

Censorship was the issue on which Marie Stopes wrote the following

17

statement about the banning of her play *Vectia*, and although there was a specific context in which she made the statement, it has a relevance to the general conditions under which plays by women were often judged:

> women have things to say which men have not the ears to hear. Women who think are often like wireless waves without a receiver. Hence women who want a hearing so often try to model their creative work on men's standards – and the result is then they are 'but lesser men' – naturally. At women as 'lesser men', the critics jibe. . . . What is the woman dramatist up against today? Men managers, men producers, men theatre owners, men newspaper proprietors, men critics, men censors.
>
> (Stopes 1926: 9)

Nevertheless, Olauson has shown that, in America, female critics were as likely to adhere to current trends in journalistic theatre criticism as were men (Olauson 1981: 1–21). The point here is that although there is a relevance to Stopes's complaint, women playwrights held their own on the London stage, and appeared to have carved a niche for themselves which expanded from the mid-1920s on. Looking at the figures in Table 1, it could be argued that, proportionately, to produce a play by a woman playwright would have been a reasonably risk-free option for a production management to take. Perhaps Kruger's point about the possibilities of absorption of 'other' as a viable commodity is right, but it does not detract from the fact of the evidence of the numbers of plays, nor from the fact that a number of the playwrights discoursed on rather than automatically conformed to dominant views on gender.

The manner in which many of the playwrights chose to discourse current debates on women's roles within culture and society was the driving force behind the writing of this book. The emergent theories on mothering, femininity, the nature of woman and so on are not directly reflected in the texts, but there are clear correlations. On a level of social and psychological discourse, the problems of identity for women and, at times, both men and women, were derived from living in a society where women were being shifted from one role to another; in turn this problematising of identity is inscribed within the dramatic texts. Many of the plays dramatise and question the fact of women's economic dependence on men, and many question the assumptions about women's roles within the family and within society as a whole. A number of the plays discourse within the narrative the fact of the 'rebellious woman', and present the limitation of her choices (Goldberg 1922: 474). This discourse takes place more often within the boundaries of a realist as opposed to an experimental dramatic form, but nevertheless it is clear.

For the sake of convenience here I have treated the women playwrights as a 'group', but stressed that the 'group' is characterised by both gender and invisibility, rather than wholly through some kind of artistic approach or aesthetic expression in their work. Many of the playwrights have in common the fact that they presented the world as they saw it, from their position as *women*. One particular case in point is the way in which F. Tennyson-Jesse in *The Pelican*, written with her husband Harold Harwood, took a real court case, the famous Russell baby case of 1921, and adapted it, giving it a central narrative position within a play about the transformation of a woman's life. In the original court case, a paternity suit between the Hon. John Russell and his wife Christabel, the judge legitimised the son, but the husband was still granted a divorce. In the sophisticated 1990s divorce is a common thing, but in the 1920s it was neither a common, nor a pleasant experience for any woman involved (Colenbrander 1984: 139). The play, however, views society through the eyes of the ex-wife, the rejected woman.

Another play relevant here is Margot Neville's witty *Heroes Don't Care*,[5] where Connie Crawford, played in the original by Coral Browne, strides around the stage and endures the sarcasm and neurosis of those around her, in order to gain herself a place on Sir Edward Packenham's expedition to the North Pole:

CONNIE: ...I am not a newspaper woman, I'm Connie Crawford.

EDWARD: Mrs Connie Crawford?

CONNIE: Yes, yes,...Look here Sir Edward, I've come up here to join your expedition....I want to go to the Pole with you...I know some woman's going to do this stint sooner or later and...I mean to be the first.

EDWARD: ...It's an undertaking completely beyond the endurance of any woman.

CONNIE: Yes, yes, I've heard all that before. They said a woman couldn't fly alone over Tibet, I did it....I'm simply asking you to let me join your expedition in any capacity you name...think of the publicity...other men have planted flags on the pole, but you'd be the first to plant a woman.

(Neville 1936: 17)

Connie proves herself to be devious, singleminded, ruthless and extremely competent in her pursuit – 'just like a man'. She is the complete opposite of Packenham's wife who, perceiving Connie as a woman, rather than an explorer, worries that Connie will run off with her husband. But Connie has a husband of her own, although he never appears in the play, being alluded to only through the fact that she is called *Mrs* Crawford. The woman aviator wants to be judged on her merits, and has to behave 'just like a man', before this can happen. Neville's play could be seen as a metaphor for the life choices of the then 'modern woman', as Connie herself says:

> If a woman competes with a man nowadays she's got everything to gain and nothing to lose . . . you want to get it right out of your head that women have to be treated as fatstock . . . or kept under glass cases, they don't.
>
> (ibid.: 44)

These two plays presented the audience with heroines who were having to make active choices about the way in which they lived their lives. Similar to many of the other plays discussed in the following chapters, neither the form nor the content appear as radical to us now. Nevertheless, as the book and the statistics indicate, it is vital that we examine the work in greater detail and within the social and cultural context in which it was created. History is not something which is fixed, it is constantly changing according to its documentors and interpreters – as Lillian Hellman's explanation of the process of pentimento indicates, when the interpreter changes so too does the picture. This book is an attempt to start the re-interpretative ball rolling, working against assumptions such as, 'she wrote numerous plays . . . with intriguing titles . . . but silly plots' (F. Morgan 1994: xvi). Such ridiculous statements undermine the enormity and variety of the work of women playwrights, re-positioning it within the margins, and disconnecting contemporary women playwrights from a historical line of women writing successfully for the theatre.

2

WOMEN IN SOCIETY
1918–1962
An overview

One thing, however, is beyond doubt: that woman is in the same process of transition as man. Whether this transition is a historical turning point or not remains to be seen. The woman of today... gives expression to one of the cultural tendencies of our time: the urge to live a completer life, a longing for meaning and fulfilment.... The woman of today is faced with a tremendous cultural task – perhaps it will be the dawn of a new era.

(Jung 1989: 56–75)

The social and economic changes caused by and felt in the aftermath of the First World War meant that 'for the middle aged, middle classes, England bore very little resemblance to the pre-war years.... The old order had passed away, the halcyon days of the privileged classes. The war had cut across everything and created an enormous gap between the generations' (Mowat 1984: 119–201). During the years immediately after the Great War the whole nation suffered from a feeling of loss, a falling away of the old order, with depression and chaos as key elements in the void. These years were experienced by many as an era of disintegration, although of course the war only provided an historical focal point for changes which had already been set into motion in the late nineteenth century, both culturally and socially.

Social change between 1918 and 1962 affected women's own expectations, the social expectations which others had of them and, at times, even the defining of the sign *woman* itself. Women's role within the home and the workplace changed immeasurably. Thus, by the early 1960s, a middle-class woman may have been a mother, lawyer, teacher, graduate; she could vote or become a parliamentary candidate; get a divorce and re-marry; and make choices about the number of children she wanted. Her lived experience as a woman was unimaginably far removed from that of her foremothers. Two world wars, legislation and ideological change had gradually produced an altered role for women.

21

During the 1914–1918 war women were moved into the visible public workplace. Although their wages were not at the same level as those of the men who had been conscripted, they were nearer to male wage levels than ever before. This gave many a taste for an economic independence which few women had experienced beforehand. After the war many women wanted to maintain their new-found independence through work. However, the post-war economy demanded that work be made available for men. Public fear of women's desire to work outside the home promoted numerous debates as to whether a woman could work and still be considered a *feminine* woman. Carl Jung was greatly concerned in 1927 with what he saw as the *masculinisation* of women, a symptom of both the economic need and their desire to work. Jung proposed that, through doing the jobs once expected only of men, women would upset the 'natural' male/female balance within culture. His perception and affirmation of what was desirable female behaviour was based on the notion that a woman ought ultimately to be able to fulfil her ambitions through the love of a man and family; women's creative urges would be realised through child rearing. His view differed little from late nineteenth-century Victorian ideology, where it was thought that a woman's place was in the home. However, Jung asserted that women *were* changing, partly as a result of their relationship to the changing needs of the economy. He saw that the effect this had on society was inescapable, very real and in need of constant analysis and re-appraisal.

The sequence of events leading up to the two stages of women's enfranchisement are seen by many to be one of the primary causes of the change in twentieth-century perceptions of womanhood and femaleness. The depth of change not only increased but also caused much discussion and analysis, both offensive and defensive, during the period which spans the end of the nineteenth century to the early 1960s. The suffrage movement involved both male and female potential voters and existed inside a period of general social and political change.

> From the vantage-ground reached by human beings in the middle of the twentieth century, with the sky stormy and the path arduous, the years before 1914 seem to lie in the background, like a golden valley, where all is order and contentment. . . . Yet it is possible that in reality the years before 1914 were neither quite so golden nor quite so prosaic as they appear today. . . the claims of women to equality were all established by 1914. But if the last was established it was certainly generally not accepted.
>
> (Fulford 1958: 9–10)

Certainly the suffragist movement inspired much humour and cynicism aimed at the New Woman who, rather than stay at home or look after her widowed father, wanted independence, education and the freedom to come and go as she wished. The campaign for suffrage which runs roughly from the late 1880s to 1918 was a hard and bitter fight. Through this battle many women developed 'a social consciousness and political understanding, along with great abilities as organisers, writers, propagandists and lecturers'. Yet abuse, 'derision and social ostracism were often their lot. "Warped old maids", "destroyers of the family", "the shrieking sisterhood", "viragos and disappointed cast-offs of the marriage market" were amongst the printable epithets that were hurled at their heads' (Ramelson 1976: 171). Even though women were not given the full vote until 1928, the semi-franchise in 1918, whereby women of property aged thirty or older could vote, meant that women had moved into a position of relative power within the social system.

THE WOMEN'S MOVEMENT AND SOCIAL CHANGE

When the initial franchise was granted in 1918 to women over the age of thirty who owned property, amid great scares of an impending 'petticoat government', women who had fought for equal rights did not simply disappear. Using different strategies and working within a different agitational structure the fight continued, albeit in a fragmented form. Even when the vote was finally given to women on an equal basis to men in 1928, the 'struggle for equal rights', contrary to some popularised histories of the women's movement, continued. During the inter-war years and into the early 1960s there was still 'a vigorous and varied women's movement which addressed similar issues and conducted similar campaigns to those which we (as modern women) have engaged in' (Spender 1984: 2–6). The 'woman question', birth control, women in education and work, were still very much subjects for public discussion. The nature and force of the debates changed so that, for example, what was unacceptable in the public eye during the 1920s may have gained support by the 1940s. Women's role within society was, however, consistently a point of public and private debate.

Thus the years after the war and up until 1928 represented a period of re-assessment and change for women. After the initial franchise was granted in 1918, women's organisations and groups which had focused on the fight for the vote began to organise around how the vote should be utilised. The publication *Time and Tide*, founded and initially run by women, created a journal in 1920 which, among other things, publicised campaigns aimed at increasing the numbers of women in parliament, printed book reviews, theatre reviews, articles on education and the new legislations which would affect women's lives. It was a journal 'devoted to an examination of society and the specific part played by conventional politics . . . from a women's perspective' (Spender 1984: 2–6). Many of the women who attained positions of political power continued to agitate and organise around women's issues after the vote was won. Some, despondent about the distant relationship between legislation and actual social change, continued working at a grass roots organisational level; others believed that the only means of change was through legislation (Alberti 1989: 220–226).

There was a growing tendency during the inter-war years to recognise the vital relationship between the personal/private and political/private. The difficulty of these oppositional relationships became a major concern within the fragmented women's movement, which no longer had one political aim in mind, that is to say, the affirmation of equal citizenship through the vote. The issues around choices for women were frequently discussed in newspaper articles, women's magazines, and academic or social treatises.

> Marriage and work? Marriage or work? Education – for what? The difficulties of maintaining a home, rearing children – and having this work valued by society – of entering the paid workforce, of being financially and psychologically dependent on men; the problems of not enjoying the same opportunities in education, in the home, in the workplace, of not earning the same pay or enjoying the same legal rights as men.
>
> (Spender 1984: 15–16)

Discussions of these issues within the popular press more often than not prioritised men's needs over those of women. They were, however, clearly issues which concerned women activists of the era and the discourse around these concerns often informed the basic narrative through-line of many of the plays which are examined later.

Gaining the vote did not prove to be more than a starting point for a shift in the relationship of women to the power structure. Ironically women, who had been treated as an homogeneous group to a large extent, did not vote on a block basis: many, it is thought, did not even use their vote for some years. Equally, when women did use their new-found voting power, party political attitudes to 'women's issues' were not the only basis on which they voted. Clemence Dane, actress (under the name of Winifred Ashton), writer, journalist, sculptress and one of the most prolific and successful of the women playwrights in this study, wrote in 1926 of how she felt a great sense of disappointment at women who, even when given the opportunity to do so, did not use their vote. Dane depicted these women as evading the responsibilities of citizenship, refusing to see women as having a place outside the home, and she pointed out that, 'If they will not take their share of national housekeeping they run the risk of having their private housekeeping threatened by forces – laws, wars, strikes and revolutions – outside their control' (Dane 1926: 9). Clemence Dane believed that any woman should be happy to 'assert her disagreement . . . by means of the vote that she has not yet bothered to use' (ibid.). There was a great deal of legislation which women needed to be informed about as it directly reflected their relationship to both the work economy and home life. Dane's concern was shared by many, and this is reflected in the issues discussed on the 'women's pages' within the national press, issues ranging from how to manage your home without domestic help to the ways in which women can be integrated into male-dominated professions.

Although a number of laws aimed at equalising women's position within British society were passed during the period in question, they were often open to interpretation and were rarely originated, worded or practised without a gender bias. The bias was grounded in an assumption of women's 'natural' inferiority, irrationality or passivity. It is not my intention to detail all the relevant legislation, but rather to indicate some of these laws which had a significant influence upon both the personal and working lives of women. These laws also provide the historian with an indication as to the perceived and received ideas about both the nature of woman, her role within society and 'femaleness' itself.

The Sex Disqualification (Removal) Act of 1919 stated that:

> a person should not be disqualified by sex or marriage from the exercise of any public function or from being appointed or holding any public function or from being appointed or holding any civil post or from entering or assuming or carrying any civil profession or vocation.
>
> (Lewis 1984: 199)

The Act suggested a move toward equality in the labour market, but it was no *guarantee* of employment for women. More often than not it was interpreted negatively and, along with the less egalitarian Marriage Bars, was often used as law to keep women out of the job market. The Marriage Bars, which many women fought against and which were not generally removed until the years which followed the Second World War, meant that women, once married, were easily removed from employment. This was especially significant for women teachers who, despite in some cases taking local authorities to the courts, often lost their jobs in favour of younger, less experienced men: 'it was taken for granted that a married women did not work unless there was some special reason' (Branson 1975: 212). This rationale was based on discrimination backed up by so-called 'scientific theory' which claimed that because of their biological make-up, women were unsuitable for responsible posts in education or industry. For some, it was obvious that the Marriage Bars were more a symptom of the economic system than anything else. During the depression, which maintained a stronghold from the mid-1920s into the 1930s, employment for men was a priority. Many feminists and campaigners for women's rights accepted this view to a large extent, and concentrated their efforts on improving women's lives within the private sphere, namely the home. It was not until the Factories Order Act in 1950 that there was any real governmental attempt to adjust the conditions of work to the condition of women's lives by the official introduction of twilight shifts and so on (Lewis 1984: 153).

The Married Women's Acts, which went through many changes and adjustments during the inter-war years, were concerned with the legal rights of matrimonial property. By 1935 married women were given the right to attain, dispose and hold property as chosen, but it was not until well into the 1940s that matrimonial property rights were equalised, and again, the benefit to middle- and upper-class women was often greater. The Divorce Laws, which had gradually been changing since the late 1900s, were 'liberalised' by the late 1930s. Although the divorce rate rose continuously from an average of 832 in 1910–1912 to 4,249 in 1930–1932 (Mowat 1984: 213–216), steadily rising as the law became more equal in its treatment of the sexes, divorce was not generally seen as positive and it is not a subject which widely featured in plays of the period. A divorced woman was often seen as having somehow failed in her 'proper' duty as a woman.

Educational opportunities improved, especially with the provision of free education for all until the age of fifteen, but girls were still not taught on an equal basis to boys; it was assumed that education should be divided by gender, with girls being encouraged to take non-scientific subjects or to train for low-skilled, low-paid work.

Despite much legislation and new primarily ideological and practical reforms, such as the contraceptive movement (which at least gave women some amount of choice as to the frequency of pregnancy), by the late 1950s and into the early 1960s women were still paid on unequal terms with men, educated to different levels, and expected to want to become mothers, housewives and so on. The commercialisation of femininity through the mass media and the new consumer society promoted traditional feminine roles, keeping women's interests focused on the home and family life. This had a growing effect on both the way in which woman as a signified was perceived and for the way in which women saw themselves. Yet, because of the demands of the economic system, especially during wartime, women were supposed to shift back and forth through single generations from work and public life to home and private life and back again.

The many women's magazines founded and flourishing from the mid-1920s onwards promoted home life and the idea that women could contribute to the welfare, growth and development of British society through their work in the home and through child rearing. There was no one single image stronger than that of the housewife, confined to the private sphere, encouraged to fantasise about being more wealthy with more leisure time, just like the glamorous women in Hollywood films. Although some women's magazines ran articles on training men to help in the home, the domestic sphere was presented as the woman's kingdom.[1] As a popularly utilised term, the 'flapper' denoted a fairly androgynous image of female independence. The associations of sexual promiscuity with this image – in *fin de siècle* Germany it was a word used to describe a young prostitute – existed alongside the fact that, during the 1920s, a woman with a burning desire for independence was frowned upon and seen as somehow a signifier of all that was problematic within the social order: 'in the early 1920s "Flapper" was a term of abuse which could be used against independent women who sought to consolidate upon women's wartime gains and upon the partial suffrage victory of 1918' (Beddoe 1989: 40).

The 'perfect lady' of the late nineteenth century was transformed into the loyal and dutiful housewife by the 1930s. Elizabeth Wilson has noted that the Second World War had a 'total domestic impact because it was global' and that 'its effect in emphasising at once Britain's world imperial role in defence of democracy, and the breakdown of class division at home was contradictory' (Wilson 1980: 13–17). This contradiction was reflected in women's lives: just as women were driven back into the socially re-evaluated home after the First World War, so were they encouraged to 're-build' the nation from the home base after the Second World War. Beveridge's post-Second World War *New Deal For Housewives* showed that although the situation of the 'tired housewife' was recognised as being socially significant, there was no real desire to see women fill gaps in the labour market. The idea of housewifery and motherhood as careers in themselves was promoted, with working-class women being encouraged once more to go into domestic service by the early 1950s. Women's magazines now focused on motherhood, rather than simply marriage, as a career.

A number of women theorists, journalists and writers questioned this ideology, pointing out that housewives were becoming the new proletariat, and that the professionalising of the domestic sphere for middle-class women did not hide the fact that the home was outside the market economy. In the mid-1940s Viola Klein and Alva Myrdal stated that:

> the anachronism between the economics of the household and those of society at large is to a considerable extent responsible for the sense of frustration and futility which fills so many housewives today when going about their daily tasks.
>
> (Myrdal and Klein 1956: 186)

Combined with the fact that in many respects, even in the early 1960s, the graduate wife was seen as something of an embarrassment, it is possible to see why the relationship between the private and public, so crucial for women during the inter-war period, transformed into the growing recognition of the personal as political, in turn one of the ideological focus points of the 'reborn' women's movement in the late 1960s.

During the 1950s the popular press in general took the view that women should move back into the home: some have suggested that this was connected to a growth in the availability of home consumer products and a need to market these products especially to women. Yet in reality many women had sustained their wartime position of being a part of the workforce outside the home. Myrdal and Klein wrote of women's move into the workforce as being revolutionary in that it would bring about 'a more equitable division of labour between the sexes such as existed before the beginning of industrialisation'. But they also recognised that this 'revolutionary' move was at one and the same time problematic for women as well as being in the 'interest, not only of women, but of the community as a whole' (ibid.: 189). However, by the mid-1950s it was once again accepted on supposedly scientific grounds that woman's *rightful* place was in the home. Woman was praised for her ability to function as part of the public economic workforce, but only in times of national need. Ultimately the role of mother and child rearer was seen as belonging to woman alone. Some social theorists and political activists alike saw that conditions within the home had to be improved, and from the 1930s through to the 1960s domestic life became more scientifically based both

28

in terms of the increased numbers and general availability of technolo-gical domestic appliances, and in terms of the number of theories around housewifery as the female art of the private but vital workforce.

FEMININITY AND SEXUAL DIFFERENCE: THE INTER-WAR YEARS

The key issue around which notions of femininity and sexual difference were based was that of the oppositional forces of biology and culture – in other words, the nature versus nurture argument. Many women were actively involved in attempts to prioritise either one or the inevitably inextricable nature of both. Winifred Holtby, writer, journalist and social theorist, was concerned with the traditionalist view of woman which she saw as having, through history, been internalised by both sexes. Holtby was perplexed by the negative response of young women to the movement for social equality between the sexes:

> Why in 1934, are women themselves often the first to repudiate the movement of the last one hundred and fifty years, which has gained for them at least the foundations of political, economical, educa-tional and moral equality. . . one of the great virtues of the militant suffragette movement was its mastery of the art of ritual . . . pageants and processions.
>
> (Holtby 1934: 96)

Her view was that a traditional perception of the male as the active, strident, ruling breadwinner was so strongly a part of culture that it necessitated an automatic inferiority complex in women, and the opposite in men. The positive aspect of 'pageants and processions' was that they validated women in large numbers, both in terms of identity as a group and as a body with its own history and vital place within culture.

Single women in the early 1930s found it easier to get jobs because they were cheaper to employ than men during the economic 'slump'. This automatically turned women as a group into a direct threat both to the earning power of men and to the potential of emotional stability gained from knowing one's place as the breadwinner which came from that earning capacity. Holtby saw that the 'slump complex' – slump being a euphemistic term for a time of national economic difficulty – encouraged a 'narrowing of ambition and a closing-in alike of ideas and opportunities for women' (ibid.: 116). Along with the all-consuming power of the 'inferiority' and 'slump complex', Holtby identified the 'chivalry com-plex', a phenomenon whereby an active masculinity could only exist

29

through the maintenance of its binary opposite, a passive femininity: she recognised that the acceptance of this binary opposition contributed to the confusion of identity felt by many women of her generation. The popular media presentation of the 'modern girl' made her out to be selfish, uninterested in public matters, impatient with authority and uncontrolled in her habits. Again, as with the flapper, any identity of the feminine which was associated with independence was seen ultimately as being negative. Holtby's fear was that, with fascism and right-wing ideologies which saw women's inherent and natural role as being that of the wife, mother and homemaker gaining a renewed credibility and popularity in Europe, there would be a new generation of fatalistic women who would accept this proposed passive and private role rather than fight against it. For Holtby, the choices were clearly polarised: either one chose to be the fashionable 'womanly woman' or one chose to fulfil one's own ambitions and self-identified potential (ibid.: 118–121).

Winifred Holtby felt that it was imperative to recognise and re-state the ideological links between her generation and that of the women of the late nineteenth century who had fought for women's political rights. In her view the revolution for women had only just begun. Certain parallels can be drawn between Holtby's analysis and Reich's observations of post-revolutionary Russian family life, where Reich points out that the 'revolution, in the ideological superstructure fails to take place, because the bearer of this revolution, the psychic structure of human beings, was not changed' (Reich 1951: 157). For Reich it was individual attitudes and psychology which needed to change in order for the ideological super-structure to undergo a process of revolution. In the same way, Holtby stressed that women had to learn to see themselves as different from the representations of the feminine which became gradually popularised in the decades which followed the First World War. Economic factors were vital to the shaping of ideological notions of femininity; the relationships between the economy and the defining of the female and the feminine were inextricable.

Other more widely accepted movements than fascism, seen at the time as radical in outlook, especially with regard to women's status, proposed and promoted the idea that a woman's place within culture was that of child bearer and home keeper. The eugenics movement, founded on the notion that in order to prosper a nation must produce healthy babies of so-called good stock, was ultimately aimed at creating an imperial race to compete with other fast-growing European imperial races. Initially, the basic tenets of eugenics were applauded by both extremes of the political spectrum. Integral to the eugenics movement was a desire for population control, more than environmental improvement (Weeks and Rowbotham 1977: 170–179). One of its founders, Francis Galton, was an 'arch-conservative' who was greatly concerned by the rising working-class birth rate. Other initial supporters came from a more liberal standpoint. Havelock Ellis who, although he was against fanatical eugenics, saw the movement as

> the ultimate movement for social reform.... It was now necessary to purify the 'stream of life' at its source, and to concentrate on the 'point of procreation'.... It was only possible to develop a negative eugenics, designed to eliminate the unfit... he believed that this would only come about through education, not direction.
>
> (Weeks and Rowbotham 1977: 170–179)

The new education in sexual responsibility was to be aimed at women and, although in his earlier writings Ellis promoted an equality of the sexes, this was inevitably incompatible with the emphasis which he placed on the ideal woman's role within the monogamous, heterosexual couple. Her role was to be that of co-parent in a family unit, which in turn was to be the basis for both change and stability within Ellis's vision of a new and healthy society. For Ellis, gender roles were of equal importance to the social structure but not naturally interchangeable within it. The birth control movement, both in England and America, ultimately proposed the search for a socially acceptable disassociation of sex from procreation, as well as trying to control the class of those babies which were being born. This supposedly scientific approach put women into an uneasy position. The new radical ideas around child bearing and child rearing did not converge with the new economic freedom which women had experienced and enjoyed during the First World War. Again, the change in Ellis's emphasis on the family as opposed to the individual bears a strong relationship to the change in society's needs because of the shift in the economy.

Havelock Ellis was, however, much more than a follower and supporter of the eugenics movement. Jeffrey Weeks provides a concise analysis of Ellis's role as one of the first sexologists:

> In the first place it is important to recognise Ellis's role as an *ideologist*. The purpose of his works was to change attitudes and to create a new view of the role of sex in individual lives and in society. He set out to rationalise sexual theory, and in doing so helped lay down the foundation of a 'liberal' ideology of sex. The essence of this was a greater toleration of sexual variations.... Its greatest

weakness was its inability to ask *why* societies have continued to control sexuality.... He recognised the question of the social roles of the two sexes was of paramount importance in the new century, particularly because of the influence of the women's movement. He therefore attempted to suggest guidelines for more humane and equal sexual and social relations and behaviour. The particular forms these guidelines took now seem among the most reactionary aspects of his work – particularly his view of woman's role ... yet, for a long period, his preoccupations were shared by all progressive tendencies, including revolutionary socialists.

(ibid.: 181)

A number of women, in particular Stella Browne and Margaret Sanger, pioneered Ellis's work, partly because it brought discourse on sex out into the open area of public debate. His later work was consumed by those wishing to raise the status of the family and bring it into the range of state support. However, his idea of the reformed family was one whereby partners had supposedly equal rights which manifested themselves in the fact of *fixed* roles within the family unit. Through the ideas of Ellis and other sexologists, women were encouraged to put their faith in science, and although many professionals who were far more 'scientific' in both their approach and methodology found Ellis's ideas to be simplistic and rarely founded on anything more than conjecture, his theories fed into a 'cultural fixing' of biologistic definitions of gender traits and characteristics.

Sexology became popularised as part of the 'new psychology' for a new age. Ellis, among others, promoted heterosexual, monogamous partnerships, and by the 1930s those who praised the movement assimilated its ideals as part of their own. Stella Browne absorbed Ellis's ideas of sexual inversion as a means of promoting heterosexuality through denigrating other sexualities. Spinsterhood was often aligned with frigidity: if a woman chose to be single her choice was perceived as somehow abnormal; independence from a marital relationship was not seen as being healthy.

The *feminine* woman was passive and motherly; man was the hunter, woman the hunted. Women could have power but rarely within the public realm. The interest in 'ideal love' and marriage was fed by numerous publications such as Van de Velde's *Ideal Marriage* (1928), which sold enough copies for it to be published and re-published well into the 1960s. Such publications were aimed at promoting heterosexual sex both within and without marriage, but again refused to encourage any real level of independence; 'the correct form of marriage ought to be male domination and female submission' (Jeffreys 1985: 183). Feminism and feminists were associated with man-hating and 'abnormal' desires for power and independence.

The basic tenets of psychoanalysis had filtered through to British middle-class intellectuals by the 1920s. Many of Freud's ideas were based on the primacy of the 'sexual instinct'. The sexologists, for whom Freud had little patience, often aligned their work with his on the basis of his emphasis on 'sexual instinct'. A number of British psychoanalysts found this emphasis difficult to accept and

> expressed reservations about certain of his doctrines...what was accepted was the energy model of the psyche, notions of unconscious mental processes and unconscious motives, repression, regression, mental conflict and complexes. What was discarded, explicitly or tacitly, was the conception that libidinal energy, or the 'sex instinct', was the organising principle of mental life...together with the associated doctrines of infantile sexuality and the sexual origins of neurosis.
>
> (N. Rose 1985: 182)

Rose labels the 'new psychology' as a body of knowledge and practice which came from a number of sources. One of the initial practical applications of this knowledge was in the treatment of the thousands of shell-shocked soldiers who came back from the First World War.[2] The details of the differences between Freud and the new psychologists are beyond the bounds of this book. However, as Rose points out, the 'new psychology' enabled 'an alignment between the register of personal happiness, that of family relations, and that of social adjustment. And where Freud was to write, in 1930, of the unease inherent in civilisation, the new psychology was to be a science of contentment. Personal happiness and social adjustment were now two sides of the same coin' (ibid.: 184–186).

Among many of the earlier psychoanalysts the women's movement caused concern. Women who wanted to follow what were traditionally seen as 'male' pursuits, encompassing independence and a professional life, were problematised and seen as having an unresolved relation to the castration complex as proposed by Freud – the perception was often that, effectively, independent women wanted to be men. However, by the early 1920s there were a number of psychoanalysts, among them Karen Horney, who stressed 'the effect of culture upon psycho-sexual development' (Garrison 1981: 687). In the mid-1920s Horney challenged Freud, asserting that the developmental context of psychoanalysis had been a world dominated by the needs of the male, as was the law, morality and religion. She saw that, historically, men and women had related to each other as master and slave and pointed out that there was no empirical proof that, for example, a small girl would experience 'penis envy' any more than a young boy might experience 'womb envy'.

During the 1930s Horney moved to the United States where she further developed her theories of female development by proposing that men experienced great conflict between their longing for woman and their dread of her (ibid.: 683). Horney has been criticised by many recent feminists because of the fact that her theories were biologically reductionalist in nature; she saw the desire for motherhood as an imperative. Horney was, however, important because of her work on female development, and because she was one of the first to criticise Freud, making a distinction between

> those ideas of Freud's which were based on his ingenious, though subjective, speculative imagination and those derived from his experiences and observations of patients.
>
> (Rubins 1979: 132)

Horney stressed the connections between the psychological state of womanhood and the demands which were made upon women by the culture in which they lived. Although she perceived woman's psychology as inscribed within her biology, she refuted the possibility of defining femininity without the consideration of cultural determinants:

> It would not be going too far to assert that ... conflicts confront every woman who ventures upon a career of her own and who is ... unwilling to pay for her daring with the renunciation of her femininity.
>
> (ibid.: 34)

As Weskott has pointed out: 'Horney's early criticism of Freud can be interpreted as an attempt to rescue instinctual femininity from a theory in which it is devalued' (Weskott 1986: 57). It is also interesting to note that Horney proposed that power should somehow be de-sexualised and that, because woman had internalised cultural ideals of femininity, both the problem and the solution for women was to be the breaking-through of a fear of what she was, rather than concerning herself with what she should be (ibid.: 213).

By the end of the inter-war period arguments around the defining of femininity and sexuality were in decline among psychoanalysts. During the post-Second World War years various theoreticians, whether consciously or not, once again framed femininity as dependent on 'natural' connections between women, the home and motherhood. John Bowlby, among others, stressed the importance of the constant presence of the mother for children under five. Although the approach of Bowlby, Donald Winnicott and Benjamin Spock appears to be rather conservative and traditional, in their time their ideas were seen as radical because their approach was 'child centred and permissive' (E. Wilson 1980: 189). The effect of their work in terms of an idea of women as independent humans able to work *and* be mothers, was to legitimise state control over women's working hours and indeed state encouragement for women to return to the home. Again, although the ideas of Bowlby and others of his generation were not originated as a means of oppressing women, they were derived from an ideology which did not consider gender roles as either interchangeable or equal.

> Their work was an indictment of elitist upper-class forms of child rearing – nannies and boarding schools . . . and implicitly working-class warmth and spontaneity towards children were validated. Their conservative views on women were accepted as part of this package.
>
> (ibid.)

The Butler Education Act in 1944 limited the number of adolescents available for work, as a result of which married mothers were seen as a source of replacement part-time, low-paid labour. The Marriage Bars were largely lifted during the immediate post-Second World War period, and yet, as well as wanting women to join the workforce on a part-time basis, there was fear of a lack of provision for adolescents with new-found leisure time. As the keepers of the home women were made somehow responsible for the guardianship of this fairly new social group of unemployed youth. Again this legislation put women in a difficult position, whereby the benefits of one choice equalled the difficulties inherent in the other.

For women, then, the social changes which took place between 1918 and 1962 were often problematic because the social needs incurred by these changes rarely correlated with either women's desires, or their lived experiences. On many levels life changed rapidly, too rapidly for relevant cultural precedents to be set.

> Profound changes in the roles of women during the past century have been accompanied by innumerable contradictions and

inconsistencies. With our rapidly changing and highly differentiated culture...the stage is set for myriads of combinations of incongruous elements. Cultural norms are often functionally unsuited to the social situations to which they apply. Thus they may deter an individual from a course of action which would serve his own, and society's interests best. Or, if behaviour contrary to the norm is engaged in, the individual may suffer from guilt over violating mores which no longer serve any socially useful end.

(Komarovsky 1946: 184)

The defining of the feminine and femininity came out of the context of this society which, because of war and fast economic change, was in a constant state of flux. Similarly, by the end of the First World War, the class system, although still rooted in a late nineteenth-century ideology, had undergone a transformation because of the speed of change and variation in the economy. Even though there was not a feminist movement which focused on an agreed social and political strategy for change, the women's movement continued to be a cultural phenomenon, whether negatively or positively proposed or received. Before the Great War, the feminist movement existed in a world which was far less fragmented than the world of the years between 1918 and 1962. These years provided a context for a women's movement which, by 1928, had gained voting power but very little real political power. It was a period when the reality of issues fought over before the war were either re-stated or underwent a continuous process of re-evaluation. Despite disagreement among women and within society about the role of woman, there was a degree of consensus among those for whom the 'woman question' was still a very real one. The fact was that women were still not equal on a social or economic level with men in a patriarchal and capitalist social structure.

It was generally accepted by those who fought for equal rights for women, on whatever level and in whatever context, that in a society

whose standards are predominantly masculine women form an 'out-group', distinguished from the dominant strata by physical characteristics, historical tradition, social role and a different process of socialisation. As in the case of other groups in a similar situation, preconceived opinions are applied more or less summarily to the class as a whole, without sufficient consideration of individual differences... 'out groups' are subject to collective judgements instead of being treated on their own merits.

(Klein 1989: 4)

The plays which are examined in the second section of this book are selected from the group of women playwrights whose work was produced between the years 1918 and 1962. My intention is not to provide a collective judgement, but rather to examine the content and nature of their work. What is important is the way in which, as women playwrights, they represented 'woman' in the public arena of the theatre at a time when woman, the feminine and femininity as cultural definitions were constantly undergoing a process of negotiation. When talking of history and of women's contribution to culture and knowledge, it is perhaps important to note that a social system which relies on the supremacy of one group over another will not provide historical links between one generation and another of the socially inferior group. Division is synonymous with control over the possibilities of uniting a minority group. Although the group in question here has many differences embodied within it, these women playwrights provide a strong link in a chain which represents a continuum of women's literary contribution to the social and cultural phenomenon of theatre in Britain during the twentieth century.

3

THE LONDON STAGE
1918–1962
An historical context for women in theatre

Richard Findlater's *The Unholy Trade* remains the most detailed and inclusive, albeit brief, account of the state and history of theatre in London during the first half of the twentieth century. Findlater outlined the structure of British theatre and production patterns in a way which allowed for a pluralistic definition of what theatre as a cultural phenomenon signified. His approach was one which insisted on the stating of a number of cultural, political and aesthetic positions. Thus it was as important then as now to stress the variety of theatres, and in turn contexts, for which the women playwrights whose work is examined in this book wrote.

> There is no one kind of theatre, and no one solution to all its problems.... The theatre exists by compromise, and feeds on contradiction. It exists to explain life, and to deny it, to decorate it and to strip it bare.... The theatre is a weapon, a magic, a science; a sedative, an aphrodisiac, a communion service; a holiday and an assize, a dress rehearsal of the here and now and a dream in action.... It is the most conservative and the most ephemeral, the most opaque and the most transparent, the strongest and the weakest of arts. It is everything and nothing, all or none of these things. The theatre is what you make it.
>
> (Findlater 1952: 13)

Writing after the demise of the club and subscription theatres which had thrived during the inter-war period, Findlater was concerned that theatre, in particular the drama, had reached a point of crisis. Yet, the 'theatre society' about which he wrote had been undergoing constant and significant change throughout the first half of the century. If we take theatre as a sign which signifies or embodies an institution within society, which both reflects and effects change, then it is possible to see theatre as a

38

generic term for an institution which is in flux, a institution whose significance and definition is entirely dependent on cultural and economic change, as well as changes in aesthetic taste. Thus the crisis which Findlater identified as being specific to his time was arguably as relevant to any point in theatre history between the wars and into the 1960s. The crisis concerns the incongruities of a theatre devoted to the development of drama and the dramatic text, and a theatre which operates as a commercial enterprise.

As historians interested in re-defining women's historical role within theatre, it is imperative that we re-assess assumptions which promote absence of women's work from history. Thus, while taking into account pre-existing key points in theatre history, it is important to see the period in question as some kind of whole, when attempting to define the context in which women playwrights between 1918 and 1962 worked. This whole can be characterised largely by its exclusion from analysis, and by the fact that the theatre system for which the women playwrights in question were writing differs in many ways from that of the pre-1914 years and that of the post-1968 years. The purpose of this chapter, therefore, is to investigate the particular nature of the structure and social context of the 'theatre society' in which plays by women were produced.

OWNERSHIP OF THEATRES: MONOPOLY

The aftermath of the First World War saw a change in ownership of the commercial theatres in Britain, and specifically in London. The theatres closed for the first few weeks of the war and, when they re-opened, it was clear that they were catering for a new audience: 'soldiers on leave sought escapism' (Pick 1983: 110); similarly, women moving into the public field of work might seek an evening's entertainment in the West End. Theatrical revues became popular, arguably as a result of a new theatre clientele, and it would seem there was great concern that these 'new audiences showed signs of ill-breeding', in other words a new class of audience was frequenting the theatres during the Great War, and new managements programmed shows accordingly (ibid.).

During the years which span 1918 to 1962, in the majority of cases the running of theatres moved from actor-managers, who were both business-men or women *and* performers, to the investor, or financial speculator. 'As early as the 1914–18 war we hear complaints about the activities of speculating middlemen, who bought up theatre leases with the object of re-letting at a profit to the producing managements' (Sandison 1953: 52). During the late nineteenth century, theatre as a cultural art form had become more acceptable to the moneyed middle classes, and the new drama of the *fin de siècle* demanded smaller casts and more intimate theatre spaces; actor-managers could profitably produce the plays in which they sought to perform. However, after the Great War, the rents in London rose to such an extent that it was no longer viable to be an actor-manager on a grand scale. Thus the immediate ownership of performance spaces changed and the means of production were no longer owned by performers. Pick has pointed out that this meant an inevitable distancing between managers and audience. The class composition of the audience had changed, or at least the range of classes going to the theatre had widened yet, 'ultimately the view of what was "lifelike" came from a deep armchair somewhere in London's club land'. Whatever the cultural bias or impetus behind the choice of what was being produced in the London theatres, to the disdain of a number of critics, a 'new business man of uncertain theatrical pedigree entered management' (Pick 1983: 114). Theatre had become an economic investment for those who were less interested in the aesthetic content of plays than they were in the financial viability of a play in production. Numbers of historians and critics were chiefly concerned with the fact that during the inter-war period and into the late 1940s the theatre system, through company buy-outs, gradually came under the control of a small number of investors and company directors; the drawing-in of theatre ownership to an 'elite group created a fear of monopoly and control' (ibid.).

The 1920s and 1930s were characterised by frustrations and vexations arising from the vested and usually conflicting interests of the theatre managements (owning the buildings) and the production managements (presenting the plays). A number of key problems resulted from this relatively new divorce between business and aesthetics. Some interesting innovatory ideas were put into practice, one of the best remembered being J. B. Priestley's takeover of the management of a West End theatre, the Duchess, where he backed and produced his own plays to give some coherence and independence to their production. But the most significantly successful manoeuvres in the mainstream, commercial theatre were concerned with a series of takeovers, amalgamations and consolidations between property-owning and play-presenting managements. By the early 1940s these had led to the creation of a small cartel of companies, linked by the mutual inclusion of a number of individuals who re-united in their operations both entrepreneurial functions. The cartel of companies, often referred to as the Group, had by the late 1940s manoeuvred themselves into a position where they either owned or ran most of the profitable theatres in London.[1] The list of West End theatre buildings connected with the Group is astounding; it includes the Apollo, Aldwych, Drury Lane, His Majesty's, St James', Lyric, Phoenix, Shaftesbury, Hippodrome, Fortune and the Ambassadors theatres. Principal producing names and managements directly connected with the Group included H. M. Tennent Ltd, Stuart Cruickshank, Tom Arnold, Emile Littler and C. B. Cochran, among others.

So by the late 1940s in any one week one may have found sixteen London theatres occupied by the Group or its associates, out of which eleven were owned by the Group. Similarly, one may have found that out of twelve theatres occupied by major independent production companies, four were owned by the Group (Sandison 1953: 77). By the early 1950s, including the number of damaged or non-operating theatres, there were eighty-five British theatres in which the Group had an interest, less than a fifth of the country-wide number. However, they had either control or interest in 42 per cent of the London theatres, which contained over 50 per cent of the seats country-wide. Of the larger theatres, fifteen out of twenty-four were either controlled or run by the Group.

For some the Group represented only a quasi-monopoly. For example, the Group were not entirely responsible for forcing up London rents, because property prices in London had risen enormously since the end of the First World War. When the Group did lease some of their venues to independent production companies, their prices were in line with other property owners. Thus, when a boom in theatre meant a rise in rental costs, the Group were not in competition with the independents because they owned their production venues; rises in rent did not affect their costs, only their income (ibid.: 27). Nevertheless, in real terms, the Group and H. M. Tennent Ltd, along with their associated and satellite companies, owned or controlled by the late 1940s the most potentially profitable part of the theatre industry. They were largely responsible for the fact that the British theatre had 'been put on a proper industrial footing, employing all the devices of horizontal and vertical combination that this involves' (ibid.: 7).

In terms of the control of venues, many dramatists were critical of the system of management and ownership of the West End theatres. J. B. Priestley was very clear about the consequences of the monopoly of ownership:

> Theatre at present is not controlled by dramatists, actors, producers or managers, but chiefly by theatre owners, men of property who may or may not have a taste for the drama. The owners ... take too much out of the Theatre ... it is not that the owners are purely

'commercial', but that they cannot help satisfying their own particular tastes.... What I condemn is the property system that allows public amenities and a communal art to be controlled by persons who happen to be rich enough to acquire playhouses.

(Priestley 1947: 6)

Ownership of the theatres in the West End was concentrated among a few who were closely 'linked in a network of companies and the outsider cannot unravel the tangle' (Findlater 1952: 41). This factor not only had consequences for the West End, but also for theatre production around the country in both a professional and amateur context.

The new piece they describe with enthusiasm at the Ivy Restaurant to-day will probably, within the next three years, be applauded from Torquay to Aberdeen.

(Priestley 1947: 36)

There were smaller management concerns such as Wyndham's Theatres Ltd, run by Bronson Albery, and a number of independent theatres. In the provinces smaller theatres not under the control of the Group were run on a purely profit-making basis (Findlater 1952: 40–45). As a parent company H. M. Tennent Ltd re-invested in less profit-oriented theatre, co-operating with the Arts Council in its promotion of educational theatre (Tennent Productions Ltd) and subsidising the productions of the Company of Four at the Lyric Hammersmith, and also giving a contract to a chosen RADA graduate every year. The directorial and board management connections between the independents, H. M. Tennent Ltd and the Group created a serious concentration of power within the British theatre production system.

Tennent Plays Ltd was the brainchild of Hugh Beaumont – some believe that it was thought up as a means of avoiding payment of the Entertainment Tax. In order to legitimise non-payment of the tax, the organisation had to be educational and, later, partly educational. There was, however, a clause in the ruling which demanded that if profit was made and the company wished to stop trading, any profits could be handed over to another non-profit-oriented production company (Black 1984: 70). The drawback of this system is obvious and until Tennent Plays Ltd very few companies other than the Old Vic took advantage of the exemption. Tennent Plays Ltd came about as a means of preserving capital and avoiding tax by starting up a non-profit-making distribution company. Operating from the Globe Theatre offices and with the support of CEMA (Council for Entertainment, Music and the Arts), the company was allowed to charge a £25 management fee per production. According to Kitty Black, who was employed in an administrative capacity by the company, Tennent Productions Ltd received no subsidy from the government, simply their 'support'. The criticism of this project was that it simply extended the range of control which H. M. Tennent Ltd had over what was or was not produced in the West End theatres and ultimately in the provinces. As such, many felt that the government was, whether intentionally or not, giving sanction to monopoly.

H. M. Tennent Ltd launched another production company in October of 1945, the Company of Four; the first production was *The Shouting Dies* by Ronda Keane. Originally the idea of Rudolph Bing (who was later the general manager of Glyndebourne Opera, then the first administrator of the Edinburgh Festival), this was seen as a means of presenting 'experimental theatre of quality in London', the venue for which was the Lyric Hammersmith. Other members of the original administrative and managerial body included Murray MacDonald and Tyrone Guthrie. The principle behind the scheme was to rehearse a play for four weeks, tour it in the provinces for four weeks and then give it a four-week run at the Lyric. It was 'experimental' in that the aim was to 'produce new plays with new directors and designers and to provide jobs for actors returning from the Forces' (Black 1984: 112–114). Within the first year, all the productions had run at a loss and many of the original board members had withdrawn. Where the critics slated a production, often the audience, many of whom worked the local markets, would applaud that production, which highlights the fact that there were often huge discrepancies between the way in which plays were received by the audiences and the critics (ibid.: 119). The programming was a never-ending stream of rehearsing, touring and so on, with three plays in preparation at any one time. The company produced classic English and European drama as well as new plays and works by American authors such as Arthur Miller and Lillian Hellman.[2]

The monopoly of ownership and production control created a peculiar irony in that, by the early 1950s, the average production of a West End play was influenced and shaped by the aesthetic tastes of a small group of owners and managers. To an extent, therefore, the identity of West End theatres, seen by a number of critics, historians and even playwrights during the immediate post-Great War years to have been lost, was reestablished, albeit that the control of identity had changed hands and the impetus was clearly more financial than artistic.

A CRISIS OF IDENTITY

Over the period in question, critics share the view that this change in ownership of the means of production had a distinct influence on the development of British theatre, but they vary as to the degree of effect which they are prepared to blame on the investors. James Agate seemed in 1926 to be more concerned about the loss of identity, complaining that, 'in our commercial theatre... you cannot be certain today of finding any particular type of entertainment at any particular theatre always of course with certain exceptions' (Agate 1926: 26–27). He cites Daly's, the Gaiety and the Winter Garden as 'remaining faithful to the musical comedy' but points out that a play-goer could expect to see anything from 'revue to Tchekov' in any of the main West End theatres. Cicely Hamilton, the feminist playwright who had worked for the Actresses Franchise League, characterised the tendency of the average London playhouse as having frequent changes to programme, indefinite policies, loss of distinctive character, generally no settled method of attracting the public and no definite policy in the choice of plays or actors. Hamilton disliked the fact that the theatres changed hands from backer to backer, losing the chance of being governed by a permanent authority, as well as losing a sense of tradition or character (Hamilton 1926). She was writing specifically about the Old Vic and the need for tradition and permanency, but nevertheless, her critique was shared by many others.

For Pick, however, the problem .originated in the fact that theatre managements were mounting productions which were more fitted to the nature of the late nineteenth- and early twentieth-century theatre, that in fact they refused to move away from tradition. The promotion of what he sees as an effectively archaic lifestyle and class system, which was fast becoming anachronistic, meant that costs rose not from the demands of the art itself but from the 'social rituals surrounding it' (Pick 1983: 97). Other critics and historians saw the economic constraints on the production of theatre as being the basis from which the history of twentieth-century British theatre was to develop. Findlater stressed that although after the Great War theatres went into the hands of 'unscrupulous profiteers and speculators', economic factors came into play as much as the aesthetic taste of the new owners. Costs went up by some 600 per cent, and rents rose by, at times, as much as 1,000 per cent, yet admission prices rarely rose by more than 50 per cent. After the Second World War there was little improvement in this economic situation:

> West End rents, unchecked by the government, have soared since 1939, and a powerful combine, linking production and distribution,

has entrenched itself without intervention from the state. Post-war social changes have brought new customers to the cheaper seats but they have whittled down the income of the middle-class playgoers and of the private patrons who kept the theatre arts alive between the wars.

(Findlater 1952: 15)

GOVERNMENT INTERVENTION: THE ENTERTAINMENT TAX, CEMA AND THE ARTS COUNCIL

The government did not intervene with financial aid for theatre until the 1940s, and governmental policies had a problematic effect on theatre production. There were a number of taxes which caused concern to theatre managements and again influenced the nature of what they perceived as financially viable productions. The key tax was the 1916 Entertainment Tax, primarily a wartime emergency, which meant that the government could make money from the run of a play, even if the production lost money for the management. In 1924 the tax, based on gross box-office receipts rather than profit, was abolished on all seats under the price of 1s 3d but this was more beneficial to the cinema than to the theatre. By 1942 the Entertainment Tax was being charged at 33.3 per cent. The amateur movement was virtually tax free, which could account for the ability of amateur production organisations to be more adventurous and experimental in their choice of plays and styles of production.

In 1934 the Old Vic was able to claim tax exemption on the basis that it was an institution founded on a non-profit-making basis, and 1942 saw the decision to give exemption to production companies who made no profit on what were seen as 'partly educational' productions, although by 1946 this exemption was based on the company concerned establishing partly educational policies. This change in governmental policy only really helped already established large production companies. Thus, under the auspices of a partly educational policy, sub-companies of the larger corporate owners and managements such as H. M. Tennent Ltd could produce financially risky plays. The production could be made financially viable by using already contracted 'star' performers to attract audiences who would not normally go to the theatre to see a play by a seemingly highbrow playwright, such as Bridie, Eliot, Priestley or Fry. As the production was backed by a management with a partly educational policy it would not be liable to Entertainment Tax, but because the management had star actors on their books, they could make the production attractive and therefore profitable. These profits could be transferred to another satellite company, owned by or closely connected to the original partly educational company. Thus, pre-Arts Council state intervention had advantages, but in the main only for production companies who were already in a profitable position.

Some financial aid was, however, given directly to theatre organisations before the formation of the Arts Council. When the theatres closed down, as part of the total blackout in 1939, many actors who were not conscripted into the army worked alongside other actors as part of the state-sponsored association ENSA, while some well-known producers, such as Basil Dean, took part in the organisation of ENSA events providing, among other things, entertainments for the troops (see Dean 1956).

The Pilgrim Trust originally gave a grant of £25,000 and alongside the wartime coalition government helped to initiate CEMA; Pilgrim Trust aid was withdrawn in 1942. In 1940 £50,000 was given by the government to match public funding of the arts (Davies 1987: 127). Sybil Thorndike and Lewis Casson, among others, were responsible for organising and performing in CEMA-backed touring productions which took account of the provinces rather than focusing on middle-class audiences in London (see Sprigge 1971). Davies proposes that CEMA 'played down' the normally rigid distinction which separated professionals from amateurs, organising factory concerts and giving, in 1940, financial help to the Old Vic, especially when it transferred to Burnley and formed a permanent repertory company in 1942. By 1942 CEMA were funding fourteen touring theatre companies, including some of those under the ENSA scheme, and had also become a totally government-controlled body (see Dellar 1989).

The development of CEMA is interesting in terms of the speed with which it moved from an organisation whose initial efforts and finances were directed toward the work of amateurs, as part of an 'arts for all' criterion. It began as 'a morale boosting exercise with a limited life expectancy... a definite vision of the importance of the arts for all ... encouraging arts activity in every village and town' (Hutchison 1982: 44). By the end of 1941 CEMA had, however, handed over any responsibility for amateur drama to the voluntary sector. By 1946, CEMA was transformed into the Arts Council under whose auspices 'a clear distinction between amateur and professional work' had been made (Pick 1980: 12). The emphasis of Arts Council funding policy showed little if any positive bias toward drama, as opposed to other types of theatre, such as opera.[3] Thus, even when the state did intervene in the production of theatre, it prioritised certain forms of performance in terms of what it was prepared to support in the name of national art. Although many critics and theorists felt this financial aid to be significant, it was not on a sufficient scale to combat the high cost of producing new plays in a commercially oriented theatre industry.

THE OTHER THEATRES

It is astonishing how few even of the West End theatre's biggest box office successes, apart from musicals, farces and thrillers were originally created by the West End managers. For instance, Noel Coward owed his first real success both as an actor and a playwright to the Everyman where *The Vortex* was produced after it had gone the rounds of the West End managers in vain. Emlyn Williams's first London production was given him by a Sunday society which afterwards persuaded a West End management to put on the play for a run. John Gielgud established himself as a West End star through the success of *Richard of Bordeaux*, originally produced on a Sunday night at the Arts. . . . I can only think of three playwrights of any note which the West End managements discovered for themselves during these years. They are A. A. Milne, Dodie Smith and Clemence Dane. . . . J. B. Priestley's early plays were given their first performances in West End theatres [although] he could only achieve this by backing them himself.

(Marshall 1948: 14–16)

The commercial theatres constituted the financial backbone of the British theatre industry during the first half of the twentieth century. However, Norman Marshall used the name of 'other theatres' to signify those theatres which existed largely outside the economics of the commercial theatre. Some of these 'other theatres' produced revues and musical shows, but many experimented with new writers using both the form of the 'well-made play', and new forms of drama such as the expressionist play. The major criticism of the West End programming policies was that they represented the tastes of the minority and in effect constituted a 'timid and reactionary commercial theatre' (ibid.). Despite what some viewed as the 'benevolent' monopoly on management and production in the West End, both Findlater and Marshall are clear that these 'other theatres' fed into the commercial theatre market, and to some extent constituted a 'trying out' ground for new plays and playwrights. For many it was the 'other theatres' which kept the British theatre alive, with their policies of trying out new plays, new writers and new performers. These 'other theatres' comprised subscription clubs, which produced Sunday night and sometimes Monday afternoon performances, and small independent theatres, whose seating capacity would just about enable the producers to cover costs. These organisations had been formed in 'self-defence against the standards of commercialism' (ibid.). Many of the play producing companies were private and functioned as subscription clubs on a non-profit-oriented basis. Thus they were able to forgo the powers of censorship dealt out by the Lord Chamberlain's office at the same time as being able to take risks in producing plays by unknown or commercially non-viable writers. Many theatre historians see the West End as having been dependent on these 'other theatres', especially during the inter-war years. Marshall even posits that this dependency was fully revealed in the narrowness of programming strategies of the West End theatre managements after the Second World War 'put an end to the activities of this other theatre' (ibid.).

Theatre producing societies and small private theatres blossomed during the inter-war period. In London these included the Stage Society, the Pioneer Players, the Three Hundred Club and the Venturers; the small independent theatres included the Embassy, the Everyman and the Gate. The ideological premise of this group of theatres was based on a desire to keep theatre fresh and new, to provide a platform for experiment and to combat the monopoly of the West End managements for whom a prospective play held no interest unless it was financially viable. To some extent the West End managements were only interested in a play if they smelled potential profit, if it could be marketed as 'another so-and-so', in other words, it had to have a similar feel to an already successful production. 'Freshness and originality were un-sellable qualities' (ibid.).

SUBSCRIPTION, CLUB AND INDEPENDENT THEATRES BEFORE THE GREAT WAR AND AFTER

Subscription, club and independent theatres were not new to the inter-war period. The production pattern of this system of non-commercial theatre had been used during the late Victorian and Edwardian eras by individuals who shared a similar ideological perception of the social and aesthetic function of theatre to the inter-war generation. The Pioneer Players provide us with a link here as it was formed in 1911 by Edith Craig, whose work was unquestionably influenced by early associations with the Actresses Franchise League, with a final season in 1919–1920. The company revived in 1925 for a production of Susan Glaspell's *The Verge*

(Dymkowski 1992: 221–234). Along with the Stage Society it was the only Edwardian theatre society to survive the First World War. Unable to find work in legitimate theatre Craig set out to produce plays

> dealing with all kinds of movements of interest at the moment. To assist social, political and other societies by providing them with plays as a means of raising funds; and to undertake when desired the organisation of performances for such Societies by professional or amateur players . . . and to produce plays which, although they may be outside the province of the commercial theatre, are sincere manifestations of the dramatic spirit.
>
> (ibid.)[4]

The early work of the Pioneer Players reflects the political interest of the suffragist movement. However, 'scattered among the Pioneer's repertoire of plays on the oppression of women in the home, workplace and brothel, were several showing generalised exploitation of labour by capital' (Holledge 1981: 133). The twelve-month subscription fee covered the cost of hiring venues such as the Kingsway, the Savoy or the Ambassadors, and paid for around four productions per year (ibid.: 128). After the war Craig produced numerous plays by foreign writers such as Yevreinov's *Theatre of the Soul* and *The Merry Death*, Paul Claud's *Tidings Brought to Mary*, as well as numerous others by new English writers, such as Gwen John's *The Luck of War*. Before the 1914–1918 war, half of the plays produced were written by women, but by 1921 less than a third (ibid.: 143). The company experienced financial problems brought about by the increase in rents for London theatres after the war, and when in 1920 Edith Craig's mother Ellen Terry – the celebrated nineteenth-century actress – went bankrupt, financial support was limited. The Pioneer Players, however, were instrumental in setting a pattern for other play producing societies which were to follow. Primarily their interest was in political theatre, that is theatre as a means of promoting through entertainment certain specific political ideologies. But as time went on their productions reflected a wider political concern, centred around a desire to widen the artistic sphere of theatre, experimenting with new writing, which might directly or indirectly reflect a specific political ideology. Within the context of theatre at the time, however, the desire to widen the repertoire of plays available to audiences was in itself a *political* act.

Edith Craig's group, along with other Sunday play producing societies, provided the opportunity for professional and amateur to work together. In addition, many of the professional performers might be working in both the commercial and the 'other theatres' at any one time, as 'many actors already playing in West End runs spent most of their spare time from October to May rehearsing for one Sunday night production after another' (Marshall 1948: 71). It was also quite common for writers to work in both commercial and non-commercial theatres; Miles Malleson, for example, was both a film and stage actor, and a writer whose work was produced by both commercial and independent theatres.

Just as many of the plays by new or foreign writers which were later picked up by West End production managements began their performance life in non-commercial theatres, so many of the performers in the 'Sunday Theatres' later went on to West End successes. Auriol Lee, for example, who became one of the most prolific women directors in the 1930s, started out as an actress and performed in the Pioneer Players' early production of Christopher St John's *The First Actress* (Dymkowski 1992: 229).

One of the most frequent criticisms of the Sunday societies, aimed in particular at the work of the Three Hundred Club, was that they seemed to be founded on the basis of 'deliberately choosing plays which were otherwise unlikely to be produced', and that this in itself went against a notion of theatre as a popular art.[5] This is an extraordinary criticism when considering the limited accessibility of the London commercial theatres, the real hunting grounds of the critics. Marshall contextualises this attitude when he points out that 'in the 1920s most of the lesser dramatic critics and theatrical journalists were openly hostile to any attempt to cater for the minority playgoer, and that any attempt by a minority group to cater for their own tastes ... by means of theatre clubs and Sunday societies was apt to be resented by the popular press as an insolent declaration of superiority' (Marshall 1948: 79). Criticisms in many cases seem to have been tainted by a narrow perspective of what theatre should be. Even during the inter-wars years it would have been difficult to deny the importance of the Sunday societies and subscription based theatre clubs, which provided the foundations for the production of new forms of theatre, and more specifically dramatic writing, in the early part of the twentieth century.

Some of the societies were formed by professionals; some, such as the Three Hundred Club, were set up by play-goers whose taste did not agree either with that of the Lord Chamberlain's office or that of the financially oriented theatre managements. By the beginning of the Second World War, the vast majority of these societies were no longer functioning, a lack of funding and difficulties with performers' touring and rehearsal schedules being among some of the problems which the societies were up against. Nevertheless, it was the general ideological basis of these theatres which inspired and fuelled a number of small independent theatres run on a belief system of art for the sake of art rather than profit, some of whose work continued after 1945.

The Everyman, Embassy, Arts theatre (see Trewin and Trewin 1986) and the Gate, to name a few, were all theatres with a comparatively small audience capacity, which produced short runs of new and experimental plays. Wages were low and sometimes non-existent; facilities were minimal. They received no state funding and many were defunct by the end of the inter-war period, either becoming cinemas (such as the Everyman at Hampstead) or simply not being used as theatres any longer. The Gate was founded by Peter Godfrey and his wife Molly Veness in 1925 in what was essentially a small attic in Floral Street. By 1927, the Gate had moved to Villiers Street, where the stage was only 18 inches high in order to allow height for setting. Productions were put on for short runs and, because wages were low, actors often had to leave for better paid assignments in larger theatres.

There was a certain amount of inverted snobbery on the part of some theatre critics to the work produced at the Gate and at other small theatres, but just as with the societies of the Edwardian era and 1920s, many of the productions were bought up by commercial theatres and many of the actors effectively used the little theatres as a training ground. Godfrey's interest was in expressionist drama, but this by no means ruled out the production of different dramatic styles. Productions of American expressionist dramas by Glaspell and O'Neill, under Godfrey, were followed by many later productions which transferred to the West End. Some plays, such as Margaret Rawlings's translation of Elsie Schauffler's *Parnell* and Lillian Hellman's *The Children's Hour*, produced under the management of Norman Marshall at the Gate, were originally banned by the Lord Chamberlain's office, and thus could not have been produced in the public West End theatres. Yet these 'private' productions transformed the plays into 'classics' which were later adapted into films. As with many of the other little or independent theatres, the taste of the management affected policy, but there appears to have been a general consensus that the job of these establishments was to keep theatre alive by refusing to pander to commercial dictates.

> The studio or art theatre exists to prevent dramatic art from being wiped out by the commercially minded. It is a movement to keep alight the torch of drama by performing neglected works. . . . The art producer is apt to have read illustrated books about the theatre . . . may also have worked as assistant stage manager in the

commercial theatre, and possibly have played small parts on tour. . . . Unlike ordinary theatre goers, the supporters of art theatres have dramatic convictions.

(Godfrey 1933: 160–170)

Godfrey's is a statement which holds true for both the Sunday societies and the small independent theatres as much as it does for the repertory movement, another part of the industry, begun before the First World War, which was more concerned with the art of theatre and the possibilities of theatre being made available to and representing audiences which did not necessarily belong to the ruling and upper-middle classes.

There are numerous publications on the development of the repertory movement in Britain and Ireland, but it is relevant to stress at this point that the repertory theatres established in the early years of the twentieth century produced another kind of 'other theatre'. To some extent they presented a less conventional side of the middle-class drama, but they were also 'experimental theatres, avant-garde and "independent" . . . meant also for an ordinary provincial public, who were good lovers of art but not too fond of novelty' (Pellizzi 1935: 132–133). Unlike many of their European equivalents, the repertory theatres were non-government funded and were often set up by wealthy theatre patrons – the Birmingham Repertory theatre, for example, was founded by Barry Jackson, who subsidised the theatre for some twenty years, reportedly losing around £100,000 in the process (Elsom 1971: 23). The repertory managements frequently promoted the production of plays by new writers, which had more interest to provincial audiences. Before the end of the First World War, for example, Annie Horniman's work at the Manchester Gaiety had encouraged a new breed of writers for whom it was important to write about the experience of the 'common man', albeit that they kept to the formula of the well-made play.

Between the two world wars approximately 150 provincial theatres closed down and for many of the repertory companies 'keeping alive meant struggling against economic obstacles and public indifference' (Marshall 1948: 50). Basil Dean's early career, before he went on to work in the West End, was spent at the Liverpool Repertory theatre, one of the two original repertory theatres to survive the financial and other pressures of the inter-war period. As with provincial theatres such as the Oxford Playhouse, there was an interest among the repertory theatres in trying out foreign plays, classical pieces, new plays by new playwrights, providing work for young actors, encouraging experimentation in design and so on. The repertory and small provincial theatres often produced plays which were bought up by commercial London managements, and for some these London transfers were the basis of their economic survival. This in turn led to the criticism that because they were often relying on West End transfers, productions became dependent on West End tastes: the desire to experiment ultimately had to give way to financial constraints.

The sociological and to an extent the aesthetic position and function of the repertory theatres changed after the Second World War, and the building of new municipal arts centres provided newer state-funded venues for drama.

TYPES OF DRAMA

It is not only the structure of the theatre system which defined what was and what was not produced from the end of the First World War up to the early 1960s, but also the style and content of the plays. James Agate's statement that 'the drama is an aesthetic phenomenon, the theatre is an economic proposition' exemplifies the distance which was increased by the First World War theatre profiteers, between theatre as entertainment and theatre as the realisation of dramatic texts which were seen to appeal to an audience more concerned with narrative and meaning than glamour (Agate 1926: 20). Hudson's observation that at the 'end of the Twenties there were no great kinds of play and no grand manner of acting' and that the 'kind of play most popular during the Thirties was the domestic adramatic play . . . belonging to the lap-dog class' is indicative of what seems to have been a longing for both a style of presentation and dramatic content which belonged to the late nineteenth century (Hudson 1946: 59). It also shows an unwillingness on the part of the critic to positively evaluate the work which was going on in non-commercial theatres, as well as a refusal to come to terms with the fact that theatre was moving toward the economic structures of an industry. That the 'adramatic domestic play' (incidentally, usually authored by a woman or male/female team) was popular was somehow seen as a sign of its lack of aesthetic worth, and a signifier that the drama was in a state of disintegration.

The form of the well-made play changed very little during the inter-war period, but what often changed were the writers and the areas on which narratives were focused. Pellizzi's view was that 'since the war young writers [showed] signs of more direct contact with the continental and American literature, of feeling foreign influences more strongly' –

literary experiment in form rarely found success within commercial theatre (Pellizzi 1935: 145–158). On the London stage during the 1920s and 1930s there was a prevalence of historical or chronicle dramas, numerous farces and thrillers, detective plays and professional dramas about working people presented in their work environments. Although the upper and middle classes still prevailed as the dramatic and narrative centres of the drama, there was a move, adumbrated by the pre-First World War writers, towards foregrounding the lower-middle classes, those who inhabited the new suburbs, the new white collar workers and their families. The prevailing style was that of realism, the setting was very often the drawing room, the front parlour or, in the case of historical dramas, the Great Hall or Chamberlain's office.

Pellizzi asserted that the changes in dramatic writing which, it would seem, had been indicated in the period immediately preceding the First World War, gave way to a 'middle ground of entertaining but fairly uncritical middle-class oriented dramas'. For him the speed of change was halted by, and never recovered from, the social and economic consequences of the war:

> England at the dawn of the century showed signs of setting forth on these new ways confusedly; her intellectuals and artists, the advance guards of history, had reached a seriousness and serenity which seemed to announce and anticipate the birth of a new form of post-middle-class aristocracy and the wealth and power which the nations enjoyed guaranteed that the new developments would have unfolded themselves in an atmosphere of relative calm.... [However] the last phase of tragic and despairing realism, fantastic or intimate, which carries to its close the tradition of polemic middle-class drama and pushes the impulse of social realism of 'social remorse' to its extremes continues up to the present day.
>
> (ibid.: 143–157)

His view was that audiences who went to see 'well-made plays' in the commercial theatres, did so out of curiosity, a desire to experience insight into the lives of people with whom they, in reality, had little contact. He proposed that audiences endured the dramas rather than learnt from them. Although to an extent there appears to be a certain truth in his perception, it again relegates theatre history to an analysis of the production and reception of dramatic texts produced by commercial theatres, and fails to acknowledge that theatre may have a different function from one period to another. Jon Clark gives the best summary of the way in which drama from the period has been viewed:

British 'naturalistic' theatre in the first half of the twentieth century has often been criticised as sentimental, thematically dated and lacking in creativity. The plays of Galsworthy, Maugham, Priestley, Barrie and Coward are quoted in evidence to support such a dismissive evaluation: the works of Shaw (and in the 'poetic drama' the works of Eliot and Yeats) are seen as the exception that proves the rule. What is immediately striking about such assessments is that they are based on highly restricted concepts of literature and theatre, and also a narrow textual analysis approach to literary and cultural criticism.

(Clark, Heinemann et al.: 1970: 219)

During the inter-war period specifically, there were numerous critics who drew a line of distinction between the playwright, as someone who worked with the needs of the audience in mind, and the dramatist, who was inevitably a poet, a linguistic craftsman. One would therefore place Noel Coward or even Ben Travers in the first category and Eliot or Fry in the second. These distinctions are seemingly based on the refusal to define a dramatic text within the context of both theatre and the social economy. It is also interesting to note that much drama at this time was written with the amateur market in mind; the amateur movement became almost an institution, which reflected the 'growing public interest in drama as a means of entertainment and performance for pleasure without monetary reward' (G. Taylor 1976: 9).

The British Drama League (BDL) was founded by Geoffrey Whitworth in 1919 to promote and organise the 'encouragement of the art of the theatre, both for its own sake and as a means of intelligent recreation among all classes of the community' (Davies 1987: 81). The BDL also organised annual summer schools for amateurs interested in acting, producing and writing for the theatre. By the mid-1920s there were some 360 affiliated societies and the BDL was publishing its own journal and building up a collection of theatre books for use by its members. During the inter-war period guest professionals were invited to lecture, direct and so on. The most frequent criticism, as put forward by Marshall among others, of the amateur movement, is that it tended to follow West End trends, that members were not interested in theatre *per se*, but rather in the entertainment value of dressing up and performing in front of their friends and families. Even though, according to the BDL, by the late 1930s over five million people a year paid to see amateur performances, these figures have been interpreted in terms of the fact that there were so many amateur companies at this point that the audience at each production must have been very small. Despite the criticism of the amateur movement, it is clear that the *amateur* has a very distinct place in the history of 'alternatives' to the commercial theatre. The Maddermarket (Norwich), the Leeds Civic theatre and the Newcastle People's theatre, to name a few, were all theatres which began life in the hands of semi-professionals and amateurs and went on to break away from the dominant taste of the commercial theatres. The other area where the amateur movement can be seen to have contributed to a development in the variety of British theatre is in work which was carried out as part of the socialist and labour movement. There are numerous in-depth and detailed publications on and studies of the Workers Theatre Movement (WTM), whose productions often involved both amateurs and professionals (see Chambers 1989, Samuel et al. 1985 and Tuckett 1979). Many of these productions took place in non-theatre spaces and certainly provided, along with the influences of German and Russian agit-prop theatre, a foundation for the 'political theatre' movement in Britain after 1968.

Theatre work carried out by the WTM fed into and influenced small theatres. The Embassy, initially under the management of Ronald Adams, often encouraged artistic directors such as André Van Gyseghem to search for new plays which appealed to and recognised the importance of wider, less middle-class audiences. Van Gyseghem had been influenced by developments in Russian theatre, and his work with the WTM led him to promote the production of plays which looked at the position of the working classes within culture. He was also interested in new forms of drama as a possible solution to the quest for a theatre which could educate and entertain simultaneously (Gyseghem 1970: 209).

Once CEMA was transformed into the Arts Council, coupled with the fact that after the Second World War the rents for London theatres rose once more, there were fewer alternatives to the mainstream commercial theatre. It is worth noting here that plays by female playwrights were produced in all of the theatres indicated above; equally, there appear to have been significantly more women writing for the theatre in the twenty years immediately preceding the disintegration of the 'other theatres' and the establishment of the Arts Council than afterwards, although it should be taken into consideration that after the Second World War, there were fewer theatres producing plays generally.

WOMEN IN THEATRE – EDWARDIAN PIONEERS

Just as the women's suffrage movement came out of a general shift in political thinking, so the Actresses Franchise League (AFL) in many ways took the form of other similar small independent theatre organisations which were breaking away from the traditions of actor-manager-centred production. Very few of these theatre organisations saw themselves as having a specific political function. The AFL differed in that rather than just promoting 'new forms' of drama, their interest lay in the use of theatre and the use of the processes of theatre as a means of discoursing the issues which grew out of and gathered support for the suffragist cause; similarly, their work was specifically woman centred. The AFL, founded and run by women, is seen by a number of contemporary scholars as being the first feminist theatre in Britain, and although their work was before the period being examined in this book, it has an inherent and obvious connection. The AFL aligned itself with the already established suffragist cause and was begun in an atmosphere of great publicity in 1908, with advertising for membership aimed at theatre professionals, 'a neutral society working for Women's Suffrage . . . and assists all Suffrage Societies by professional services. Members of the Theatrical, Musical and Music Hall Professions are eligible for membership' (Gardner 1985: 10). Membership was made up of known and little known actresses, although Claire Hirshfield has suggested that because 'many of its earliest members enjoyed celebrity status and public esteem, the AFL was perhaps the most successful of all "professional" women's organisations in drawing popular attention and sympathy to the cause of female enfranchisement' (Hirshfield 1985: 129). According to one of the early members the 'league grew and grew until nearly every actress in the business joined' (Holledge 1981: 50–59). The headquarters were situated on the ground floor of the Adelphi theatre, and meetings were held once a week.

The AFL originally supported both the National Union of Women's Suffrage Societies (NUWSS) and the Women's Social and Political Union (WSPU) despite their different strategical approaches toward political change. Some actresses, however, left the league at an early stage because of political difference, for although the AFL supported the suffragist cause many members were not prepared to 'jeopardise their careers' through being associated with political militancy (ibid.). The actresses entertained at political meetings and trained non-professionals in the art of public speaking. The play department, set up and run by Inez Bensusan, was responsible for the requisitioning and production of purpose-made plays. These were toured at both traditional and non-traditional theatre venues, with production profits donated to relevant political organisations. Not all of their plays were written by women, and many of the productions were largely ignored by the press, except when they were full of star performers, such as the 1909 production, *A Pageant of Great Women*. Providing an endless stream of actresses who represented positive images of, among other things, exceptional women from history, the play was first produced at the Scala and then toured by the AFL. After this the play was performed by many other suffrage societies around the country (Holledge 1981: 69–75). The production was one of the key events responsible for spreading the work of the AFL into the East End of London.[6] By 1912 the AFL had become more brave in its affiliation with the suffrage movement, the plays became more complex, both in their characterisation and in the 'confrontation [of] the political issues which dominated the suffrage movement' (ibid.: 86).

By 1913 the AFL, although never cutting links entirely with the Women's Social and Political Union, put more energy into its affiliation with the National Union of Women's Suffrage Societies and their work in the East End, supporting the Men's League for Women's Suffrage. Around 1913 there was also a men's group for actors and dramatists, and the AFL began to focus on the position of its some 900 members within their own profession. In 1913, encouraged and organised by Inez Bensusan, the AFL set up an 'independent Women's Theatre Company', run, controlled and managed by women. The company produced two full-scale productions, but with the advent of the war the AFL turned its attention to entertainments for the troops. There were many cross-over points between the legitimate theatre, the commercial theatre and the AFL: some of the original writers and actresses turn up later in theatre history as writers used by the WTM and the Independent Labour Party theatre events or as writers, performers and directors working within the mainstream commercial theatre. The point here is that although the AFL is seen as the first feminist theatre, it was largely middle class and run on a similar basis to other independent theatre clubs – albeit with more fervent and focused dedication. A policy which demanded that women ran the company was innovative, but the project was fairly short lived. The work of the AFL has often been used as a springboard by feminist theatre historians, as a means of aligning current feminist practice with a historical past. This is convenient but doesn't take into consideration the events of the years between the end of the First World War and the feminist theatre which came out of the political unrest of the late 1960s.

WOMEN, FEMINISM AND THEATRE HISTORY

Within the area of women and theatre, if we are prepared to take this as a specific focus for research which exists both inside and outside the field of theatre studies, there are many areas which still need active research and analysis. There are, for example, great gaps within studies in the area of the history of performers and analyses of the history of the female performing body (Bassnett 1989: 107–112). Bassnett stresses that although the study of texts is often prioritised to the cost of any other area of study, it is still far too early in the development of the field to make assumptions about the non-existence of female playwrights in certain periods of history. Tracy Davis has also pointed out that many of the studies of women's theatre are based upon a feminist agenda (Davis 1989: 60), and it is important to note here that a great many studies of plays by women are framed by the question of whether the plays could be considered to be feminist or not.

It has become clear over the last decade or so that 'feminist' is too closed and geographically specific a term to apply to all cultures. A notion of *feminisms*, a multiplicity of identities, which have more to do with ways of thinking rather than any specific political struggle, would allow for a far less Anglo–American or even Eurocentric approach to the framing of analysis. Another factor is that many of those who have historicised women's contribution to the history and development of the dramatic text have done so by seemingly negating the existence of texts written by women in periods other than those which they happen to be focusing on themselves. For example, Sue Ellen Case quotes Nancy Cotton's study of women playwrights in England: during 'the period from 1660–1770, over sixty plays by women were produced on the London stage – more than from 1920–1980' (Case 1988: 39). In this particular case misleading information is used in order to justify a focus on a particular period of study. Here, the author justifies her examination by noting the number of performances of plays by women during this period by comparison to another. This kind of ill-informed justification should not be necessary and merely reflects a seemingly defensive position in terms of the importance of studying women's creative work in theatre. There is an inherent danger in this approach, as it often leads to a negation of much of the work it is trying to promote. Research on women playwrights, let alone performers, managers, directors and designers is, in real terms, only just beginning. It is important that we look at what was there, rather than trying to fit our findings into some preconceived notion of what it is that, for example, women ought to have been writing.

In a recent short study of women dramatists in Britain and Ireland between 1958 and 1968, Lib Taylor focuses on the work of Enid Bagnold and Agatha Christie, with a later mention of Iris Murdoch, Anne Jellicoe and Doris Lessing. She is critical of the ultimately conformist ideological stance inscribed within much of Christie's work and indirectly of Bagnold for the fact that her work 'was endorsed by the casting of established heavy-weight theatrical stars' (L. Taylor 1993: 13). Yet, within a commercial theatre system, productions with well-known performers were more likely to be successful, and whether one managed to secure contracts with 'stars' depended on which management company was mounting the production. What an analysis of Bagnold's career reveals is her class origin and, in turn, the fact that it was extremely difficult to create an economically viable playwriting career unless one belonged to the middle and ruling classes – or had one's play taken up by a wealthy production company. Taylor's agenda cautions us away from an analysis of the work of commercial and non-commercial female playwrights who are not included in the chapter. Obviously one of the limitations of the material used is already defined by the limit in required wordage and by the framework of the book in which the chapter is placed. Yet there is a clear bias which again involves assumptions about theatre or, rather, dramatic texts written by women. These assumptions are not dissimilar to those made by male theatre historians of the past. Thus women's work becomes re-marginalised by such suggestions as 'the history of women's theatre makes evident, when women dramatists have flourished, it is on the fringes rather than within the mainstream theatre. The political expediency of occupying a marginal position is not something that can be considered here' (ibid.: 18). Here, clear and rather obvious assumptions about women playwrights continue to be made.[7]

Taylor expands her argument by including Joan Littlewood's pioneering work at Stratford East and looks at the work of women playwrights whose plays were produced at the Royal Court. However although, as she says, both were theatres which worked in ideological opposition to the mainstream, it should be pointed out that certainly both were either financially dependent on the mainstream system, or on state subsidy in order to survive. The point is that if we use a closed or fixed notion of feminist as a starting point for analysis, or make fairly arbitrary or unclear disassociations between different types of theatre in order to justify an inclusion of women's creative theatre work in a history of theatre, we continue to defer their work to a marginal position and negate the possibility of re-discovering an historical continuum. Part of the problem is to do with a desire to create and be included in a canon, or to fit history into a theoretical framework. However, using this as the primary basis for historical categorising limits the depiction and analysis of history to the extent that it becomes a discipline used to verify or justify our own contemporary position. It is arguably just another way of *fixing* history.

During the period 1918–1962, plays written by women were produced in the commercial theatres, repertory theatres, club and subscription theatres, amateur theatres and as part of the work of politically focused theatre companies and groups. In some cases their work was seen as representing a real threat to the 'male hegemony' in theatre, with a number of critics, both in Britain and America, complaining about the *feminisation* of theatre.[8] Although as yet there are no extensive detailed studies of women's writing for political theatres in Britain during the period in question, there are a number of small studies which indicate the existence of either all-women groups, groups run by women or plays written by women specifically for the political theatre (see Merkin 1992).

The women playwrights whose work is surveyed in this book did not all share the same class origins, education or political ideology. Some wrote plays which were concerned with class, some about women's lives, some simply put their work on to the market in a desire to earn a living from their craft, regardless of their gender.

WOMEN WORKING IN THEATRE AFTER THE FIRST WORLD WAR: PLAYWRIGHTS, MANAGERS, ADMINISTRATORS AND DIRECTORS

Although many of the playwrights writing for the theatre of the period were not self-professed feminists, much of their work positioned perceptions of the private lives of women inside the public arena of the theatre, foregrounding the female experience in order to create the central narrative in their plays. A number of the plays received limited production runs, yet many of the writers were household names, writing serious and complex parts for actresses and creating a working wage from writing for the theatre. The evidence of these playwrights provides a strong counter-argument to Helen Keyssar's proposal that 'it was not until the last decade that playwrights in significant numbers became self-consciously concerned about the presence – or absence – of women as women on stage' (Keyssar 1984: 1–5). They also provide evidence that a creative culture which expressed and confirmed the idea that for women 'art is related to their condition as women' (ibid.) did not simply cease to exist after the vote was won. Many of the plays specifically deal with social change in relation to ideas of femininity and femaleness, exploring the transformations taking place in the social and cultural perceptions of womanhood.

Women working in theatre during the period with which we are dealing here worked within a transitional theatre system. Their ideas about the female condition filtered through into their work, in a social environment where the women's movement took on a different shape and form to that of the years immediately preceding the First World War. Very little research has been carried out in recent years on the non-political theatre of the years between the wars and up until the mid-1950s. From the point of view of theatre history, many of the female playwrights have been critically dismissed because the theatre of their era is thought to have been both middle class and lacking in either conceptual or ideological challenge. The general pattern of theatre history research negates their work; current ignorance about their contribution to British theatre is by no means entirely due to the false marginalising practices of recent feminist theatre historians. The framework for critique used by critics who were contemporary to the inter-war and post-Second World War period, however, does appear to be based on an overt recognition of and emphasis on the gender of the female playwrights in question. Equally, the form of the domestic comedy, frequently used by a number of these playwrights, was often seen as a *feminised* form in itself. Obviously, not all the plays written by women during the period were domestic, neither were they all comic. Although it is inadvisable to group their work as a whole, there are clear thematic obsessions at different junctures over the forty or so years under examination. Many inevitably promoted a questioning of both class and gender stereotypes, others did nothing to undermine these stereotypes. But to ignore their work, even if the ideological basis of that work is difficult to accept, is tantamount to writing *out* of history an important aspect of women's contribution to the development of the dramatic text.

The AFL, was the first mass effort of 'theatre women' to direct their energies towards a particular political end. However, in order to re-discover a history of women's theatre we must be careful not to take each discovery and place it completely out of context. The historical event of the AFL took place in a political and social climate that was in a state of flux, in the same way that many of the feminist theatres of the post-1968 period began life at a time of political ferment and unrest. The interesting question here is, what happens to the role of women in theatre, and specifically of women playwrights, when theatre has no one political agenda in mind and does not directly and consciously aim to reflect or promote social unrest or change? It might be relevant also to ask what happens to women working in theatre when there is no one mass political or literary movement with which to affiliate, associate or disassociate themselves.

Between 1918 and 1962 women's position within the power structures of theatre, especially the commercial theatre, did not change greatly; it was a system largely controlled by men, for men were at the centre of the power bases and at the centre of the decision-making processes in most cases. We should, however, take into account the number of women who were in secondary or tertiary positions of power, usually behind closed doors. The observation made by Kitty Black, who worked for H. M. Tennent Ltd, is relevant here:

> In the present climate of women's lib, it's quite surprising to look back and remember just how many successful women literary agents there were at that time. Margery Vosper, Joyce Weiner, Helen Gunner and Dorothea Fasset were all leading figures on the London scene, and Paris boasted Marguerite Scialtiel . . . as well as Denise Tual and Ninon Tallon. Kay Brown, Leah Salisbury, Monica McCall and Audrey Wood dominated the New York scene. Quite why females are so successful is probably hard to say – perhaps women are more temperamentally suited to dealing with private problems as well as literary dilemmas, with methodical minds to register details of contract and remember anniversaries and celebrations.

> (Black 1984: 219)

There is very little evidence to suggest that a woman literary agent is any more likely to show preference towards work written by women than her male counterpart. It is, however, interesting to note that even within the gender hierarchies of the mainstream commercial system, there was room for mobility from secretarial to management roles within the administrative areas of production. The implication here is that perhaps certain areas of the management and production process were seen as being feminine, for example dealing with customers, gate-keeping for the male boss and so on.

Prior to the 1914–1918 war a number of women had been instrumental in setting up the successful management of the early repertory theatres: Annie Horniman in Manchester, Lady Gregory in Dublin and Madge McIntosh in Liverpool are particular cases in point (see Pogson 1952; Gooddie 1990; Wyndham-Goldie 1935; Gregory 1972). Similarly, a number of women were instrumental in the establishment and running of small theatre companies which were effectively part of the circuit of independent or little theatres that thrived in London and elsewhere, especially between the wars.

Beatrice de Leon's work at the Q theatre in Kew, in London, was vital to the developmental shape of the London stage. She encouraged and taught young actors and new playwrights, as well as those who were already finding work in the London theatres. Many new plays opened at the Q theatre or ended their performance run there after a long run in the West End. She was known as being 'unsentimental, tough and honest' and in her time produced many plays, taking under her wing young performers, many of whom went on to later stardom. Because of the nature of the theatre system during her time at the Q theatre, her management skills required a great sense of adventure and willingness to take risks. Just as de Leon had originally been an actress, Lena Ashwell began her career as an actress and was integral to the formation of the British Drama League. While manager of the Kingsway theatre Ashwell was heavily involved with the work of the AFL and was responsible for organising entertainments for the troops during the First World War. After 1918 she continued to organise work for unemployed artists at the Century theatre, where she took over management in 1925, producing a number of new plays as well as her own adaptations of *Crime and Punishment* and *Dr Jekyll and Mr Hyde*. Described by many critics as an actress of great emotional power, she has been likened to both Annie Horniman and Lillian Baylis because of her active role in the development of the British theatre. Nancy Price was another actress turned manager who began her acting career in 1899 and played literally hundreds of roles, directing some eighty-seven plays during her lifetime. She founded the People's National theatre in 1930 through which she disseminated many of the ideas and influences of innovative European theatre practitioners and produced over fifty plays in seven years. During the late 1930s Price also founded the English School Theatre Movement, touring Shakespeare to working-class children, often using star actors willing to work for low wages. There still exist very few studies of the work carried out by these women, who through their desire to have some kind of control over the kind of theatre work with which they were involved, or through their desire to expand the repertoire of theatre in England, moved from the position of employee to that of employer.

The women directors whose work was either achieved inside mainstream commercial or outside political categories of theatre history, during the years in question, is also poorly documented. Irene Hentschel, for example, trained at RADA and joined the Lena Ashwell Players as actress and director after 1918. Her many West End productions include *Eden End* (1934), *Time and the Conways* (1937) and *Jeannie* (1940). She worked in both the mainstream commercial theatre and on the independent circuit, was known for her direction of classics and also worked at the Shakespeare Memorial theatre in Stratford-upon-Avon. Hentschel at one point identified the value of women as directors and producers, claiming that women had a more suitable psychological disposition to bring to the work, especially with regard to working with women (*Daily Express*, August 1937). Margaret Webster, another actress turned director, appeared on the stage as a young child performer in the famous production of *The Trojan Women* (1924) alongside Sybil Thorndike, and worked in both Ben Greet's and J. B. Fagan's companies. Productions of classics such as *Othello* (1943) starring Paul Robeson, which broke box-office records for a Shakespeare production on Broadway, made her reputation as a director. Both of Webster's autobiographies reflect, albeit in a very personalised and anecdotal manner, the depth and range of her prolific directing career and her strong desire to take theatre into new venues to audiences for whom theatre was ordinarily a luxury (see Webster 1969; 1972).

Another of the great unsung women directors of the age was Auriol Lee, who had worked for Edith Craig as an actress. She not only played an enormous number of stage roles, but was one of the most prolific directors of her time. Her skill as an actress and director was praised by many, including both Noel Coward and John Van Druten. Lee directed many West End hits during the 1920s and 1930s and was praised in particular for her productions of Van Druten's plays. Engaged as a director by Hitchcock at Elstree studios in 1932, Lee spent her later years in America, where she died in a car crash in 1941, by then an American citizen.

The memory of women such as Auriol Lee only just reaches us through scant mentions in critical histories or biographies. That they may not have been either feminist or left wing should not stop the process of re-placing them back into British theatre history (see Chapter 6). Equally, if re-defining and re-discovering a history of women in theatre is a primary aim, then we should question the validity of statements such as, 'The major assault on the male dominated stage of the day came from ... the AFL and not until the 1970s did the question of women's theatre surface once more' (Davies 1987: 77–78). Between 1918 and 1962 there was very little in the way of theatre made by women, about and for women from a specifically feminist-centred political standpoint, but there was a great deal of theatre, both facilitated and written by women. Just as the women's movement did not disappear but rather became dissipated during the years between the end of the First World War and the mid-1960s, so dramatic texts written by women displayed a multitude of ideologies and political positions, as well as being written with a variety of potential audiences in mind. Many of the texts reflect, although sometimes rather distantly, the vast social change which affected the lives of British people during the first half of the twentieth century.

SOCIAL CHANGE

Although the technological advances made in the early twentieth century arguably improved the quality of life among the lower classes, there was relatively little social mobility. The middle and upper classes still controlled the economy, were the owners of the means of production and still dominated the high status professions. In the years immediately preceding the First World War, three-quarters of all those in employment worked in the manual trades (Mowat 1984: 202). Although there was a significant increase in the number of white collar workers after the war, the education system, which did little to close the class gap, limited possibilities of social mobility until the Butler Education Act of 1944. Mowat describes the education ladder as being narrow during the first four decades of the twentieth century, and although the increase in the number of universities, following the setting up of the University Grants Committee in 1911, made a significant difference, the gap between rich and poor was still immense and the possibility of closing that gap in real terms fairly low. The new road systems, bus services and the improvement in public services in general increased the speed with which the gap between the 'haves and the have nots' could be geographically closed. Yet poverty and hardship, unemployment and a lack of prospects were the experience of the masses during the 1920s and 1930s in Britain. Economically the 'roaring twenties', as a description of an era, had relevance to only a few in the more privileged sectors of society. For most, Britain in the 1920s signified poverty, depression and a sense of frustration at having fought a war for nothing. The decade saw the General Strike in 1926 and hunger marches in Britain, so the growth of European fascism in the 1930s came about in a general atmosphere of economic depression.

During the 1930s, in particular, the north/south divide, in terms of levels of wealth, was stronger than ever and differed very little from the nineteenth century. In Glasgow, for example, at any one time, as many as half of the population could be unemployed. Ostensibly, there were, 'four Englands... old England – the southern counties with their rich middle- and upper-class families... the industrial north, with its coal tips and silent blast furnaces... the so-called twentieth-century England – the home counties with their new housing estates and suburban villas... and then there was the Britain on the dole, geographically situated in much the same place as in the nineteenth century in the north, industrial Scotland,

South Wales and parts of north Wales' (Mowat 1984: 480–485). There was great social discontent over much of the country. Yet, after the Second World War, the landslide Labour victory of 1945 and the setting up of the Welfare State, which many thought would alleviate this sense of discontent, met with its first generation of disillusioned critics by the mid-1950s, for whom the social and economic changes had not happened quickly enough, nor in a great enough number.

Despite the gloom which prevailed after the First World War, the inter-war years saw the emergence of a new 'spirit' in literature and the arts, although as Noreen Branson points out, the impact of literary work which reflected a dissenting point of view on the events and consequences of the First World War was not generally felt until the late 1920s (Branson 1975: 240). The new social sciences gained ground and credibility: 'psychology was destroying reason as a guide to conduct and the physicists, certainty in the order of the Universe' (ibid.: 202). Einstein's Theory of Relativity in 1919 came into existence alongside new and adventurous attitudes towards architecture, epitomised by the modernist Le Corbusier. The opening of Tutankhamun's tomb in 1923 created a fervent mass interest in archaeology and anthropology. The British Broadcasting Corporation began regular broadcasting in 1922 and although for many years radio drama was undeveloped most of the 'entertainment industry. . . looked on the BBC as a threat to their prosperity'. The theatre managers believed that listening to radio at home could mean a drop in box-office returns, so they banned live broadcast from theatres (ibid.: 236).

Housing conditions had greatly improved in terms of standards of housing. Building programmes set in motion before the First World War, which included projects such as Welwyn Garden City, provided new housing but generally benefited the higher strata of the working classes and the lower-middle classes for whom home-making became almost a new hobby. With each household struggling to keep up with the new home trends, the expansion in the furniture trade catered for the boom in home furnishings; three-piece suites and dining-room sets were the new status symbols which could be bought via hire purchase (see Branson and Heinemann 1971).

By 1931 home life was revolutionised by the fact that one in three families owned a wireless set. Although church attendance was fast dwindling, the BBC broadcast religious programmes on Sundays and popularised traditionally inaccessible classical music, and although there was an initial ban on broadcasting sports commentaries, it was broken by the BBC by 1927. Competition for the highest sales of newspapers, which much like the theatre were run on a monopoly basis by a minority group, reached an all-time high in the 1930s; by 1939 most families subscribed to some kind of morning paper. Communications in general had advanced unimaginably since the end of the Great War. There was an emphasis on organised leisure time for industrial and white collar workers, for whom the arts and social sciences became more accessible through the establishment of the BBC and the new publishing houses such as Penguin Books in 1935 and, from the 'left', Victor Gollancz and the Left Book Club. The late1930s saw the beginnings of the boom in women's magazines, with *Woman* being published in 1937. Leisure became a mass market fed by new technologies. Family leisure became more institutionalised and, especially in the 1930s, moved toward outside activities such as cycling and motoring, with a proliferation of cycling clubs. By 1931 there were some 2,000,000 motor vehicles on the road of which 1,000,000 were private cars, 600,000 motorcycles, 350,000 commercial vans and lorries and 85,000 buses. Yet some have argued that, overall, large businesses 'dominated and exploited entertainment and leisure, taking advantage of people's spare time and money... the commercialisation of leisure was making ordinary people more passive in their enjoyment, receiving... culture rather than making their own' (Branson and Heinemann 1971: 240–253).

CINEMA

Perhaps the most important aspect of the new mass media culture for a theatre historian is the growth of cinema which, 'rather than religion', fast came to be seen by many as 'the heart of a heartless world, the opium of the people.' Cinema had been in its infancy before 1914 but, just as with the motor trade and aviation, by the time the war had ended technological improvements meant that it became possible for cinema to be an industry in its own right. American film companies, who carried on producing films during the war, were able to buy British theatres and music halls and convert them, imposing block bookings on other theatres as a condition for allowing them to hire the most popular American films (Branson 1975: 229). Metro Goldwyn Mayer, for example, bought London's Tivoli and the Old Empire in 1919, and the Leicester Square in 1921, which they reopened in 1928 as a grand cinema (Pick 1983: 111–117). Before the advent of 'talkies', in the closing years of the 1920s, American films such as *Robin Hood* in 1922 and *The Hunchback of Notre Dame* in 1923 were both costly and impressive, and comparable in style to the great Victorian theatre spectacles. British films were unprofitable and Hollywood dominated the British screens, setting trends for fashion, promoting a star system and providing some kind of an escape from the depression. The Cinematograph Films Act in 1927 represented an attempt by the government to intervene in the rapid and almost total influx of American films, by forcing distributors to take a percentage of British films, yet Heinemann argues that it was the: 'American domination of the screen dream world which indirectly helped to weaken respect for the old British ruling class values of titles, hereditary wealth, Oxford accents and public school manners among the working classes' (Branson and Heinemann 1971: 253).

It was the cinema more than any other cultural development which most threatened theatre. As a new form of leisure it cut across class barriers, for everyone went to the cinema, largely seeing the same films; 'as a leisure activity the cinema superseded the music hall and competed not unsuccessfully with pub, church and political meeting' (Branson 1975: 229). By 1929 there were some 3,300 cinemas in Britain, under the ownership of Gaumont and British International, the two controlling chains until the establishment of Odeon in 1933. By the late 1930s some twenty million British people attended the cinema weekly, with an estimated 25 per cent going twice or more each week. The programmes would often change twice weekly and might include cartoons and news-reels. The popularity of cinema as a form of entertainment worried theatre managements, but provided a new avenue of expression for both male and female playwrights, and more lucrative possibilities of work for actors and actresses (see Francke 1994). The cinema industry took, absorbed and exploited the financial benefits of the star system, feeding on popular stage successes by making them into films for mass distribu-tion. It could be argued that the advent of cinema depleted theatre audiences, but it must also be taken into account that cinema reached a far wider and less middle-class audience than either the commercial or the 'other theatres' of the years between 1918 and 1962, as did television, which began to replace the cinema as a form of mass entertainment by the late 1950s. Many critics and theorists were already talking of the theatre as being in a state of crisis well before the growth in mass popularity of cinema.

CONCLUSION

In conclusion, theatre in Britain between 1918 and the early 1960s appeared in many different forms. The most significant difference, both in terms of economics and aesthetics, was between the commercial theatre – whose primary objective was to make money – and the 'other theatre' –

for whom the primary concern was the development and maintenance of theatre, and especially the drama, as an art form. Although on the surface the differences are immense, in reality each type of theatre was to a large extent dependent on the other. Equally, productions of plays by women were spread over the range of theatres. Commercial theatres had become popular venues of entertainment during the 1914–1918 war, at which time speculators had taken over management, much to the angst of those who believed the function of theatre to be aesthetic or intellectual. After the First World War, few new theatres were built, and those which remained by the beginning of the Second World War were owned or managed by an elite social group who had control over what was produced. The club, 'little' and subscription theatres, with their ideology of theatre for theatre's sake, grew in number during the inter-war years and provided venues for new or foreign playwrights' work. They survived because of the public interest of a minority and because many productions were bought up by West End managements and transferred into the commercial theatre. Many of these theatres and play producing societies had, however, disappeared by the end of the Second World War. Although the amateur movement grew during the inter-war period, it generally fed very little back into the professional theatre, except arguably through the work of the Workers Theatre Movement.

From early on in the period under discussion, many thought there was a crisis in the theatre. For some, it was due to the monopoly of control being in the hands of a small group; for others it was due to what they saw as the impoverished and defunct nature of the 'naturalist' and 'realist' dramatic form. For yet others, the theatre was in a state of crisis because of a lack of organisation; again, partly due to the hegemony of control, but also because theatre was not being seen as a national asset which needed nurturing and support from the state. To all intents and purposes this support did arrive in the form of the Arts Council, whose original objective was to maintain 'the highest possible standard in the arts', but by the end of the period in question it became clear that this support was financially inadequate. Arts Council policies had not created opportunities in which independent theatres could continue to flourish. With fewer theatre buildings after the Second World War and production costs soaring, the 'other theatre' was unable to thrive, without state support. Touring companies had fewer venues to play and by the mid-1950s many theatres were given over to revues or revivals.

Until the establishment of the Royal Court in the mid-1950s, there was no government-subsidised venue or company which worked specifically with new playwrights. Peter Hall took over the Shakespeare Memorial theatre in 1959 with an ensemble company, and the National theatre opened its first season at the Old Vic in 1963, representing the first realisations of the much desired national companies (Elsom 1976: 160–163). Critics and practitioners such as Marshall foresaw the danger, however, of the transformation of state aid into state control of theatre, a fear which has been confirmed in the eyes of a number of recent critics of the Arts Council.

Social and economic changes during the period under discussion were immense. The Labour party had its first government, women finally received the full franchise in 1928, the education system was developed in such a way as to recognise the need for state-funded continuing education for the young and the Welfare State was introduced. The nation experienced mass unemployment, a second world war, the tremendous acceleration of communications systems and the social and psychological impact of previously unimaginable new inventions such as the atom bomb. The cinema became the new form of mass entertainment and, by the early 1960s, television was beginning to bring entertainment back into the home.

By the mid-1960s theatre no longer had the same social function as it had in the early part of the century and, for a multitude of reasons, as early as 1947 it was feared by many that the 'race of English dramatists may soon become almost extinct' (Marshall 1948: 235). Seen as a whole, theatre as a social and economic phenomenon during the years in question was made up of the two seeming polarities of the legitimate theatre and the entertainment industry. The dramatic text more often found its home in the former. However, even within the legitimate theatre there were vast differences between venues, audience size and social group, styles of presentation and so on. The entertainment industry, characterised by the large and expensive revue shows and those of such 'theatre men' as C. B. Cochran, had much in common with the commercial side of the legitimate theatre. Both theatres were part of the same economic and social system. The situation was perhaps best summed up by Philip Godfrey:

> The nearest approach to a working generalisation of the theatre seems to be to regard it as a sort of Siamese twins of markedly different personalities, but dependent on the same bloodstream. Our theatre twins, however, differ from their Siamese originals in size as well as in character. The small one, at his best, is thoughtfully serious and creatively comic; the big one, at his worst, is sentimental, pornographic, cheaply musical . . . and commercially

minded ... it is rare for both of them to flourish at the same time ... neither is very strong; both suffer from frequent collapse ... their dissimilarities are most striking on the side of each which is farthest from their point of junction; where they merge (and they are joined by a very large area) their differences disappear.

(Godfrey 1933: 171)

4

TO WORK OR NOT TO WORK

Representations of working women

The majority of plays written by women between 1918 and 1962 focused on the lives and concerns of middle-class women, and yet issues around work and the division of labour, both in terms of class and gender, prevail in a great many of the texts. The most predominant thematic focus is on the relationship between work and the family. Interestingly, the working mother becomes almost a standard narrative feature in plays written by women, especially during the inter-war years, at a point where discourse and public debate around the status of women as employees was at its height. The nature and status of work is class differentiated but there is an assertion of the inevitable connection between the problems which arise from the incongruities of the relationship of work to national duty and family, and notions of femininity and self-fulfilment.

> But still, in 1934, with the best intentions in the world, public authorities dismiss married women employees upon marriage; factories exclude them from special processes; unequal pay is given for equal work. Still in the sacred names of motherhood and chivalry, women are obstructed in their attempt to earn a living wage; and still, because of their lower pay, they undercut men, lower wage rates, and act as unwilling black-legs throughout industry.
>
> (Holtby 1934: 82)

The First World War provided an opportunity for women of all classes to move into the public sector and take on jobs, many of which had been left vacant by men conscripted into the army. Many have argued that after the 1914–1918 war it was only, in reality, women from the middle classes who could capitalise on the opening up of work opportunities for women. For working-class women the lack of opportunities in new areas of employment was more significant. Women who had worked in the munitions factories during the war, given the accolade of being called heroines or 'our gallant girls', were dismissed within weeks of the war ending and female unemployment reached a high level during 1918 and 1919. One of the problems was that the government considered working in 'service' as an appropriate vocation for working-class women, so much so that women were not given out-of-work pay if they refused to take work in 'domestic service' (see Beddoe 1989: 51).

Whether or not a woman should work, what work she should be allowed to do and when, continued to be issues which concerned both men and women of the period under discussion. The cultural and social ideology which produced such laws as the Marriage Bar, in all of its variations, continued to connect women's perceived roles within the family and home to questions around the nature of the work which they should be permitted or expected to undertake. Many women playwrights concerned themselves with representations of and discourses around the 'real' issues faced by working middle-class women in their plays.

MOTHERHOOD, MARRIAGE AND BUSINESS

The characteristic feminine dilemma of to-day is usually sum-marised under the heading 'Career and Family'. The struggle for the right to work is no longer directed against external obstacles; no longer is there the same hostile public opinion to overcome. . . . To-day the conflict has become 'internalised' and continues as a psychological problem which may assume many different varia-tions and shades; and just because there is no longer an absolute 'either – or' to be decided on at the beginning of adult life, the pull in two directions goes on practically throughout a woman's life.

(Myrdal and Klein 1956: 137)

For women of all classes the inter-war years in particular were charac-terised by enormous pressures to choose between work and the family, and even after the Second World War these pressures continued, although, as Myrdal and Klein suggest, they had by this point become internalised. It is the internalisation and practical reality of these pressures which Sylvia Rayman foregrounds in *Women of Twilight* (1951), her hit play which focuses on the private lives of single mothers forced to work in order to support themselves and their children (Rayman 1951; see Chapter 5). The play presents a conscious critique of the way in which privileged women, and in turn society, benefit from and take advantage of this socially invisible class of women for whom, because of a lack of public support systems, there is often no choice but to work and bring up their offspring.

During the early 1920s and until the early 1930s there are a number of plays where the plot centres around the problems raised for lower-middle and middle-class women, who, having lost their husbands or fathers in the Great War, are forced into the position of having to work for a living. Dramatic focus on the lives and experiences of these women could be seen as an active strategy to subvert the assumption of women's 'natural' financial dependence on men. In Fryn Tennyson-Jesse's *The Pelican* (Tennyson-Jesse and Harwood 1926), which ran in London between October 1924 and May 1925, Wanda pretends that her son has been fathered by a friend rather than her husband. Her attempt to escape the stronghold of her husband's stultifying upper-middle-class family back-fires when they take her to court for adultery. The family wins the case through Wanda's own admissions during the court hearing. However, Wanda returns to the family home and tells her husband the truth, offering him the child to bring up as his own, stating that she will have nothing to do with the family or the child's upbringing:

WANDA: Oh – you fools! Do you think I *want* you to believe me? Do you think I want you to take him? My child! The only thing I've got left? To keep him here, where I shall never see him – here in this house of bitterness and godforsaken respectability, where I've spent the most miserable years of my life...all the unkindness, all the hatred!... The life you lead, the thoughts you think – I can't stick them at any price. (*To Lady Heriot.*) You're quite right, I *shouldn't* have married Marcus.... But I can't decide for *him* – the boy... he may be different when he grows up. He may like the things you like – he'd have lost everything – and it would be my fault.

(ibid.: 28–29)

The first act presents the audience with a critique of a specific class ideology around both family and a woman's rightful position within it, and draws to a close as Wanda leaves for a life of economic and social uncertainty, taking her child with her: the family will not be burdened with a child when they can't be certain that it is of their blood.

During the second and third acts, the action is projected from the immediate post-war year of 1919, of the first act, to the year 1936. Wanda's status as both a businesswoman and a mother and the inter-dependence of these two roles, both on an emotional and on an economic level, are the key factors in determining the progression of her actions and the plot in general. Wanda's employer, Paul Lauzin, falls in love with her, but for Wanda her role as businesswoman and mother over-rides any romantic desires. As soon as Paul tells her of his amorous intentions, and speaks of her as a prospective lover rather than a female employee, she responds by telling him how valuable her working years have been to her:

PAUL: I hate to think of these years.

WANDA: I don't. The thing I'm most glad about is that I've made good on my own – that you took me for what you thought I could do. . . . You didn't take me because of my looks . . .

PAUL: . . . I thought your appearance would help – it was an asset.

WANDA: Oh, well, I don't mind that. I don't mind my looks such as they are, being *business*. I only don't want them to be *pleasure*. . . . Is it courage? I had something – perhaps just obstinacy – something that wouldn't let me fail, that made me keep on even when I was down and out.

(ibid.: 42–43)

Wanda is able to use both the language of a 'feminine' woman and that of the businesswoman; she moves with ease from the everyday to using the language of commerce when talking to Paul:

WANDA: . . . They've really got something to sell.

PAUL: Something worth buying?

WANDA: I think so, I can show you the figures . . . I've got their working costs and their selling prices, and there's the balance sheet – of sorts . . . I don't know what their assets are really worth. . . . The valuable thing is the patent. . . . Oh I went to the bank and saw the manager. . . . They'd find 25 per cent on mortgage, if there were good people behind it.

PAUL: . . . As I listen to you now, the very words 'per cent' seem full of romance.

WANDA: *They are.* Who knows better than I? If you'd ever made your living, as I have, from day to day, you'd know just how romantic money is. Why it's the world's great daily adventure! Paul! you're not going to be silly about me – to try and stop me from working, are you? . . . It's work that brought us together – it's been our common interest. And it's part of me – I don't want to stop being myself just because I'm married to you.

PAUL: No fear of that!

WANDA: That's the mistake everyone makes – wanting people to be something else – afterwards.

(ibid.: 46–47)

Having spent almost two decades working to support herself and her son Robin, Wanda's work has become another means, apart from 'family', through which she can attain self-fulfilment and pride. The possibility of re-marriage comes relatively late in life, coinciding with the point at which her son is 'becoming a man', planning a career and no longer having the same needs of his mother. Wanda's choice of marriage to Paul is based on her feeling that this will be something for her, a marriage immediately complemented by her love of business. The traditional twist in the closing moments of the play arguably does much to undermine the narrative development of the heroine as a self-determined businesswoman, mother and a woman with her own needs and desires. Here, Wanda makes the decision to accept her ex-husband's offer of a convenient re-marriage in order to legitimise their son, who wishes to join his father's army regiment and cannot do so unless he has an 'official father'.

Ultimately, then, romance and self-fulfilment through her work are sacrificed because of the demands which result from her role as mother, within a fixed social structure regulated by the legitimate upper-middle-class family and, in turn, predominant within theatre and, it would seem, the social structure itself. Despite this fact, it could be argued that Tennyson-Jesse, by locating it in the public arena of the theatre, is promoting the idea that women can be emotionally, but more importantly perhaps, economically independent. This is certainly the case right up until the last few moments of the play. There is no 'happy' ending for the heroine, who in choosing to support a family structure which outlaws her individuality as a 'spirited' businesswoman, takes the negative view of herself and her own life as being one which is 'over'. That is to say, she chooses to sacrifice her own self-designed future in order to service her son's needs and those pertinent to the maintenance of his father's social position. The role of mother ultimately undermines individual choice within a social structure which has fixed notions of social position and behaviour. Even though he is his father's real son, Robin has no legitimacy because of a divorce granted on effectively false grounds. Thus the heroine, as mother, gives in to, but does not necessarily condone, a social system which does not cater for her needs as a woman.

Aimée and Philip Stuart's *Sixteen,* (Stuart and Stuart 1934), first produced at the Embassy and then transferring to the Criterion in 1934, provided London audiences with another heroine who has to work in order to maintain stability within her fatherless family unit. Jennifer Lawrence works in the fashion business in order to support her mother and two children. Her work means that family life has to come second to business trips abroad. Although much of the play focuses on her relationship with her daughter – whom the family doctor has diagnosed as having a 'mother fixation' – one of the most important narrative devices is the presentation of the dilemma of Jennifer's choice between continuing to work at the pace to which she has become accustomed, or marrying someone who is willing and able to provide for her and her family, in which case she will both cease having a career and alienate her daughter. Her decisions are based primarily on serving the welfare needs of her family. However, the discussions around marriage between herself and her suitor, are interesting because they embody the needs felt by many middle-class women of the time, as well as the opinions of many of those who were against women working after marriage:

> JENNIFER: I can't of course.
>
> SIR JOHN: (*Who is prepared to argue, but not to give in.*) Why not?
>
> JENNIFER: The best I can think of is that I'm going back to work to-morrow morning at nine . . . I was going to talk to you about that. Even when we do marry, I can't give up my job. It's out of the question. We should be entirely dependent on you . . . all of us . . . surely you understand . . .
>
> SIR JOHN: . . . (*Earnestly.*) Don't let's have any false sentiment about money. I can keep you fully employed looking after my interests. You'll earn as much at that as you do at your dressmaking.
>
> JENNIFER: It's not the same. You must see my side of it.
>
> SIR JOHN: I do. I'm not going to allow it. From an economic point of view mine's a sound proposition. I'm a going concern. I'm understaffed. . . . If you can truthfully tell me you enjoy your present job so much you'd hate giving it up, that's an argument . . .
>
> JENNIFER: No, I don't. But I'd hate to lose my independence.
>
> SIR JOHN: You're not independent. You're a slave to your employers, a slave to your customers, a slave to conditions. You're not the type for independence. You're essentially a womanly woman, cut out to get your own way by guile.
>
> (ibid.: 549–550)

Ultimately it is Jennifer's relationship with her eldest daughter, Irene, which makes her hesitate in taking up the offer of marriage. Irene tells her grandmother in the opening moments of the first act:

> IRENE: . . . Instead of going for my year in the convent in Paris, I want to go as an apprentice to Bouchonner's or some other good

dressmaking firm. Then I might be able to take mother's place
when she needs a rest. . . . I'm sixteen today. . . . If council school
girls can get work at fourteen why can't I at sixteen?

(ibid.: 483)

Irene has been brought up to see hard work as the *embodiment* of feminine
character. She prides herself in the fact that her mother has continued to
work and does not see that emulating her mother would invite accusations of 'unwomanliness'. However, when the doctor tells her in the final
act that she must put her feelings away in order to 'grow up', his thoughts
could be seen as representing a whole social ethos which was designed to
rationalise keeping women out of the job market once they were
married, adhering to the notion that women should only work when
they have to, rather than because they either want to or have some
philosophical need to.

THE 'WOMANLY WOMAN' AND WORK

While there are a number of permissive variants of the feminine role
for women of college age they all have a common core of attributes
defining the proper attitudes to men, family, work, love, etc., and a
set of personality traits often described . . . as 'not as dominant, or
aggressive as men' or 'more emotional, sympathetic'.

The other and more recent role is, in a sense, no *sex* role at all,
because it partly obliterates the differentiation in sex. It demands of
the woman much the same virtues, patterns of behaviour, and
attitude that it does of the men of a corresponding age . . .

Both roles are present in the social environment of these women
throughout their lives, though, as the precise content of each sex
role varies with age, so does the nature of their clashes change from
one stage to another.

(Komarovsky 1946: 184–189)

Komarovsky's statement alludes to the consistent pressure on women of
the first half of the century to choose between a 'feminine' domestic life
and an 'unwomanly' public life. This consistently enforced polarisation
haunts many of the female protagonists in plays of the period written by
women. Namely, that to be economically independent is to align oneself
with the masculine world, despite the fact that often there was little
economic choice as to whether one worked or not.

G. B. Stern's *The Man Who Pays the Piper* was first performed in London
at the St Martin's theatre in 1931 with a cast which included Diana

Wynyard and the young Jessica Tandy. The play represents a serious attempt to analyse the relationship between gender and socio-economic power – perhaps because of this factor, the play only had a short run by comparison to the success of her earlier play, *The Matriarch.*[1] It is a three-act, 'well-made' play centred around seventeen years in the history of the middle-class Fairley family. The prologue is set in 1913 and begins with an argument between Daryll, the heroine, and her father. He disapproves of her friendship with a suffragette:

> DR FAIRLEY: And now since she's stuffed you up with all this fudge about votes for women – Suffragette processions and I don't know what... the next thing is I shall have you burning down churches... throwing acid into letter boxes.
>
> (Stern 1931b: 9)

To which Daryll replies:

> DARYLL: ... Alexia's wonderful. I can't bear silly little halfwitted flappers... I wish you'd let me join Alexia's business when I've finished my training... what's the use of learning anything. I'll sit at home and be useful and cut bread and butter... I want to be independent.
>
> (ibid.: 9–10)

The foregrounded differential between the aspirations and needs of three close generations of women in terms of their attitudes to work and their social ambition, is established during the Prologue. The author also implies that the rule of the patriarch is reliant on the fact that it is he who holds the *economic* power.

The second act is set in 1926. Daryll's father and elder brother have been killed in action during the Great War and she is now the head of the family. The male characters are rather inept and their self-importance is undermined by the fact that they are as financially dependent on Daryll as the other women. Daryll's mother Rosie has a new husband, an unemployed musician, who, as such, has no economic power. The men constantly ask Daryll for financial support which she is able to provide through her job as head of her ex-suffragette friend Alexia's business, now a large West End concern. At one point while they are waiting for Daryll to arrive at a restaurant after work, two of the financially dependent men discuss women, femininity and economic power:

> SCOTT: Oh, yes. She won't even sign the bill in front of her guests.

BEN: Glad to hear it.

SCOTT: Yes, one appreciates that. She's a good fellow, Daryll, though she's a bit too lordly at times.

BEN: She's not masculine to look at. I can't bear women with gruff voices who cover half the room in a stride.

SCOTT: No nor can I. Unsexed, that's what they are. Daryll's attractive in a way...

BEN: Oh, yes... yes... but of course her mother –

SCOTT: Anthea too – she's so sensitive. Now Daryll isn't... Daryll's been wonderfully generous... to us all. Even I – let's own it – am not in the least ashamed to consult her when I want advice. She's certainly got the best head of the family.

BEN: (*suddenly*) She *is* the head of the family, and I don't like it!

(ibid.: 41)

The men make a direct correlation between economic power and masculinity. Daryll herself feels that she can't get married and take on the feminine role of wife and mother, because she already has such a large family to support. She sees herself, albeit rather uncomfortably, as the 'father' of this family:

DARYLL: ... in this house... there isn't a father... not one single father except me.... Of course I come home and behave abominably.... It's got into my bones.... And all the men come to me as man to man and thank me rather resentfully for what I've done.... I'm not going to wish this on any daughter of mine.

(ibid.: 60–65)

Stern creates her heroine in complete contrast to the other women in the play, especially so in the case of her sister Fay, for whom the fact that it is 1926 means that 'independence and work and bright young bachelor girls' are not as preferable as living at home (ibid.: 70). Nevertheless, when Daryll's mother inherits a fortune from one of her dead husband's patients at the end of Act Two, Daryll turns to her long time fiancé and tells him:

DARYLL: ... take me, marry me, smash me, begin me all over again, and make me into the usual sort of wife... it's not too late... I don't care how you do it... but break me.

(ibid.: 77)

Daryll's ideas change again after two years of marriage, by which point she is bored and frustrated by domestic life and feels intellectually unchallenged. When she discovers that the business which she helped to build up is in a state of collapse, Daryll goes against her husband's wishes and decides to go back to work, telling him:

DARYLL: Oh Rufus ... you're being quite unendurably silly and such a cave man. This isn't the time to stand with folded arms and a rocky scowl. ... If I hadn't been bored from morning till night do you think I'd have been so wildly frantically glad to get back again ... back to my business ... oh to have something to do again ... something continuous and constructive ... I'm no good for marriage ... it's the war, we had to take over then ... I expect there's a whole generation of us. ... We're none of us fit for marriage, we *fathers* of nineteen fourteen ... I'm a freak. We're all freaks my generation of girls.

(ibid.: 97–99)

Rufus insists that they can't both work, that is to say, take on the 'masculine' role, and so offers to become a 'house husband', saying that it is just traditional prejudice which insists that men must work and women must weep. Daryll rejects his suggestion as being 'unnatural' and because of this reaction he tells her that she is *perfectly* conventional, perfectly *feminine* at which point she falls into his arms. That might be the end of the play except that Daryll does go off to 'save' the business and the ending of the play is left open with her leaving saying, 'just this once, we can arrange things differently afterwards' (ibid.: 110).

Stern's play brings up all kinds of questions about the nature of femininity in relation to the need to work. The heroine's femininity has been constructed by social and historical imperatives. She represents a whole generation of middle-class women who were required to leave their traditional feminine roles behind, take control during the First World War, and were then literally dropped from the public domain when the war was over. One of the key questions which Daryll asks, and others ask of her, is whether she can be both economically powerful *and* feminine. She struggles to find an acceptable feminine identity which fits her *actual* fragmented experience of being a woman. The play centres around recognition and a need for transformation in terms of women's roles. Both genders discuss female social roles in terms of their social constructedness rather than their biological innateness. Daryll's confusion and fragmented experience of femaleness are seen as a symptom of a political and economic system based on the supply and demand of labour. The dénouement suggests negotiation as a device for the management of gender roles.

Arguably, Stern's heroine is a victim of patriarchal attitudes – structured by their location within a capitalist economy. The author foregrounds questions around whether woman's personal fulfilment will be achieved through family or marriage alone and suggests that a woman should have the opportunity of recognition in the public as well as the private sphere. The play exposes a desire for emergence, a need to break out of constructed roles into ones created by need and experience.

The question of career or marriage was an all-pervasive one for women. That one chose to work at all was often used as a contributing factor to a process of defining gender boundaries; at times women who seemingly chose to work were seen as being somehow 'manly' or 'unsexed' women, even if the choice to work came out of necessity. Working-class women were as susceptible to the prejudice of the popular press as middle-class women. The debate over whether or not women should work, taking jobs which could be given to men, to a large extent transgressed class boundaries. As the twentieth century progressed, the level to which women's working lives were controlled by state intervention and the needs of the economy increased. At times of high levels of unemployment women's jobs were given over to men, no matter what their class.

Even in the early 1960s a play like Muriel Spark's *Doctors of Philosophy* (1962) reflects within the narrative a social attitude to the relationship between femininity and work which associated a woman's need or desire to work with some kind of abnormality. Many of the reviewers found the setting for the play to be too unreal:

> Straightforward farce is one of the most difficult of all forms....
> Miss Spark is writing about a society she knows very well – the academic world – the play's idiom gets the upper hand and forces her to exhibit a society that has no existence outside the theatre, and certainly deserves no existence inside one.
>
> (*The Times*, 3 October 1962)

Any interpretation of this critique must take into account the fact that both the narrative focus and dramatic action of the play concern women. This adds a further dimension to the critic's point of view, that is to say, the play is as much if not more a treatment of the 'female condition' as it is that of the world of academia. In the opening scene Leonora, cousin to Charlie Delfont's wife Catherine, appears before him asking him to give her a baby. He reports this to his wife thinking that he must have been dreaming. In Charlie's opinion, Leonora's academic work has made her repress her sexuality.

CATHERINE: After all, if I don't know my own cousin, I

mean ... we grew up together. Leonora's not that type. She's a *born* virgin. I ought to know.... No-one would believe that a university teacher like Leonora –

CHARLIE: That makes her more dangerous than ever. Remember Sarah Desmond ... Senior Lecturer in Comparative Religions. The author of *The Life Force*. She was discovered in the bath with a wine waiter in a Folkestone hotel. It was hushed up, but she had to resign. What's more they were both naked.

CATHERINE: Leonora doesn't teach Life Force, Greek is an old sound subject.

CHARLIE: It comes to the same thing in a woman scholar.... - Once they break out, they break out.

CATHERINE: I've got as good a degree as Leonora has, and I don't go round inviting men to give me a child.

(Spark 1963: 4–5)

When the two women discuss the different directions in which their careers have moved, it is clear that both see Leonora as having taken on a male profession, and for Catherine, Leonora has, as a result, developed a persona which does not align itself with socially acceptable notions of feminine behaviour:

LEONORA: When you come up to visit me in college you have a hankering look. I feel sorry for you – the knowledge that you had it in you to become a distinguished scholar – and have become merely the mother of an average student and the wife of a second class scholar. ... A woman of intellectual capacity has a certain manner and expression all the time. They are the manner and expression of detachment, and you can't pick them up overnight.

CATHERINE: I wouldn't want to pick them up at all. I like to please men. Do you think it pleases a man when he looks into a woman's eyes and sees a reflection of the British Museum Reading Room? I don't envy your expression and your manner.

LEONORA: ... I admit sometimes I get tired of being treated as a scholar and a gentleman.

CATHERINE: You ought to have got married, Leonora, if only for the pleasure of pleasing a man. Hundreds of women academics are married these days. They teach in the universities, run their homes, have babies, write books and feed their husbands – I don't know how they do it all.

LEONORA: ... Badly.

(ibid.: 14–15)

Both the form and content subvert any idea of a *fixed* normality. Leonora becomes more and more self-conscious of her position as a woman academic and as a member of a family. She says of her request to Charlie that it was a 'dramatic urge', that in fact she has been playing a part which they have already devised for her, and that it is through a glimpse of reality that she has developed a 'dramatic sense of herself'.[2]

> LEONORA: I have occupied the role in which you've cast me. At times of low spirits when one is tired one behaves largely as people expect one to behave. It has been expected of me that I should be envious of you, Catherine, and should want Charlie to give me a child. I've instinctively played the part in your minds of Leonora the barren virgin.
>
> (ibid.: 61)

Although discourse around the possible feminine attributes of a woman scholar may at first seem removed from the specific thematic discourse on women and work found in many of the earlier plays of the period in question, Spark is clearly positing Leonora as a working woman whose field of employment happens to be academia, a traditionally male bastion. Thus the implication is that when a woman moves into a traditionally male area of employment her level of femininity is put into question.

In the vast majority of plays where a working, middle-class woman is central to the action, issues around the relationship between gender, femininity and work prevail. The differential in the representation of working-class women reflects the difference in comparative status for working-class and middle-class women as much as it is a reflection of the fact that the majority of the plays under examination were written by middle-class women for largely middle-class audiences.

WOMEN AND WORK–1918 TO THE EARLY 1960s: THE POSITION AND PERCEPTION OF WOMEN IN THE LABOUR MARKET

> The graduate wife seemed an embarrassment rather than a welcomed addition to society, even when there was an acute shortage of teachers and nurses.
>
> (E. Wilson 1980: 57)

Elizabeth Wilson has noted that, even with the changes in form and access to the education system, employment for women was still dependent on cultural perceptions of femininity as much as it was dependent upon the demands of the economy. During the 1939–1945 war, women had been re-introduced into the labour market on a similar scale to the First World War. Even though the legislation affecting wages and long-term employment rights was not as strict as during the Great War, women were still discouraged from staying in the same areas of employment after the war was over. Although the war opened up new possibilities of careers for middle-class women, and despite the fact that in the mid-1940s many, such as the Fabian Group in 1946, felt that the housewife was 'rapidly becoming the oppressed proletariat of the modern world', the prevailing cultural image projected onto the average British woman was that of the sexy, bright and willing housewife for whom marriage and family management could become a career in itself (ibid.: 21).

In terms of various legislation, during the mid-1940s work and marriage were still seen as *alternatives*. The unwillingness to remove the Marriage Bars was a symptom of a social ideology which saw women's role as being centred in the home and family. However, it was perhaps the immediate post-Second World War fear of a labour shortage which encouraged policy-makers to promote the idea that women could manage part-time work as well as family responsibilities. Some legislation was even aimed at encouraging employers to design their labour needs to fit into the life patterns of married women. From the census report in 1901 to that of 1951 the number of married women in insured employment had gone from 13 per cent to 40 per cent of the total female workforce. These figures, however, do not account for the vast number of women working outside the home in jobs where there was little security of tenure, or insurance, that is to say, working-class women in part-time, short-term employment, widows on low pensions in part-time work and so on (see Lewis 1984).

By 1951 women made up 30.8 per cent of the labour force; 52 per cent of working women at this point were single, 40 per cent married. Census figures show that the number of working women between the ages of thirty-five and fifty-nine increased from 26 per cent in 1921 to 43 per cent in 1951. The number of women under thirty-five who were part of the labour market in 1951 had decreased from 69 per cent in 1921 to 52 per cent in 1951. The nature of 'typical' women's work had changed, although again historians such as Lewis and Beddoe stress the fact that the regional, class and married status variants mean that it is difficult to ascertain a general picture over the country as a whole. Nevertheless, it would seem clear that certain trades had become *feminised* by the early 1950s. By 1951, the distribution of women working as clerks or typists had risen to 20 per cent compared with 1 per cent in 1901.

The number of women working in domestic service was fairly sustained during the inter-war years, but had dropped significantly by the 1951 census. This was not so much because domestic service had somehow become de-feminised, but rather was due to the growth in 'new industries' and in the number of white collar jobs available to women, such as teaching, retailing, office work and so on (Lewis 1984: 158). It is also important to note that the decrease in the numbers of women working in domestic service was partly due to the growth in the availability of new domestic appliances and the diminishing size of the average family in terms of the number of members living in any one household. As 'new light industries' grew in number, so did the number of women working in them, although the highest increases for percentages of women's employment are in the non-manual trades. Even though women in non-manual trades tended to earn wages which were proportionately more equal to their male counterparts than in other trades, they often worked longer hours and so, similar to many other areas of employment, women were paid less for the same level and, often, more hours of work than men.

Despite some legislative changes which affected the position of working women, the ideological basis on which they were allowed to work was one which to some extent justified the enormous differentiation between men and women in the employment market. Although women were encouraged to work in times of social and economic need, and although they may have found themselves doing much the same work as their male counterparts, they were rarely paid the same wages, nor did their jobs have the same legislative protection as those of men. Underlying this was the assumption that women were secondary wage earners chiefly responsible for the private domain, their duty being to bear and nurture children and to supply a comfortable home for their husbands: 'women's labour was treated by employers as adaptable, interchangeable and temporary' (Glucksman 1986: 29).

Single women were in a consistently difficult position within the job market. During the inter-war period, for example, while there was a shortage of available men to marry, so there was a shortage of jobs for men. Many married women resented a situation whereby they saw what they considered to be men's jobs being carried out by women. Similarly, single women resented married women who worked, perceiving them as being already financially supported by their husbands. For single women the job market narrowed as they grew older; in the service trades, for example, middle-aged, single women were in danger of being replaced by younger, single women, and yet their pension rights were not equal to those of men. Lewis notes that 'The National Spinsters Association, formed in 1935, believed that 5 per cent of unmarried women aged between 55–65 were already in receipt of poor relief', and points out that over 10 per cent of charwomen or cleaning ladies were elderly, unmarried women (Lewis 1984: 155).

There are differences of opinion as to why a situation whereby women are more likely to be employed in low-skilled, low-paid work still persists. There is no doubt, however, as to the fact that this was the general situation from the turn of the century onwards.

> The press, and the public opinion it purported to represent, were outraged that women wished to hang on to factory work when what the country needed most was wives, mothers and domestic servants.
>
> (Beddoe 1989: 51)

Even when working-class women moved back into the public labour industry during the inter-war period, it was in the main into the new 'light industries' which were mass producing goods to feed the fast growing consumer market. Women moved into these industries as a 'preferred source of labour for firms which introduced methods of mass production, machine powered tools and assembly lines' (Glucksman 1986: 7). Despite this, Beddoe argues that domestic service and 'office work', the nature of which could be anything from the clerk in a small shop to a private assistant or an administrative manager, continued to be the key areas in which women worked, certainly during the inter-war period. Beddoe also points out that although the 'office girl' became a glamorised figure in the Hollywood film industry, her wages rarely ever covered her living costs. Office work was low paid and generally held low status. It is interesting to note, at this point, that the unmarried secretary or personal assistant became almost a stock character in many of the plays by women of the period 1918–1962 (see Chapter 7).

There were wide class and regional differences in the employment situation of women after the Second World War. As I have already noted, middle-class women found new openings during the 1940s and, once the Marriage Bars were largely removed, it was more acceptable for them to go back into work, albeit mostly on a part-time basis, after their children had reached school age. The vast differential in employment possibilities for women became more obvious during the inter-war period as more middle-class women moved into the labour market. It was very rare, for example, that a working-class girl would have the opportunity to train as a teacher, even though an upper-working-class or lower-middle-class girl might have been able to do so. Social mobility through employment was unlikely for those at the lower end of the job market. There were also often differences in the ways in which low-status jobs were perceived by the women who did them. A shop girl, for example, even though she might not receive significantly higher wages, may have frowned upon the factory girl, seeing her as being of a different social class *because* she worked in a factory. A shop assistant may have seen her work as being better than that of a domestic servant in a large and established family house, even though her hours would have been longer and the financial benefits of her job fewer. In the same way, to work for a large, upper-middle-class or upper-class family was seen as more secure and desirable for a middle-aged woman than to work in a shop, as the family would possibly feel some kind of responsibility for her as she became older and less able.

A WOMAN'S PROPER PLACE

Under the heading of *Marriage and Career*, a letter from a reader of *Time and Tide*, printed in 1927, goes a long way towards summing up the general attitude toward the issue of women and work and in turn, a woman's rightful place within society:

> Under the guise of fitting herself to be a better wife, a better mother, the young girl is urged to train herself for a career. And why? Solely that, when the physical act of motherhood is ended she may not be bored. Not a word about the moral duties of wife hood and motherhood, duties which increase, not decrease, as the children grow older. What more beautiful picture can there be than the mother, the centre of the home, the rest for the husband from his hours of toil, the never failing fount of comfort, of sympathy and of help to the children, of all ages. And this is to be sacrificed for a career? A career which must take her out of the home, must keep her where neither husband or children can depend upon her help, where she can, indeed only help herself.
>
> (Spender 1984: 203)

Until the years which follow the end of the Second World War, the questions raised with regard to women's employment were largely based on the assumption that work somehow disrupted and undermined a woman's 'natural' role as a woman and so challenged 'typical' female behaviour. The fear was based upon the assumption that a woman's first duty was to be a wife and mother, and that the desire to fulfil these roles was a *natural* feminine trait. Although the situation changed slightly, and despite the fact that working-class women had invariably always worked, albeit relatively invisibly, any woman choosing a career rather than motherhood and marriage was considered to be somehow abnormal. The post-Second World War changes in economy and ideological positions on women's social roles held the greatest benefits for middle-class women looking for openings in particular careers 'who had the means to buy child-care, domestic appliances and often, domestic help' (Lewis 1984: 222).

With the setting up of the Welfare State, government intervention became more relevant to family life, and so legislation around issues of employment was bound up with governmental notions of what it was that women should be doing, that is to say, especially in the case of married women, it was assumed that they could serve their country better through home and family management, rather than through being part of public industry (here, there are many parallels with the employment situation in which women found themselves after the First World War). Even though, by the early 1950s, it was generally accepted that a woman could have a career, be a wife and a mother, underlying this acceptance was the belief that the career would not be one of great opportunity or status. Winifred Holtby felt in the mid-1930s, that it was 'acceptable' for a woman to be a doctor or lawyer, to be a part of the 'professional' workforce on a higher level than ever before – but in terms of real increase, women's position in the professional job market did not really improve until the late 1960s.

A sociological analysis of facts and figures reveals similar issues in terms of women and work, which many of the female playwrights of the period under examination brought to bear in the thematic and narrative focus of their plays. The distinction between the private and public sphere is foregrounded alongside a questioning of the *real* relationship between femininity, gender and work.

BUSINESS OR ROMANCE

There are a number of plays during the early years of the period under examination where the female protagonists are seen as choosing to work rather than marry for the sake of convenience. This comes at a time when, partly due to the aftermath of the First World War, eligible men are in short supply. The idea that one should marry for love rather than convenience, and that marriage itself could be based on a partnership of souls as much as mutual economic interests, was in fact relatively new. Marie Stopes's *Married Love*, with its advice on how marital partners could live as soul-mates, work as a team, and should be allowed to expect sexual and emotional fulfilment from intercourse, sold thousands of copies to willing buyers in search of a blueprint for what Stopes herself defined as the ideal marriage (Stopes 1918). Her work as part of the contraceptive movement was in its time radical, although she was at the time (and is still) criticised for her eugenicist beliefs. Just as she believed that women could gain economic independence from being able to control the number of children they had, so she also believed that certain classes needed the frequency of pregnancy to be controlled for them (see Rose 1993). Stopes received some success on the West End stage with her play *Our Ostriches* (Stopes 1923), which, propagandist in nature, was essentially about the need for the legal introduction and social acceptance of contraception.[3]

Despite the way in which we may interpret her work now, Dr Marie Stopes's ideas were absorbed by a generation of middle-class women especially, for whom the separate spheres in which husbands and wives functioned during the late nineteenth century were no longer seen as representing a satisfactory way of conducting a married relationship. These concerns reverberate in many of the narratives in plays written by women, especially during the late 1910s and well into the late 1920s. Equally, for many young women, work was seen as an alternative to the drudgery of married life and motherhood, as one character in Aimée and Philip Stuart's *Nine Till Six* (originally produced at the Arts theatre under the direction of Auriol Lee in 1930) tells her prospective employer when asked why she would want a career in dressmaking:

> GRACIE: I want to see life. I don't want only to be at 'ome. It's either that or being a typist.... Gettin' married only means a lot of kids and no time to yourself the whole blessed day!... It's getting their breakfast and washin' up; then it's getting their dinner and washin' up; then it's getting their tea and washin' up – then you haven't properly started in!
>
> (Stuart and Stuart 1930: 11)

For women like Francis Llewellyn in Kate O'Brien's *Distinguished Villa* (O'Brien 1926), working in a library and refusing to marry a handsome man with a fast car are priorities. The priorities are presented as being vastly superior to those of her landlady, Mabel, for whom a home, husband and housekeeping provide the *real* career challenge for a woman. When her husband Natty tells Mabel that he doubts very much if Francis Llewellyn is the type to rush into marriage she responds with,

> MABEL: Well, what girl would choose to go on listing up books in a free library when she could be married to a smart young gentleman? Woman's sphere is in the home. I've always held that Natty, and always will.
>
> (ibid.: 16)

For Mabel's sister, Gwen, whom the author describes as having an 'ill-educated tone', marriage appears to be the only escape from a life of working in a typing pool, even if it means marrying a man who is neither in love with her nor the biological father of her unborn child. In this play, which was first produced in 1926 and ran for sixty-four performances, the choices for women are shown to be between work and marriage or love and social respectability. In other plays of the period women are presented as having to make ideological choices about what kind of marriage they would want, negotiating the terms on which they can both work and be in a married partnership. In Elizabeth Baker's *Partnership*, Kate Rolling finds romance with a man who actually insists that she keep her business concern, as well as fighting off an impending buy-out by a former suitor (Baker 1921).

Elizabeth Baker, born into a lower-middle-class family, began her working life as a cashier and stenographer and moved into professional playwriting after the positive reception of a number of her first pieces (see Stowell 1992: 100–128). She was actively involved in aspects of the suffrage movement and was connected with 'innovative repertory companies in London, Manchester and Birmingham' (ibid.). *Partnership*, as with her play, *Edith*, has a female protagonist who is an unmarried, successful businesswoman (Baker 1927). Kate Rolling and Maisie Glow run a successful business close to the Brighton seafront: Rolling & Co., Milliners and Costumiers. Kate Rolling – played by Laura Cowie in the original London production at the Court theatre in 1917 – is made a proposition by one of her suppliers, Mr Goodrich. He tells her that he has made an offer for a small firm which she agrees could prosper if handled appropriately. Goodrich also tells her that one of the local businessmen is buying out the neighbouring shop to her own:

GOODRICH: ... We smaller fry must make a stand against him, Miss Rolling. ... He'll swamp us – but there, I oughtn't to say that of you. You're a clever woman ... and now this brings me to what I came to say. (*Gets up and brings his chair down level with Kate and sits.*) I've got a proposition to lay before you. Why not put our two businesses together? ... Yours and mine. (*Kate is too taken aback to reply.*) This thing of mine is a dead cert. I've got the cash alright, and with this biz and yours we could get the pick of the trade ...

KATE: Do you mean a partnership? –

GOODRICH: (*Interrupting buoyantly.*) I do, Miss Rolling. And I mean it in another way too, if you'll allow me to out it before you, but I put the business consideration first, knowing what a businesswoman you are. I ask you to marry me, Miss Rolling, and have a partnership that way... I've a genuine admiration for you, quite apart from business and all that. You're a woman any man in the land might be proud of, and I'm sure you before this have seen something of what I feel – (*Kate rises and stands in front of her chair.*)

KATE: I've seen nothing of the kind. This is nonsense Mr Goodrich. I'm not thinking of marrying –

GOODRICH: ... (*rising and speaking earnestly*) ... You're afraid of the risk – you think I'm offering you a speculation in the business I've put before you, and that it isn't worth your while.... Well that's a natural feeling in a businesswoman like you...

KATE: My business satisfies me, and it would require something certainly very great to make me think of any change.

(Baker 1921: 17)

Goodrich is oblivious to the seriousness of Kate's overt refusal and insists that he'll come back in six months to ask her again, despite the fact that she does not hide her dislike for him. At this point in the play her business is of the utmost importance to her, although she is not entirely against the idea of a partnership. When Maisie Glow suggests to her that she might partner up with Pillatt, who is buying the shop next door, Kate is not against the idea in principle; she sees that it would be a good business move, and as Maisie points out, 'It would be better than fighting him.' When Pillatt does in fact make the suggestion that they should join their businesses together, marriage, but not love, is a part of the deal:

PILLATT: Has the idea of a partnership ever entered your head? ... Your business and mine. We two hold the pick of the trade here. We do very well separate, no doubt. Together we could top the lot. ... You have style, and not only style but brains – and one can prophesy success for the person who has them ... I very rarely make a mistake in these things ... I want to suggest, to propose a partnership – in another sense, and that is – marriage. ... Being a plain businessman I wish to be quite frank in the matter, and so I have not hesitated to put the business part of the plan foremost. I am sure you, as a businesswoman thoroughly understand this ... I'm not a sentimentalist, but then you, as I say, a woman of business, do not wish for any expression of sentiment.

(ibid.: 27)

They then continue to discuss the logistics of how they would arrange their shops together and the way in which the partnership might work. Kate becomes absorbed in thinking about the shop's future, but then comes 'to attention' and re-frames the discussion so that they are clear about exactly what is being proposed. She points out that although a business partnership might be a good idea, she had not thought of getting married. For Pillatt, however, there is little difference between considering a business partnership with a woman and marriage:

PILLATT: But that part of it will make no more difference than the other.

KATE: It is an important thing to give up one's independence. Marriage must mean that – for someone.

PILLATT: (*earnestly*) Not at all, not at all – in this case. You would have your part of the concern. I should have mine. We should each be responsible for its management, just as two men might. The difference is that in our case the contract is a slightly closer one – which is an advantage ... I thoroughly admire you and – er – respect you – and ... I would never have thought of making my proposal if I had not felt that if you could accept it, it would be to our mutual satisfaction and happiness, I may say. ... Well no, to put things on a clear and proper basis, I have drawn up a statement of what I propose. Perhaps you would run your eye over it now and tell me if it seems to you sufficiently good (*hands her paper and rises*).

(ibid.: 26–29)

Pillatt treats Kate 'like a man': he takes her seriously as a business manager and gives her a contract, offering to cover the costs of converting the two shops. Maisie Glow warns her colleague that Pillatt's offer is not one to turn down lightly. Kate, however, is unsure of what it is she wants. For her the dilemma is between building up her business and continuing her search for another sort of partnership, one which involves a validation of her 'womanliness', not just her 'manly' business sense. When she talks of losing independence she clearly implies that both financial and emotional independence would work on a different level in an ideal partnership rooted in mutual interest.

Romance comes along in the form of Fawcett, who unlike his friend Pillatt has taken risks with his inherited fortune, financing experiments in dyes. Fawcett holds a fascination for Kate, as he is not ruled by business hours, preferring walks on the Downs. He notices the rose on her desk: he prefers the sentimental and the picturesque to convenient time-keeping and business tasks. He tells Kate, 'Whenever I am in danger of giving too much up to work I always come and see Pillatt as a warning!' (ibid.: 59). Fawcett also advises Kate that whoever the 'chap' is that Pillatt has persuaded to go into business with him, he will be 'swallowed up', and encourages Kate to take time away from her business and go hiking on the Downs. When Kate tells Maisie that she has fallen in love with this character who is so incongruous with their world, Maisie suggests that she do all she can to create a partnership with Pillatt and see Fawcett in secret. Kate's response is a clear condemnation of the way in which her life has become ruled by contracts and businesslike behaviour.

> KATE: Before I met him I was an automaton ... Everything I had was up for sale – my brains that helped to make my business, my good looks, even the way that I smiled and laughed – all arranged to bring in the best interest. Then at last I did the worst thing – I gave my soul – for a bargain, a mere clause in the contract. A woman can't give her body without giving her soul. Then – he – came and the very thing I had been ready to throw in as a mere item made the whole bargain impossible.
>
> (ibid.: 105)

Fawcett finally offers her the partnership she has wanted and, with it, the support for her business – not financial, but emotional support based on a romantic partnership and friendship:

> FAWCETT: It's you I want and to do what you wish. If you'd rather throw everything up and come off with me, we'll go tomorrow if you like. If you'd rather keep your little show here and fight old Pillatt, I'll stand in with you ... I'll be there, anywhere, when you want me. So long as you don't get swallowed up by it.
>
> (ibid.: 107)

Baker's play offers a critique of a certain view of life as much as it presents on stage the lives of a specific class of working women. Much like *Chains* (Baker 1911), Baker's earlier perhaps best-known play, the female protagonist is strong and independent, wanting more from life than a marriage of convenience. The independence goes beyond relationships with men, and the protagonist finds a vision of a possible world which to her social equals seems either illogical or simply crazed. Baker's heroines in these two plays both have aspirations which set them apart from those around them. In *Partnership* Kate finds an ideal in that she can put time, thought and energy into both her work and her romantic life. Throughout the play she suggests that there is a false dichotomy between the 'manly' and the 'womanly' businesswoman, as much as she promotes what could be seen as a socialist ideology for the world of commerce, where life and business run in parallel, the importance of each being balanced by the requirements of the other.

Many of the other plays of the period in question, through choice of narrative focus, represent an attempt to somehow close the distance between the public and the private spheres. On one level, business or work, and romance or emotion, are presented as being successfully intertwined, albeit farcically as in *Love Goes to Press*, written by two women war correspondents, Martha Gellhorn and Virginia Cowles; one of the authors has recently commented that she remembers the play as a 'dotty farce'.[4] The play involves two women journalists as the heroines whose mission to 'tell the public the truth' gets mixed up with their amorous adventures (see Chapter 6). On another level, there is what can only be seen as a conscious attempt to subvert the idea that women are not biologically or psychologically designed to work in the public world of business, by using their femininity as the main reason for their success. This is certainly the case in Aimée and Philip Stuart's *Her Shop* where Lady Torrent tells her husband that she intends to make 'pots of money' from her shop and when told that she is being ridiculous, she replies,

LADY TORRENT: . . . You're afraid I'll succeed where you can't, anyway. . . you've never made a penny piece in your life! You happen to have inherited money. That's luck.

(Stuart and Stuart 1929: 39)

He proposes that they make a bet that she won't be successful, her response is to ask him not to bother her, insisting, 'I don't intend to live at home while I run my shop' (ibid.). Lady Torrent buys a dressmaking business and proceeds to incur multiple debts, mainly because her friends don't pay their bills; she knows a great deal about dresses but nothing about running a business. Her so-called feminine wiles help her win the day as she is cautious about transferring her shop to a different part of London when the suggestion is made by the two men who originally leased her the building.[5] Lady Torrent is then made an offer by a property firm and pays her debts, wins her bet with her husband and tells him to come and take her home.

Although the play is rather tame compared to many others written by women of the period, it is interesting for the way in which it to some extent demystifies the functionings of the world of business, as well as for the way in which it attempts to undermine the argument that women cannot function in the public world. Another play by Aimée and Philip Stuart goes a great deal further – both to expose on the public stage the workings of an essentially woman's world of work, that of the dressmaker's shop, and in the way it represents a woman's method of running a business. That is to say, in *Nine Till Six*, which ran in London for 229 performances, Mrs Pembroke handles her business with a similar set of criteria and ethics to those which she uses within her family (Stuart and Stuart 1930).

THE WOMAN'S WORLD OF WORK

Aimée and Philip Stuart's *Nine Till Six* was originally produced at the Arts theatre in 1930, and then reproduced by Mrs C. B. Cochran at the Apollo. The critics had mixed opinions: some thought it 'an attractive little play' (*Sunday Times*, 29 January 1930); others felt that it was essentially 'less a play than a study of women at work'. It was arguably because of this that the same critic felt able to criticise it for the fact that,

> As a view of unfamiliar life, nothing could be better. As a play, all that can be said of it is that it had the pathos and some of the sentimentality of melodrama without the plot and movement.
>
> (*Daily Telegraph*, 30 January 1930)

It is interesting that the following letter to the *Sunday Times*, written by a woman who had herself written and had produced one-act plays in the 1920s, depicts the play as having a far greater significance, both historically and theatrically:

> Sir – *Nine Till Six* has nothing to complain of in the warm welcome accorded it alike by Press and public, but its importance as a sociological contribution has possibly been a little under-stressed. Surely no play in modern times has presented so searching and fair-minded an analysis of women's place in the world of industry? It sets out to give a faithful picture of a fashionable dressmaking establishment; there is not a trace of propaganda about it. Here is life humorously perceived as it is lived today. You see a girl from a Council school side by side with the daughter of a lord, each equally keen on her job as an apprentice with its salary and prospect of adventure. But while the girls from the working classes have some faint perception of loyalty to their employer, the Society girl has only a sense of good-natured camaraderie with her fellow-manne-quins... Miss Louise Hampton's unforgettable picture of the head, with her acutely modern daughter, played by Marjory Clark with all

the outside hardness and hidden sympathy of to-day, show women's growing sense of responsibility. We see them over burdened by financial strain, their private happiness and peace inexorably set on one side in the immense strain of their business venture. . . . Mr James Agate prophesies a nine to six months' run for Aimée and Philip Stuart's play. There are those who say that this is a women's counterpart of *Journey's End*; its field of battle is the business world; its privations are the ruthless denials of ease and beauty; its sex problems, as incidental.[6]

Much of *Nine Till Six* centres around both an examination of the nature of work, the lived experience of a working life, different class attitudes to work and the relationships between employer and employee. Fifty-five-year-old Mrs Pembroke, who has worked in the retail trade since she was twelve, tells her staff that in her youth one was expected to work till midnight, or simply until the work was done. She refuses to allow her daughter to let her moods over-ride her responsibility to the family business, pointing out that whether or not her daughter is 'one of the firm', they cannot afford to offend the customers – a life in work or business is hard whether you are the boss or the cleaner:

MRS PEMBROKE: . . . Have you any idea what our expenses are here? . . . We have four driving months; six when we just manage to jog along, and two when we're so slack that we think the world's come to an end. In the meantime the expenses go on. Do you know the rent of this shop? . . . We pay by the inch. The workrooms are extra. For the shop alone we pay a yearly rental of seven thousand five hundred pounds, with rates and taxes . . . I only just manage to make both ends meet. With all my responsibility, I make very little more out of it than you do. I sometimes wonder if it's worth going on. It takes all our time to keep pace. Since the War we shopkeepers have had much to fight against. Everything hits back – weather, strikes, political situations . . . cost of production, cost of a roof over our heads, and it gets worse and worse . . . wages are not high enough – nothing like high enough! But they're too high for those that have to find them at the end of the week. The fault lies with conditions that cripple the employed and employer alike . . . . You're quite right to feel resentment against conditions that make the day's work seem a drudgery. I feel resentment against conditions that make me seem a tyrant.

(Stuart and Stuart 1930: 75–76)

In such a way, when Mrs Pembroke has to deal with two of the staff who have 'borrowed' some old stock, she treats them with the same leniency as she might her own daughter. In doing so she goes against her saleswoman, Miss Roberts, who somehow represents an 'old', less humane style of doing business. Mrs Pembroke gives both Freda, her senior employee, and Gracie, her junior employee, another chance, hoping that they've learnt their lesson. Although Pembroke believes it to be her duty to sack dishonest staff, she cannot do so after her daughter speaks up for one of the employees in question:

> CLARE: I understand what it means to be your age and not to have had any life. You and I don't live. We just go on, day after day. So does Miss Roberts. But she doesn't care. She didn't expect anything anyway. It's lucky for her. You and I rebel against what we'll have to put up with. She's content just to be what she is.
>
> (ibid.: 78)

When Mrs Pembroke realises that her own daughter, her own flesh and blood, could have behaved with the same dishonesty as her employee, she has the good sense and humanity to overlook the matter of the theft. She also persuades Gracie's mother to see reason when they learn that Gracie has been lying about where she's been going in the evenings, thus transgressing class boundaries and speaking up for the 'new' class of the younger generation, whose needs, expectations and aspirations she recognises as being different from women of her own generation. The suggestion is that women employers, because of their gender, have a significantly different way of overseeing their staff, one which is based on a kind of 'maternal–matriarchal' ethics. Mrs Pembroke is also interesting for the way in which she consciously negotiates class issues within her business dealings. When her daughter wants her to give one of her friends an apprenticeship, Mrs Pembroke is cautious:

> CLARE: Her grandfather's the Earl of Glendarran.
> MRS PEMBROKE: ... That's nice for her... Lord's daughter or no, don't you give her credit unless you're sure she can pay...
> CLARE: She wants to come on our staff.
> MRS PEMBROKE: That's absurd...we're not in business for fun.
> CLARE: Lots of girls of good family are learning to do something useful these days. Other firms take them on.

MRS PEMBROKE: That's probably why so many other firms come to grief.

CLARE: ...Why shouldn't they be as capable as anyone else.

MRS PEMBROKE: Because they don't HAVE to work.

(ibid.: 20–23)

Mrs Pembroke states her regret at having sent her youngest daughter to an expensive public school, feeling that she might have learnt more about working life and ordinary people at an ordinary school. She herself was educated in a council school, and is against the snobbery which her daughter has developed from being part of an upwardly mobile family. Clare's friend Bridgit wants the job because she's bored, sees no future in staying at home and basically needs 'something to do' while waiting for a wealthy man to come along and marry her:

BRIDGIT: ...There's no point in my staying at home. There's absolutely nothing for me to do. Daddie's trying to let Avonlaye. We can't hunt; we can't entertain. I'll probably have to earn my living pretty soon – so I might as well get down to it.

(ibid.)

Much of the talk between the shop girls is based on discussions of work conditions, pay and prospects. The authors foreground class differences between the workers and the way in which those class differences influence the manner in which the young women see themselves. For the young women who come from lower-middle or working-class backgrounds, work is a way of helping their families financially and breaking the pattern of labour for women within the family unit.

One of the most interesting aspects of Dodie Smith's *Service* is her representation of the way in which two different classes of family cope with financial crisis and the way in which it affects their lives. Gabriel Service's family, faced with the possibility that their established firm will have to sell out, only rally round at the very last moment, worrying about the loss the buy-out will cause them personally. His young wife even leaves him and becomes involved with a richer younger man. In contrast the family of the sacked employee, Timothy Benton, spring into action. Mrs Benton heads the household of a lower-middle-class family, giving her charlady extra hours because she's a widow managing a family on her own. The extra hours are withdrawn when Timothy Benton gets the sack. As she says, 'It's no use thinking of her now – we've got to think of the home' (Smith 1933: 273). By the first scene of the third act, the Benton's front parlour has completely changed:

Gone are the aspidistra in the bay window; in their place is a makeshift stand for the display of confectionery. . . . Near the window are two small round tables and chairs – a very immature café. . . . The armchairs have disappeared. . . . The room is now a curious mongrel, half shop, half sitting room.

Mrs Benton has become a cook. Her young son sees himself as the business manager and is in awe of his mother's secret culinary talents:

WILLIE: What beats me is the way you've known all about this posh cooking for years and never let on.
MRS BENTON: . . . You always knew I was a baker's daughter.
WILLIE: Yes but what's a baker – just loaves and things. Tell you what you are, Mum – you're a speciality cook.

(ibid.: 322)

Willie has aspirations to build the business up into a chain of stores, on a smaller scale to Service's, the business from which his father was dismissed. Mrs Benton is quite clear however that: 'It's all very well getting these classy orders, but it's the regular trade that keeps us – the girls going to business and such' (ibid. 322–323). The Benton women are drawn in sharp contrast to the women of the Service family who don't join in the family workforce until the last moment – for the Bentons the distance between wealth and poverty is far greater.

Many of the plays so far discussed were catering for an essentially West End audience who would rarely have been drawn from the working classes, and as such reproduced fairly stereotypical versions of working-class women. However, many of the plays written by women which do focus on issues around working life seem to be consciously presenting what was a private world of working women, on a public stage.

Governmental policy, especially during the inter-war years, did not favour the working woman. The Anomalies Act of 1931, for example, stated that a married woman had to prove that she had left insured employment for reasons other than marriage in order to gain any state benefit. Most employers would not employ married women, other than in domestic service, which was of course uninsured.[7] Although policy changed according to the needs of the economy after the Second World War, women's work was still seen as being of secondary importance to that of the male bread-winner. Ideological bias against women working was also strong, especially during the inter-war years, and it is interesting to note that, around this period, a great many plays are written by women where the protagonists are working women – the stage settings are the environments in which women work. Camillo Pellizzi saw the

101

preponderance of plays which looked at the lives of lower-middle and middle-class working people as constituting a category of their own, naming them 'professional drama' or plays of 'professional realism' (Pellizzi 1935: 284–285).

Overall the 'professional realist' plays written by women promote an ironic mixture of conservatism and feminism. The conservative element is most pronounced in the class of women about which they chose to write. The 'feminism' comes out through the conscious portrayal of women working in the public sphere, whether through choice or necessity and in some cases through both. Although they do not represent on stage the many women's strikes or, for example, the dilemmas of the married woman teacher of the inter-war period, many do write positive images of the woman at work, and centre narrative around a discourse which aims at presenting an argument for women's employment, sometimes despite and sometimes *because* of the fact that they are women.

During the years in question, it was almost impossible for a woman to be seen as a prospective employee without the fact of her gender or marital status being taken into account. Nevertheless, playwrights like Dodie Smith and Aimée and Philip Stuart turn the working woman into a signifier of *Britishness*, whether she is a shop girl or a businesswoman. The question of whether a woman should work outside the family becomes theatricalised into a questioning of the method by which a woman may find personal fulfilment beyond marriage and motherhood. Equally, that a woman ought to work is bound up with an assertion about the possible ways in which a woman can serve the nation.

George Herbert Mead's radical idea that women should train while parenting but that they should also have the employment opportunities to put that training into working practice, integrating work with mother-hood, went against the ideas of a number of his female colleagues for whom an educated woman should have to *choose* between career or motherhood (Diner 1978: 407–408). It was the middle-class woman who attempted and in some cases succeeded in breaking into the job market in Britain during the early and mid-twentieth century. Albeit rather con-servatively, it is this fact and the dilemmas which surround it which is often theatricalised by the playwrights in question. To some extent these plays represent a dramatic culture which is largely, although not solely, inhabited by women whose 'conservatism' and 'feminism' appealed to the theatre audiences of the day. In turn, the theatrical idea of the working woman appealed greatly to the imaginations of both audiences and, especially, women playwrights of the time.

It is important to remember that in terms of feminism and the women's movement, after the vote was gained, the issues were more diverse than those of the years of the suffrage movement. Women were struggling to be seen as equal to men in terms of the importance of their roles within British culture, wanting to be seen as equally responsible within society and the economy, whether in the home or at work. The post-First World War feminist saw her political agenda as being different from that of the previous generation. Thus it is possible to argue that the writing of working woman as a theatrical sign was, consciously or not, part of an attempt to re-position both woman and the 'woman question' in a theatre world where power and choice of discourse lay traditionally in the hands of men.

5

MOTHERHOOD AND THE FAMILY

From matriarchs to refusing mothers

GRETA: Rails, rules, laws, guides, promises, terms, guarantees, conventions, traditions: into the pot with the whole bloody lot. Birth! Birth! That's the thing! Oh, I shall have hundreds of children, millions of hundreds and hundreds of millions.

(Jellicoe 1985: 168)

The mother is a dominant figure in many of the plays written by women during the period under examination. Women playwrights appear to have had an over-riding interest in the relationships between women of different generations with differing status, both to each other and to the society in which they function. Thus the mother figure varies, both in terms of her position within the narrative, and in terms of the definition of her character and nature. When representations of mothers and motherhood of the period are examined *en masse*, it appears that women playwrights were taking on board and at times challenging both the new perceived social, ideological and psychological ideals of motherhood and definitions of, in turn, the 'good' and 'bad' mother. The polarisations of 'good' and 'bad' mothers are far less clearly defined than in nineteenth-century stage representations of mothers, although during the period examined here the stage mother was also often used as a means of positing and sometimes questioning a particular relationship of women to both public and private social structures. In mid-twentieth-century theatre the stage mother, as written by women, often exposed, sometimes affirmed, sometimes challenged, the relationship of motherhood to an idea or proposed ideal of femaleness, femininity and the family.

In terms of social-ideological and semi-scientific tracts, focus during the twentieth century has largely been on motherhood from the child's point of view. Thus some have talked of the twentieth century as being the 'century of the child' (see Ehrenreich and English 1988). The new middle-class mother of the 1920s was in a completely different position from her foremothers, as to some extent was the mother of the 1930s, 1940s and so on. Over the fifty or so year period, mothers were required, for example, to be protective without being too protective, directive without being too directive, permissive without being overly permissive, to breast feed and enjoy it, to not breast feed and enjoy it, to fulfil her own ambitions but never to let them get in the way of the job of nurturing her child. The women playwrights writing during this time often foregrounded the difficulties which women experienced in adhering to the various new popular theories of mothering, with the emphasis being on the difficulty of dealing with the inherent problematics and realities of putting into practice ever-changing ideas of how mothering should be done.

As numerous feminist theorists and historians have identified, there were fairly clear cultural and historical shifts which influenced the role of the mother from the industrial revolution onwards.[1] During the period with which we are concerned here, new 'theories' on mothering arose in part as a backlash to those of the late Victorian and Edwardian eras, and as a result of the changing requirements of the economy. Freudian and other psychoanalytic theories on the nature and the pathology of the mother, and in turn the 'nature of woman', also influenced the emergent social theories on mothering and motherhood, mainly from the 1930s onward. It is interesting to note that many of the theories of motherhood are frequently impossible to separate from the varying ideas on the *nature* of the female and so-called prerequisites of femininity.

The latter years of the industrial revolution saw motherhood, as a social and ideological concept, slowly becoming more dependent on so-called scientific theory. This had consequences for all classes of women, although the target groups were largely among the literate middle classes and bourgeoisie. The making of motherhood into a scientific proposition was,

> according to the experts ... to bring the home into harmony with (contemporary) industrial conditions ... mothers were supposed to seek their ideals as well as their methods in the laboratories and commercial centres of the 'outside world'.
>
> (Ehrenreich and English 1988: 211)

Methods of mothering became a public issue, the solution of which was to be found in so-called scientific theorising.

By the mid-1920s middle-class family size was shrinking, with the nuclear family as a smaller social-domestic unit replacing the extended family. Equally, the function of the family was becoming as much to consume as it was to produce, with more households relying on shop-bought foodstuffs and goods. As a result, some feminists have argued that motherhood and child rearing had, for the middle classes, become perceived as being an end in itself, both emotionally and practically; a situation which invited women 'deeper and deeper into a shadow world of feelings and suspected feelings, guilt, self-analysis, and every nuance of ambivalence' (ibid.).

Although Ehrenreich and English are largely concerned with cultural shifts in the United States, there is clearly a similar pattern in Britain, certainly on a general level. By the late 1920s motherhood was seen as a job, for which women were seen to be most 'naturally' suited. As a result women were becoming more and more isolated from the public world, and this is reflected in the plays through the predominance of the private domestic sphere as a key stage environment. The 'shadow world of feelings and suspected feeling' is one which is dramatised particularly in plays of the late 1940s and 1950s where the mother is the protagonist.

The identification of motherhood as work ran in parallel with an economic situation where work in the public sphere was in short supply. The legal prohibitions against married women working, such as the Married Women's laws, coincided with a social backlash against the notion of independence for women. This was in line with the thinking that marriage was a forerunner to motherhood and so retirement from the public workforce.[2] In terms of popular debate, woman was seen as being characterised by her biology. She was naturally passive, irrational and nurturing, and it was taken for granted that 'for her personal happiness, her social status and her economic prosperity, marriage was for woman an indispensable condition' (Klein 1989: 10).

The biological reduction of femininity to a defined series of character-istics, inherent in the 'natural' woman, was used again and again as a means of persuading middle-class women to give up the work to which they had become accustomed during each of the two world wars. Yet the reduction of femininity to a series of biological determinants could arguably be seen as a reflection of economic strategies more than anything else.[3] But as the twentieth century progressed, the 'experts' on mother-hood centred their attention more and more on the child's needs rather than those of the mother. If a woman found that being a mother, wife and 'household engineer' was not enough in terms of fulfilment of her ambition, then she was in danger of moving into the range of the abnormal, becoming a 'bad' or a rejecting mother. The grounds for defining and analysing the phenomenon of the rejecting mother were based largely on popular interpretations of developments in psycho-analytic theory during the first thirty or so years of the twentieth century. E. A. Kaplan's observation that there 'is no overnight, uniform change either in relations of production or in cultural/ideological discourse' is important here (Kaplan 1992: 17–19). She points out that we can see the link between industrial and cultural ideological change from a historical perspective, but that we need to take into account the fact that practices of mothering, in reality, vary enormously. Thus, 'mother-representations in any one period are also contradictory, multiple and many-sided; a variety of images exists at the same time' (ibid.).

The playwrights we are concerned with here made reference to these theoretical and cultural shifts in relation to the mother, but rarely in a direct way. Most of the settings for representations of motherhood, with very few exceptions, are middle-class domestic environments; the domestic realm being a private world in which very often women have either direct or implicit control. One of the most common criticisms of these playwrights, both by their own contemporary critics and too often by those of our own age, is that their plays were merely domestic comedies or melodramas which refused or neglected to take on the *real* world – the public world with its political issues and social change. What many of these playwrights did, however, was to dramatise the lived experience which resulted from the *consequences* of changes within the public world. It may also be that the form of the dramas did not allow for direct and overt social critiques: many of the plays borrow from the melodramatic form, albeit in a twentieth-century context.

Christine Gledhill has argued that the early Hollywood film industry was heavily influenced by the European melodramatic tradition. The melodrama was re-moulded into a form which brought it from the Victorian age into the popular film culture of the early twentieth century:

> As regards television, soap opera is commonly only seen as the last resort of melodrama. But soap opera, like the woman's film, has an affiliation with women's culture, the elision of which with melodrama should not be assumed.
>
> (Gledhill 1987: 2)

Kaplan also notes that the melodramatic film form made use of 'popular materials' which addressed a wide audience (Kaplan 1992). In terms of theatre there are certain comparable points to be observed.

It was not until the late 1960s that melodrama began to attract more serious critical attention.[4] Some critics see the emergence of melodrama as being specifically linked to cultural change produced by a particular stage of industrialisation. Beyond the theatrical genre, melodrama can be seen as a generalised type of aesthetic experience which produced specific emotional effects in the spectator; the growth in popularity of the melodramatic form was a response to the 'loss of tragic vision', itself a result of the new society which emerged after the industrial revolution, bringing with it a 'society without organic and hierarchical order'. Melodrama could thus be seen as a type of 'sense-making', with its characteristic 'extreme states of being, suspense, dark plots rewarding of good over evil', and so on (Brooks 1976; Kaplan 1992: 62–64). In terms of the texts under examination here the element of 'melodrama' is one which has been transformed, where the discrepancies between good and evil are less clear, where there are fewer 'dark plots' and where characterisation and plot lines arguably reveal, if not more complex readings of the human condition, then certainly ones which are more applicable to the twentieth-century experience than that of the nineteenth century. Many of the playwrights used a popular form which took account of the developments in bourgeois and social drama of the late nineteenth and early twentieth century, but in terms of representations of motherhood, statements of good or bad were replaced by a more investigative attitude. The plays under examination were not just melodramas, they were also plays of ideas, some of which were implicit rather than explicit, but which were readable to their audiences as more than simple domestic narratives: the domestic realm has a different significance for women, especially at this point in history.

Representations of the mother and the family are prevalent in the vast majority of the plays written by women during the period under discussion, with the relationship of woman to mother, mother to daughter and family, and family to state often centralised. Mother as protagonist is almost always either portrayed with some psychological or social reference to marriage, motherhood or the family. When thematic emphasis is on the mother and family life, discourse on the fragmented experience of being both a mother and a woman is often present.

Often, female characters were portrayed as being dissatisfied with the supposed automatic link between femininity and the desire for an experience of motherhood. More often, though, there is a celebration of an expanded perception of motherhood. Here, a mother is shown as also having to work outside the home, or her role within the domestic sphere is shown to be not simply that of a nurturer but also the role of an overseer of emotions and group organisation, often protecting her family from the outside world, at the same time as creating a family which somehow represents a building block in an attempt to strengthen the nation.

Many of the ideas which the early psychoanalysts – Karen Horney, Melanie Klein and Helen Deutsch among others – were processing, were also, in a much simplified form, part of the social and popular discourse on 'the woman question' in newspapers and various other literature of the age. In dramatic texts where the mother persona is created with seemingly more direct reference to emergent psychoanalytic theory, she is rarely condemned or presented as being 'abnormal'. Rather, there is often some social or historical rationale for her position presented within the dramatic narrative. This is not to suggest that the psychoanalytic theories on motherhood and femininity are directly reflected in the dramatic texts, but rather that some parallels could be, and in some cases are made.

During the inter-war years in particular the debate on femininity, to which discourse on the mother was central, raged. The pivotal issue concerned ranking the importance of either nature or nurture in terms of sexual difference. Strangely this debate is one which still divides feminist theorists, with those such as Chodorow, Cixous and Irigaray being heavily criticised for the way in which their argument relies too heavily on the body and on essentialist notions of 'woman'.[5] However, some of the earlier psychoanalysts, especially Karen Horney, had begun to assert and investigate the importance of cultural influence on female development. A very brief and basic comparison of Karen Horney and Helen Deutsch's position in relation to Freud's theories of female 'nature' indicate the two major camps of thought (see Freud 1937; 1977).

> During the last 30 or 40 years there have been contrasting evaluations of the educational capacities innate in mothers. About 30 years ago the maternal instinct was considered an infallible guide in the upbringing of children. When this proved inadequate it was followed by an equally over-stressed belief in theoretical knowledge about education. Unfortunately, equipment with the tools of scientific educational theories proved to be no more perfect guarantee against failure than the maternal instinct had been. And now we are in the midst of a return to stressing the emotional side of the mother–child relationship. This time, however, not with a vague conception of instincts to be relied upon, but with one definite problem: What are the emotional factors that can disturb a desirable attitude and from what sources do they originate?
>
> (Horney 1967a: 175)

The general cultural environment in which Horney developed her ideas was one whereby women were expected to become emotionally and socially fulfilled by marriage and, in turn, motherhood. One of the many criticisms against Horney is that in her attempt to rescue female psychology from Freud's idea that female psychology is based on lack, she tried to 'assert separate female instincts' (Weskott 1986: 54–55). Horney's ideas are significant in part because of the emphasis she placed on the sociological causes of sexual difference. Some would argue that she 'feminised' psychoanalysis:

> If Freudian theory reflects the male stereotypes in its emphasis on instinct and the supremacy of the ego, Horney's reflects the female experience... Freud's instinct theory... reflects the narcissism of the rebellious son and the triumph of the modern, detached managerial man, Horney's sociological explanation reflects the wounding of the devalued daughter and the hope for a new woman.
>
> (ibid.: 64–65)

The Viennese psychoanalyst Helen Deutsch was also involved in the discourse around the nature of female psychology which prevailed during the 1920s and 1930s, but her ideas followed Freud's more closely.[6] There are certain cross-over points with Horney and Klein, but Deutsch did not, unlike Horney, see motherhood as an inherently contradictory role. Deutsch was interested in the differentials in roles of the male and female in reproduction and in the nature of the heterosexual 'sex act' itself. Unlike Horney, and to a certain extent Klein, Deutsch re-emphasised the primacy of penis envy. For Deutsch feminine psychology was bound by a lack, a situation of loss, as a result of which women were formed on a basis of 'castration complex'. By the early 1930s she outlined key character traits of female psychology as being those of masochism and passivity. The implications of Deutsch's theories, although simplified here, can be seen to be far reaching: 'the key elements of Deutsch's reinterpretation of Freud became widely perceived as the Freudian orthodoxy after the Second World War' (Appignanesi and Forrester 1993: 400–441). Primarily, although she became one of the vanguard in psychoanalytic discussions on female psychology, she has been criticised both by her contemporaries – for her lack of desire to deviate from Freud to any great extent – and by feminists – for her contribution to a dominant ideology that women are naturally passive and masochistic. Other critiques have been based on her emphasis on biology rather than cultural imperatives.

For Horney, cultural imperatives were integral to the development of personality and especially to the development of female personality. Nevertheless, although there are great differences between Horney, Deutsch and Klein, all were susceptible to the influence of the cultural background of their time, much of which was designed to create, or at least had the effect of promoting and validating, a notion of acceptable hierarchies of both gender and class. Mitchell points to the difficulties of positively evaluating Deutsch and Horney's work because of their search for an 'essential' and therefore 'natural' woman (J. Mitchell 1983: 128). This search was, however, acceptable in the intellectual climate within which they were working; one in which a search for the 'natural' and 'essential' dominated. In much of the work of women playwrights during a period of fifty or so years which encompass that era where the debate on femininity and motherhood raged fiercely, it is precisely this confused relationship between nurture and nature which is consistently foregrounded in narratives which focus on mothers, motherhood, femininity and the family. There is a recognition that the biological origins of motherhood often function in opposition to the social and economic forces which shape the experience of both mothering and the choices of social roles for women in both the private and the public world.

THE IRON HAND IN A VELVET GLOVE: THE MATRIARCHS OF THE 1920S AND 1930S

Originally an actress, G. B. Stern was a popular novelist who also worked as a journalist and film scriptwriter: she was also a close friend of the novelists Sheila-Kaye Smith and Rebecca West.[7] Described by one critic in the mid-1930s as a 'pantechnicon novelist (saga school)', Stern found great success with her Rakonitz novels, of which *The Tents of Israel* was adapted for the stage in the form of *The Matriarch* (*Evening Standard*, 16 November 1935). The play, which ran at the Royalty theatre for 229 performances, provided one of the last British stage roles for Mrs Patrick Campbell, as Anastasia Rakonitz, the matriarch of the title. *The Matriarch* provides an implicit investigation of motherhood as both a biological and culturally defined experience. The narrative gives a history of three generations of the Rakonitz 'tribe', a wealthy Jewish family based in London with contacts and family members all over Europe. The economic basis of the family originates from their dealings in precious stones, which gained momentum after the Napoleonic Wars. Anastasia is 'head' of the family and, as such, controls the decision-making both within the business and within the extended family unit. The play opens with a Prologue, set in 1902, in which Anastasia's daughter Sophie reveals to the audience that she has adopted the illegitimate child fathered by her soon-to-be estranged husband, Oliver Maitland, and mothered by a local barmaid, 'Plymouth Nell' (who, coincidentally, never appears in the play). Sophie adopts the baby out of necessity rather than kindness, as she tells her husband,

111

SOPHIE: I've told you a hundred times, I must have a son to show
Mamma!... She'll never take any notice of me if I don't have a
son! I might as well never have been born – I might as well die, if I
don't have a son. A daughter would have been no good.

OLIVER: No. Girls don't count for much in the tribe of Israel do
they?

(Stern 1931a: 7)

Maitland disappears before the arrival of Anastasia, who brings her
unmarried sister Wanda, treated as a servant, with her. Anastasia has
already organised for her grandchild Danny to become part of the family
business. She plans to take them all back to London, where her granddaughter Toni was born on the same day as Sophie's 'son':

ANASTASIA: ...For in London we will all be united. For the
babies, they must be considered first.

(ibid.: 15)

Act One takes us forward in time, to 1921, to the drawing room of a
Georgian house in Holland Terrace, in London, lavishly decorated with
chandeliers and Eastern carpets, and with two portraits of the founders of
the Rakonitz family, Simon and Babette, hanging in a prominent position
on the wall. The family are all waiting for Danny's imminent return from
Vienna. Anastasia's brothers, 'the uncles', are waiting in the drawing
room. Toni has asked Anastasia to order Danny back from Vienna, about
which he is not pleased, and when she tells him that, because Sophie died
when he was a baby, she will always back him up, as it must have been
awful for him not to have had a mother, Danny points out that he has no
such attachment to family: 'Oh, Toni, you sentimental ass!... I like being
without a mother. I only wish I was without a grandmother, too. Without
any relations at all. That would be perfect. Paradise...' (ibid.: 20).

The two grandchildren are characterised as opposites: Toni, the
daughter of a non-Jewish woman, is the eldest child of Anastasia's eldest
son. She has a romanticised vision of and deep attachment to *family* as an
ideal, and to family roots in terms of her position within the Rakonitz
tribe. Danny, on the other hand, has little affiliation with the family and
wants to travel; his attachment is to Toni and to the financial support
which the family provides. Although she understands the criticisms which
are constantly aimed at Anastasia, Toni is protective of her, and understands that her role as the matriarch is defined by cultural necessity as
much as biological fact.

Toni's cousin Val represents another opposition, this time female to female. Val is an artist who has been socialising outside the family parameters, much like Danny. When he asks her what she's been occupying herself with in his absence she replies,

VAL: Everything I shouldn't. Bobbing my hair, smoking, drinking cocktails, using my solemn art on advertisement posters, loafing about in France without a chaperone.

TONI: Ineligible young men: daring clothes, debts, extravagances, *crimes passionelles*, and cheeking Aunt Elsa – isn't that it, Val? I wonder you weren't afraid to come today.

(ibid.: 21)

Used as one layer of a dramatic device which aims to represent the necessary differences between the two generations of matriarchs, namely, Anastasia and Toni, this opposition in characterisation is also re-focused in the different ways in which each of the three cousins takes responsibility during the family crises of the play.

In the Prologue, Anastasia Rakonitz, whose resemblance to a Chekhovian matriarch is uncanny, is a woman of fifty who looks no older than a 'voluptuous forty', with an accentuated central European accent. She is an archetypal image of a 1920s 'Jewish mother' who continues to control her children even when they have matured into adulthood. She covers up any cracks in the illusion of family respectability, justifying Oliver Maitland's disappearance as being almost an act of God, because he was not Jewish, therefore allaying any possibility of her daughter Sophie's loss of face at 'losing' her husband. When Anastasia's son Ludo steals a significant sum of money from the firm of a great family friend, Mr Cohen, she insists that Ludo was borrowing the money, that no criminal act could have taken place within the boundaries of family and family friends. For the first act, Anastasia's world is that of Vienna during the late nineteenth century, a world which she has re-created for herself in London. According to her younger sister Elsa, Anastasia has taken all the best family possessions as her own, only loaning them out to family members, to recall them later when she herself has suffered financial losses. Other women in the family have little access to information about the financial state of the business, but Anastasia is fully informed:

MAXIMILLIAN: Anastasia! Oh yes, she is different, she is our field-Marshal. Her energy is stupendous.

(ibid.: 36)

Equally, Anastasia Rakonitz has control over the daily lives of the other women in the play, especially her sister Wanda and her daughter-in-law Susan, who is Toni's mother.

Act Two takes place six months after an economic devastation has caused the collapse of family investments. The scene is more bare – gone are the lavish rugs and ornaments of the first act. Anastasia is busy ordering everyone about, possessions have been sold and the family is on the move to a smaller house in Ealing. Toni has been working in a dressmaking establishment, and it is implied that her father committed suicide after their financial crash. Anastasia is concerned for Toni's health, complaining that her employers do not feed her regularly with chicken-soup, and do not let her rest every few hours. The main point, however, is that Anastasia cannot accept that Toni is working for a living, and the opening lines of the scene bring the difference between the two generations of matriarch into the foreground:

ANASTASIA: No Rakonitz woman has ever before earned money! No Rakonitz woman has ever worked before! (*Puts some linen in hamper down R. and goes behind table again, sorting linen.*)

SUSAN: (*Brusquely.*) Work? Look at Wanda! They've worked like slaves, but not for money. That's the only difference, if you ask me!

ANASTASIA: ... It's not right for my granddaughter to be brought up without travel and languages, without conversation with brilliant people, who have influence, who have *savoir faire*, who can make her future for her! ... It is not likely that Toni will meet anyone either, with these Woolfs or at the evening school where she learns to draw the fashions, whom could she possibly marry!

SUSAN: Marry? At her age? She's a child!

ANASTASIA: When I was Toni's age I was already married three years!

(ibid.: 40–41)

Anastasia wants to 'save' Toni by bringing her home and feeding her copious hot meals. Her character, described by the reviewer for the 1950 radio production of the play, is one of an 'indomitable' woman, who 'storms, persuades, domineers and cajoles', and she is described by Danny as being 'like nine people' (*Radio Times*, 17 November 1950). However, this description of Anastasia is only applicable to the first two acts of the play. By Act Three, where the action has again been moved, this time by five years, she has had a stroke and is an old lady in a wheelchair, still giving orders but with less effect and fewer results.

By the end of the third act, Toni, who has being saving in order to pay back into Mr Cohen's family business the money stolen by Ludo, is effectively running the family. She is living in a cottage studio in Chelsea with Val and wants to take over the fashion business from the Woolfs, who are about to retire, but lacks the capital. Toni felt it her duty to take on the family debt, and preserve the family honour. When the time comes for her to pay off the debt, she does not have enough money. She considers using the money which she has saved to buy the Woolfs' business from them, but eventually prioritises the family reputation over her own ambition. When Danny's estranged father turns up unexpectedly and gives Danny £200, explaining that he is not a real member of the family by blood, Danny proposes marriage to Toni, emphasising the fact that they are not blood cousins, as were Anastasia and her husband. Toni's initial reaction is that she will marry him and have 'fun at last'. That is, until Danny asks her what she plans to do about paying the debt. At this point Toni makes what she sees as the only decision possible, that Danny's cheque should be used to pay the debt, and that they will get married but delay leaving the family fold until they can save enough money to make sure that everyone is 'safe' and taken care of. In her eyes the family has to come first. This is the point at which Danny accuses her of being a matriarch:

> DANNY: (*as though he were just waking from a nightmare*)... and I never saw it until now... it's been going on all the time, getting stronger!... if I married you I'd never be free of the family.... You're the Matriarch over again, you are exactly like her and know it... afraid to behave as she behaves. You try and think you're cool and logical and modern – but all that passes away, and you'll be more and more like the Matriarch as you grow older... you'll be the bully of the family... and yet they'll all come to you, as head of the family... because you care about them most.... There'll always be a Matriarch in your family.
>
> (Stern 1931a: 74–75)

Danny then leaves all connection with the family behind him, following in his father's footsteps. Toni is left alone, shocked that she should be thought of as being like her grandmother with whose personality she considers herself to have very little in common. When Mr Cohen arrives to collect the debt money, he instead offers the sum as capital for Toni's business venture, and she then decides that she will buy a house so that she and her mother, brother, aunt and grandmother can all live together. When she tells Val the response is less vehement, but along the same lines as Danny's:

VAL: Well, I'm damned...Toni you're the Matriarch all over
again.
TONI: (*very simply*) Am I ?

(ibid.: 79)

To a certain extent the narrative of the play fits into the 'maternal
sacrifice paradigm', based on Kaplan's perception of representations of
motherhood in popular culture and melodrama, as characterised by,

> dominant representations, even in forms that specifically address
> women, satisfy unconscious male desire more than any possible
> unconscious female ones, pleasure is gained through the fantasy of
> surrendering all for the phallus.

(Kaplan 1992: 106)

If we substitute family for phallus, then there is an interesting dilemma.
The particular family in this case is matriarchal in structure. Position
within the power structure of the family, by the end of the play, has nothing
to do with biological motherhood. *The Matriarch* is not so much a play
about mothering as it is a play in which changes in the form and structure
of a matriarchal family are examined. Anastasia is the biological mother
and head of the family. Toni, on the other hand, is not a biological mother,
and the implication is that she has traded possibilities of romance and
marriage with Danny for what she sees as being her matriarchal 'role'. For
Toni, the position of family matriarch has to be maintained and
modernised. Her maternal sacrifice is to make it her job to provide for
the needs of those around her, through work rather than through
negotiation and favouritism like her grandmother. She finds romance in
her role within the family. Originally described as being frail, Toni
develops an ambition to run her own company almost as soon as she
ventures out into the public world of work. This ambition is both the result
of a desire to be 'successful' in the 'male' public business world and a
fulfilment of the need to provide for the family.

There are very few male characters in the play. The old uncles
disappear after the first act, and Danny and his father, who are both
written as having rather shallow personalities, have very little real action
other than to provide the audience with further insight into the position of
the women within the play. The abundance of mothers can be contrasted
with the absence of fathers. Stern creates an historical distance between
the matriarch of the nineteenth century and that of the twentieth. In doing
so, the role of matriarch becomes far more of a cultural and economic
imperative than a biological one; Toni may be the eldest grandchild, but

she is not fully of the 'tribe' in that her mother was not of the Jewish faith. Toni does see herself as having a duty to the 'tribe'; she is related by blood. Yet her choice is to remain within a powerful position in a 'female' world, rather than be married. Thus it is a choice between being located in a position of power, or being married and relatively powerless. Married life is not as appealing when her potential husband, Danny, makes such statements as, 'I think Toni needs to be bossed and bullied for a bit' (Stern 1931a: 62). Stern has written a complex play which, although on the surface promises to provide a biological imperative as the rationale for the dénouement, fails to do so. We should note, however, that at the same time as questioning and criticising the structure of this culture-specific family unit, she affirms its necessity. This was not an uncommon strategy.

Family Affairs by Gertrude Jennings and *Dear Octopus* by Dodie Smith are two plays particularly notable for the use to which the matriarch figure is put.[8] Both plays are set in the private sphere of the home, both are concerned with the events in the internal family life of the upper-middle classes, and each featured actresses who were well-known 'stars' of the West End theatre as matriarch figures. The matriarch is the central figure around whose behaviour and emotional complexities the actions of the other characters revolve.

Gertrude Jennings was no stranger to the West End by the early 1930s, nor was she unknown to audiences more concerned with non-commercial theatre. Born in 1877, Jennings was the daughter of I. L. Jennings, one-time editor of the *New York Times*, later MP for Stockport, and Madeleine Henriques, an American actress known for her work at Wallack's theatre in New York. Gertrude's professional career as an actress began with touring work for Ben Greet's company, also working in New York as Gertrude Henriques.

Her one-act play, *A Woman's Influence*, was one of the most frequently performed in the early years of the Actresses Franchise League (see Gardner 1985). She wrote numerous one-act plays, and although she is often mentioned for her popularity among amateurs, she achieved a number of successes with her West End plays during the inter-war years. Directed by Auriol Lee and starring Lilian Braithwaite as Lady Madehurst, the first act of *Family Affairs* takes place in the drawing room at Lady Madehurst's house in Queen's Gate, London. Jennings uses what appears to have been a familiar format: the family gathering; revelations of superficial dilemmas; discovery, by the maternal figure, of the 'real' family problems. The plot includes, as seems to have been the general pattern, the revelation of family secrets, followed by the re-instatement of both the matriarch's position as head of the family and the re-solidifying of family

unity. *Family Affairs* is both about 'romantic' affairs and the affairs involved
in the overseeing or managing of the complexities of family life.

We are introduced to Helena Warwick who, it turns out, is having an
affair with Harvey Madehurst, one of Lady Madehurst's sons, the other
two being Sydney and Herbert. Helena complains that Harvey is rarely
on his own and always surrounded by 'such a barrage of family' (Jennings
1934: 584). Lady Madehurst's grandson Nevil has a wife, Rose, who is just
about to sue him and run off with a hairdresser. Herbert's wife Julia is
reprimanded by Lady Madehurst for not paying enough attention to
family matters:

> LADY MADEHURST: My mother, dear Julia, lived for her home
> and her children, as I did for mine! She never thought us one too
> many!
>
> (ibid.: 600)

The family secret revealed at the end of Act One is that the estranged
son Sydney is back from Jamaica and needs money to support himself.
When he turns up in the second act, his brother Harvey tells him that he'll
find the money if Sydney promises to disappear again. Act Two continues
with Lady Madehurst's admission that she knows all about Rose and is
trying to bribe the amorous hairdresser to vanish. She also tells Harvey
that, instead of marrying Helena, who by now has come up with plans to
divorce her husband which will leave her with a large income, he should
marry his secretary who is a 'nice dear girl'. An outsider, Helena has few
romantic notions either about family life or about Lady Madehurst. She
tells Harvey that when they get married she wants to move and she wants
him to sell the family home:

> HELENA: ... No house, however large, would hold your mother
> and me. The British Museum wouldn't do it. I've gone all 1870
> to please her. I've listened to all her tales... entirely on your
> account, and now I've done with the lot of it. ... Put the house in
> the agent's hands as soon as ever you can, won't you?
>
> (ibid.: 638)

Lady Madehurst plans to put Helena off marrying Harvey by 'be-
friending' her; she fantasises with her about how they will spend their
evenings together once she becomes her daughter-in-law. The realisation
that Harvey is inescapably entwined with the family discourages Helena
from continuing the relationship. In Act Three Lady Madehurst discovers
that the reason Sydney disappeared in the first place was because he had
been embezzling money. Rather than spurn him, she helps him, saying

that she will find the money to pay back what was stolen. She tells him to forget everything and reminds him that, after all, she is his *mother*, then she helps him to go into hiding from the police. When Lady Madehurst is sure that Harvey will marry Margaret, the secretary, she offers to move in with her daughter and let him sell the house.

The matriarch in *Family Affairs* is considered as the head of the family, even though she is financially supported by her children, who humour her but still need her approval. Lady Madehurst is opinionated, romanticises the value of the family and always, in the end, seems to know best. The maintenance of family bonds is of the utmost importance, and morality is not shaped by the outside world, but rather by what is required to keep the family together. A mother's love for her children means that she will do anything for them, even break the law, but in return they must obey her and must also prioritise, not themselves, but the needs of the family unit.

Dodie Smith's *Dear Octopus* provides a contrast of character in the matriarchal figure of Dora Randolph, the mother of an upper-middle-class family who have come to celebrate their parents' golden wedding anniversary. Dora believes that women should not be independent and certainly should not be businesswomen. She disapproves of the fact that her daughter Hilda is a businesswoman and when her grandson tells her that her daughter is,

> quite a big pot really Granny. I read an article on her the other day in a Pioneer Woman series.... She's an estate agent. She's put through one or two pretty big deals in house property.

Dora rather scathingly replies, 'It's a surprise to me that Hilda knows the back of a house from the front' (Smith 1966: 292–293).

Dora Randolph does not, however, show any real disapproval of her daughter Cynthia, who is living in Paris with a married man. Much like the relationship between Lady Madehurst and Sydney in the Jennings' play, Dora's relationship with Cynthia is bound by blood and, as far as she is concerned, it is more important for Cynthia to be a part of the family than to be judged and outcast because of the choices she has made in her personal life. Smith makes some attempt to show Dora outside her connection to the matriarchal role, through her relationship with her husband's ex-fiancée Belle, who has been invited to the golden wedding celebrations. Belle is bright and garish but full of character and individuality, and through their relationship the 'younger' Dora is revealed as jealous and highly competitive with other women.

The play is interesting because it provides an extremely idealised picture of upper-middle-class family life and of Englishness, and as such

contains innate statements about the necessity of the family unit and its
indestructibility. The 'dear octopus' of the title symbolises the family, a
treasured but feared institution. In the closing scene of the play, the speech
made in honour of the celebrating couple is both coercive and patriotic:

> NICHOLAS: The family isn't what it was. And there...lies its
> strength. It is, like nearly every British institution, adaptable. It
> bends, it stretches – but it never breaks.... To the family – that
> dear octopus from whose tentacles we never quite escape, nor, in
> our inmost hearts, ever quite wish to.
>
> (ibid.: 379)

Upper-middle-class matriarchal figures can be found again and again,
especially in plays written by women during the 1930s. These grand old
dames were often feared or despised by their families, such as in Clemence
Dane's *Moonlight is Silver* (Dane 1934), where Dame Agnes Ronsard almost
breaks up her son's marriage because of her desire to keep him in the
family home. Stage representations of the all-powerful and fearsome
matriarch, such as the popular American playwright Rose Franken's Mrs
Hallam in *Another Language* (Franken 1933) or Mildred Surrège, with her
'thin, restless face and...discontented mouth' in Dorothy Massingham's
The Lake, abound (Massingham 1933: 10). They are sometimes humoured
but more commonly they are revered. Here Franken describes Mrs
Hallam as follows:

> Outwardly she presents the picture of a sweet and appealing old
> lady, but one gradually becomes aware of the incessant functioning
> of an alert mind, a quick discernment and an indomitable will.
>
> (Franken 1933: 11)

These plays are more concerned with the institution and historical
foundations of motherhood and the psychology of a particular generation
of mothers than with the conditions of, or issues which surround,
motherhood. There were, in fact, a stream of plays about families and
family life during the last decade of the inter-war years, including
Gertrude Jennings's *Our Own Lives* (produced in 1935), and Dodie Smith's
smash hit, *Call it a Day* (Smith 1936). Contemporary critics were quick to
see these plays as being 'of strong feminine interest' (*Daily Mail*, 23 August
1934), as 'dramas of the home' and as being vehicles for the 'stage
grandmother' who,

> is a distinct species with two principal varieties – the wisely tender
> (with lace and bugles), the shrewdly dictatorial (with ebony

stick)...for, though not real, she has on stage a reality of her own...and is often an endearing and even a persuasive creature.

(*The Times*, 23 August 1934)

The matriarchal maternal figures represent mothers as the resolvers of family conflict, and the maintainers of order within the family. They are the 'household engineers', serving what they perceive as being the needs of their children, controlling access to family information and indeed the structure and activities of the family unit itself. The matriarchs are often shown to be in conflict with the next generation of women, especially those who come from outside the family unit and marry their sons. The plays provide dominant representations of this figure, which during the 1930s was given wide circulation, especially in the commercially oriented West End. It is rare to find any critique of this family figure except from younger generations of women in particular, who object to the control which the matriarch figures wield over their lives.

During the 1930s there appear to have been two prevalent representations of motherhood in plays by women which, to some extent, are polarised in terms of generations. Where motherhood is thematically linked with work and the public sphere, the mothers are younger and the plays are more about the relationship between work, family responsibility and 'womanhood' or motherhood. These are plays where the lives of 'modern' mothers are foregrounded rather than being entwined with narratives that are more concerned with theatrically visible generational differences between mothers of one era and mothers of another. This is not to say that the two polarities are mutually exclusive, but where two generations are in opposition one often finds what Kaplan has identified as a resisting text, whereby 'it is a matter of distinguishing some texts that at least recognise certain discursively constituted female positions as oppressive as against those that simply validate the structure' (Kaplan 1992: 125).

Certainly, if we substitute child with family and mother with matriarch, then the paradigm is such that the private family unit as presented in these plays is at times an idealised and extended version of a perceived socially ideal relationship between mother and child, whereby the mothers' needs as individuals are fulfilled through their relationship to the child. In turn the possibility of an ideal relationship is often questioned – there is a notable lack of the kind of obsessional attitude about 'ideal' mothers with which, for example, Ibsen's Nora in *A Doll's House* was met in the late nineteenth century.

PHALLIC MOTHERS AND REFUSING MOTHERS

The phallic mother as propounded by psychoanalytic discourse is basically a controlling and forceful woman whose 'natural' femininity has somehow been overcome by what were seen as being essentially male desires for control and dominance. As such she 'refuses' to be a subservient mother, and becomes manipulative and overpowering, often projecting her own desires onto the way she nurtures her child. Although there are a number of 'refusing mothers' in plays before the 1950s, they are few and far between. Kaplan returns to Melanie Klein for theoretical discourse on the mother in the unconscious in her quest to find a psychoanalytic basis for the 'phallic' mother. Klein

> stressed the child's unconscious fantasies of being devoured by the mother... Klein also theorised that early on the child has two internalised unconscious mothers which emerge from its experience in relation to the breast.... It is easy to see how these two unconscious mothers later become the alternate 'ideal' nurturing and evil 'phallic', denying mothers. It is also clear that, from this psychoanalytic perspective, the mother in the social cannot hope to satisfy the infant, no matter what she does or how nurturing she is.
>
> (Kaplan 1992.: 207–208)

Kaplan also points to the fact that Freud did very little work on the mother/daughter and mother/child relationship during this pre-Oedipal phase. For him it was a period to which only the woman could have experiential access and data on. During the 1920s, Deutsch was concerned with the way in which women whom she effectively classed as abnormal developed traits which she saw as being masculine, that is to say, non-passive. But it was Horney who, even though she often entangled the psychic and the social, suggested that women were given negative images of womanhood from birth. As a result women may develop negative feelings about being a woman and so develop characteristics which are considered as being masculine. This, of course, may result in a woman having the desire to be domineering. What is interesting about these ideas when we apply them to the matriarch figure, is that she *has* to be domineering in order to fulfil her feminine role. It may be possible, therefore, to see the maternal matriarch texts as providing at one and the same time very conservative female constructs who, through being represented in the context of their 'power domain', provide a social rationale for existence rather an innate biological one. If the social role of the mother is instinctively to maintain and protect the family, the required behaviour may be more 'masculine' identified than 'feminine'. As such the 'maternal' mothers of the previous section are to some extent also 'phallic' mothers, by necessity.

Joan Morgan's *This was a Woman* (Morgan 1946) had its first try-out at Beatrice and Jack de Leon's Q theatre and then transferred to the Comedy theatre in 1944 where it ran for 380 performances. Morgan was described by West End critic Beverley Baxter as

> one of those light skinned, fair-haired girls...whose healthy vivacity at tea would turn any potential lover into a pal. For sheer wind-swept normality and British girlhood let me commend Miss Morgan as she appeared to us on the stage.
>
> (*Evening Standard*, March 1944)

The description of the erstwhile child film star and West End actress is in complete contrast to a narrative breakdown of her play, in which we find lust, murder, frustration and a son who has just taken a course with psychoanalytic analysis as the key component. Morgan was criticised for not re-writing a Hedda Gabler or Regina Hubbard with more depth, yet, although Olivia Russell bears some resemblance to the 'anti'-heroines of both Ibsen's and Hellman's plays, Morgan could only ever be accused of a vague re-working of similar archetypes within a completely different social and cultural context (*Sunday Times*, 19 March 1944).

The narrative focuses on the transformation of Olivia Russell from the rather wistful and bored wife of Arthur Russell – shipping clerk and keen bird watcher – into a power-hungry murderess whose devious actions are discovered by her medically trained son, Terry, in the final act of the play. The play is set in 'suburbia', and Olivia, with her tumbling curls and artistic taste, is middle aged and middle class; 'her voice is as complex as her appearance' (Morgan 1946: 6). We first meet her in the Turret Room of her Gothic house, talking to the housekeeper who intends to leave the household and join her husband in his new business:

OLIVIA: I think you're sacrificing yourself to a man's whim...I only hope you won't regret it.

(ibid.: 7)

Olivia questions her own husband's lack of ambition and social status and is concerned that her son will just marry on a whim, rather than find someone whom she considers to be suitable; she is ambitious both for herself and for her son. Olivia also projects her own feelings about men and marriage onto her daughter, Fenella:

Oh why must I feel like this, as if the whole horror were my own to be gone through all over again? Why must my children be so close to me, part of me, that I feel everything that happens to them as though it were my own tragedy... (men)... you wouldn't understand... beasts they are all beasts.

(ibid.: 18–19)

After giving her new housekeeper *Lady Chatterley's Lover* to read, Olivia encourages her to flirt with her own daughter Fenella's fiancé and future husband. When Austen Penrose, family friend and old friend of Mr Russell, comes to pay a visit, the audience are shown a man who has the status and ambition which Olivia would like to find in her own husband. Her open admiration for Penrose instigates a tense conversation where he assures her that she has the perfect family 'set-up', and asks her what more a person could possibly want from life:

OLIVIA: Power. (*the word drops like a stone into a still pool... there is a long silence*)

PENROSE: Power is an unknown quantity... according to how it is used. No... no, on balance I wouldn't say that power was a desirable factor in life.

OLIVIA: (*holding his eyes*) No one realises the *full* of a thing unless they've had it. A loaf only has meaning for a starving man... (*Terry watches his mother intently*).... Authority is power. I envy you that. I envy you. I'd have enjoyed power... (*there is a curiously tense atmosphere*)...

OLIVIA: (*presses her fingers to her brow*) This sense of frustration... mediocrity... knowing one's potentialities. Knowing one might have been... accomplished... with the right man...

(ibid.: 40)

The third act takes us to a point six months later. Olivia's husband has been taken ill. Austen has been helping Olivia to look after him and now reads Olivia as a self-sacrificing, nurturing woman. When the children return from a working cruise, they are full of apprehension and find their mother with dishevelled hair, '*her mouth a gash in her livid mask-like face. She moves as though walking in her sleep*' (ibid.: 50). In the last scene of the play, Olivia tells Austen that she is in love with him, and entreats him to acknowledge her innate power:

OLIVIA: ... I know my power... a woman's power. How many of the women who've destroyed men, cost them their thrones, how many of them have been beautiful? The great courtesans of

France . . . they had the same power at fifty that they possessed in their youth. The eternal mystery of woman. Our power is beyond analysis. . . . Myself? What do you know of the sleeping dark potential that is a woman's soul?

(ibid.: 60)

Penrose has no romantic intentions towards Olivia, whose son turns on her when she reveals that she has been slowly poisoning her husband. Terry describes her as 'interesting subject matter . . . a study in ultimate egotism', and when they are left alone together, analyses her behaviour as being that of

The animated waxwork of a devoted wife and mother, the kind mistress, the sympathetic friend. . . . Then the undercurrent, the brilliant woman stifled by mediocre surroundings . . . frustrated, seeking sublimation or outlet. The suburban Aspasia. . . . The-power-behind-the-throne . . . stronger than her environment in will, in personality. . . in intellect.

(ibid.: 61–63)

Olivia's rapid and pleading response is that he was her sublimation, that no great man can exist without a woman, that 'women have the seed of greatness within them', that while poisoning her husband she experienced what it is like to have power, with his life in her hands. Her son's penultimate speech is conclusive:

TERRY: I know you're not mad. You're evil. There is evil in everyone. . . . You're a conventional woman . . . busy with your role of devoted wife. . . . If you'd been born into a different world you'd have got your power easily. You weren't, you were middle class, so you had to build up your ego on cruelties.

(ibid.: 63–64)

The play ends dramatically as she says to her son, 'I am too strong for you! I've beaten you all. I've won, I've won!', at which point Olivia gives a wild cry and jumps from the balcony to her death as the curtain falls.

Played to great acclaim by Sonya Dresdel, Olivia Russell is constructed by Morgan as a 'complex woman'. In the opening moments of the play one of the servants observes,

Many's the time I've come in and found her standing out on the balcony looking out. She once said, ' . . . space . . . space Mrs

125

Holmes. Have you ever thought how stifled we all are'... that's her all over though, unexpected.

(ibid.: 6)

Morgan is very clear to distinguish between Olivia's mannerisms and those of the people around her; she repeatedly fingers her brow and seeks prolonged eye contact with others and so on. Her behaviour and general demeanour set her apart from the other characters in the play. Olivia makes constant references throughout to the fact that she feels she has wasted her life by devoting herself to one man. We are encouraged to think of her as an exception, as somehow an outsider, yet, at the end of the play, her son, a trained analyst, assures her that she is a *conventional woman*. Her suicide provides the dramatic, fatalistic ending to the play. But she commits suicide in order to avoid the legal consequences of her previous actions, and in this way she has taken control of the situation in the only way open to her.

Certainly Olivia Russell is founded on a notion of a neurotic and masculine woman, and Morgan makes great use of psychoanalytic terminology and concepts, especially in the relationship between mother and child – Morgan also makes it clear that her anti-heroine has no means of expression inside her social setting other than through her familial role. Although perhaps not presenting us with the most positive of images of woman, Morgan shows a recognition of character and context rather than transformation and in this she is not alone among the women playwrights of the era under discussion. The only way in which Olivia can step outside of the 'suburban Aspasia' is to destroy herself. The entire play has an atmosphere of containment, of suppressed desires and rigid social roles; Olivia is the only character who provides any challenge to this situation. When commenting on her hospitality, Penrose's lines, 'You've given me my first glimpse of English home life. Charming... really charming,' strike rather an ironic note, if we take into account the constant mood of dissatisfaction and suspicion which simmers just below the surface of the play (ibid.: 33).

Among the key signifying characteristics of the 'phallic mother' are manipulation, resentment and over-attachment to offspring. As previously noted, these characteristics are similar to those found in representations of the matriarch in plays of the 1920s and 1930s. Although a sense of having sacrificed one's own life and ambitions for the sake of the family could also be seen to be part of the same model of motherhood, there are few other examples of an interpretation of the 'phallic mother' as strong as Morgan's. Here, Olivia's personal ambition works against her role as mother and she perceives herself as having been the cause of her own downfall. For her family it is right that she has to sacrifice her personal ambition for the sake of the family unit.

The sacrificing mother is more readily identifiable in those plays where an ideal mother is being foregrounded. Where the previous matriarchs constantly sacrificed their needs to those of the family, sacrifice was integral to the role of the good matriarch. However, in Margaret Kennedy and George Ratoff's *Autumn,* produced in 1937 at the St Martin's theatre, the element of sacrifice normally associated with the ideal is the key element of a non-conforming mother in the shape of Lady Brooke, played in the original production by Flora Robson.

Again the setting for the play is an English upper-middle-class family based in London. The play is far more grounded in the English domestic drawing-room drama tradition than Kennedy's two earlier plays *The Constant Nymph* (1926) and *Escape Me Never* (1933). Monica Brooke is a young eager student (played by Victoria Hopper) who has communist friends, and 'new' ideas about women:

NANNY: ...Women as you might say are born to suffer.
MONICA: That's a very old fashioned idea....Women have
    more sense nowadays. They refuse to put up with suffering.
(Kennedy and Ratoff 1939: 111–112)

Lady Catherine Brooke has been nursing her ailing husband, Brian, to whom she has been married for ten years. We discover that until his illness they have not really spent all that much time together, as he has been devoted to his work. Someone sends an anonymous letter to say that Catherine has been having an affair with Mark Seeley (played by Jack Hawkins). Catherine twists the facts and tells her husband that actually it's their daughter who has caught this young man's attention. Monica, however, has no time for Mark; she sees him as being insincere, with 'one eye on God and the other on the main chance' (ibid.: 132). Catherine manipulates the situation and of course Monica begins to see Mark in a completely new light, as a result of which she gives up all her notions of female independence:

MONICA: What you do...What you are–that will be me.
    Everything I used to believe in...oh, I suppose I believe it
    still...but it just doesn't matter any more.
(ibid.: 164)

By the end of Act Two Monica has found out about her mother's affiliations with Mark and runs away to stay with her communist friends.

127

Catherine confesses to Brian that she is jealous of Mark and Monica. By doing so she keeps the marriage together and then manages to stabilise her relationship with her daughter, also ensuring possibilities of continued contact with her ex-lover. The play ends happily as husband and wife are re-united and the family is kept intact. Catherine Brooke breaks out of her mothering role in search of fulfilment, but the family and her role as wife to a busy but sick man overcome her.

In Lesley Storm's *Black Chiffon* (1949), the mother, played again by Flora Robson, makes the ultimate maternal sacrifice of choosing to go to prison rather than have family secrets used as a defence in a court case. When arrested for shoplifting a few days before her son's marriage, the lawyer proposes that they use her close relationship with her son and her fear of his impending marriage and flight from the home as her defence. Both the lawyer and the husband use a psychoanalytic framework to question the nature of her relationship with her son. However, for Alicia Christie, to love and protect one's son, in a home environment which is made hostile because of her husband's jealousy of her son, is only natural. By going to prison for her crime, she disrupts the smooth running and respectability of the family, but maintains the sanctity of the relationship between mother and child. Storm's implication here is that the family is a complex and unhappy environment and that when the children leave, the dysfunctions of the family are revealed. Thus Alicia's refusal to plead not guilty is an implicit as well as an explicit means of disruption as well as a maintenance of family bonds.

SINGLE MOTHERS – FALLEN WOMEN OR REFUSING MOTHERS?

Virtually all of the plays so far examined focus on motherhood and the family without great reference to the social and economic structure. Although there is an emphasis on the psychological effect of proscribed motherhood roles, there is very little examination of the social construction of motherhood and mothering outside the family unit. With exceptions such as Kennedy's *Escape Me Never*, there are very few unmarried stage mothers up until the early 1950s, and so the social problematics of motherhood are rarely examined. The fallen woman as a stage icon does not appear to have had the same theatrical marketability as it had had in the nineteenth century.

In Sylvia Rayman's first and most successful play, *Women of Twilight*, written while she was working in a London snack bar, motherhood as a role for women is explored on a social-economic rather than a social-psychological level. The play was originally staged at the Embassy in 1951, later successfully transferring to the Vaudeville. It was made into a film, produced by Daniel Angel Films, in 1952 and directed by Gordon Parry with a screenplay by Anatole de Grunwald. In Rayman's play there is a deliberate subverting of the image of 'charming English home life' so beautifully portrayed in plays like *Dear Octopus*. Rayman is interested in moving from emergence and recognition to exposure and critique.

Women of Twilight is a tragic but socially observant tale of the life of single mothers living on the margins of society, in the twilight zone. The action takes place in a semi-basement living room of a large house near London, a place characterised by neglect, untidiness and squalor. Helen Allistair is a widowed middle-class woman who at first glance appears to be a well-meaning philanthropist, providing shelter and child care for women who cannot find homes because they are single mothers. During the first act we are introduced to the women who live in the house – for example, Laura, who proudly presents herself as a willingly unmarried mother: 'I don't want no man tied to me . . . all I wants is my baby', and Rosie, an eighteen-year-old factory girl (Rayman 1951: 14). Sal is the ex-maid who now looks after the children. She has aged prematurely and is rather slow, hardly featuring in the play until her dramatic revelations in the final act. Vivianne is expecting a child by a man who is on trial for manslaughter, and Christina has just arrived at the house with her very young son. The women are unsettled and unhappy, and although they are from a variety of social classes they are all caught in the poverty trap. Their wages only just cover the rent and child-care fees; few of them manage to save any money and the only escape is provided by the hope of either the return of the estranged fathers of their children, or through finding another man to marry. It is not long before Vivianne reveals the true nature of Mrs Allistair's supposed altruism:

> VIVIANNE: . . . I didn't want this baby. . . nine out of ten are like
> Rosie and they're better game for Allistair than the wiser ones.
> She takes every penny they've got and lets them live in squalor
> and talks to them like the salvation army. . . all her saccharine
> talk about taking the homeless in off the street and giving them
> shelter; shelter's just about all at three guineas a week with a quid
> on top if you want her to look after the kid.
>
> (ibid.: 23)

The first act draws to a close when one of the lodgers, Rosie, comes in from a day out with her boyfriend to reveal that she has been told that her child has malnutrition. Helen Allistair's response is that the child's weakness must be 'the result of generations of squalor and ignorance and unwholesome stock'. In her opinion, 'some mothers [are] not in a condition to produce model babies ... healthy trees produce healthy fruit' (ibid.: 34).

Similarly the second act ends when Christina comes back from a week away to find her child on the brink of death; the implications of this build to a crescendo in Act Three where Vivianne has a conversation with Sal who tells her,

> SAL: ... one day Nellie (Allistair) 'it 'im with a stick and 'e just lay there on the carpet. I wanted to put 'im to bed but Nellie said it weren't no use, 'cos he was dead ... she says girls like me didn't ought to have babies and if they found out they'd put me in prison.
>
> (ibid.: 78)

Vivianne's suspicions are re-affirmed when Sal tells her that, 'Nellie used to take in babies the nice ladies who 'ad'n't any babies of their own would take them away.' She says,

> VIVIANNE: A lot of things go on that the public don't want to know. So they look the other way – the same as the Welfare people do when they come down here. They're not really fooled by the show you put on for them, but it's easier not to look too closely. I've seen so much dirt I'm not squeamish anymore.
>
> (ibid.: 81)

When Allistair overhears Sal's confession, she turns on Vivianne and violently pushes her down the stairs, leaving her about to go into labour. When we come to the last scene of the play, the whole of the basement has changed; it is now bright and clean. Christina – whose baby has by now died through Helen Allistair's neglect – returns to the house to be told by Allistair that Vivianne has had her child and is unable to see anyone as she is so close to death. Finally, Helen Allistair's evil intent is revealed and her final words are spoken centre stage, just before her arrest:

> HELEN: *(centre stage)* ... sluts all of you with your rotten little bastards. I took you off the streets, when decent people wouldn't look at you. God when I think what I've done for you; slaved morning and night. What have I kept for myself since my husband died. I gave up my house to you, and this is how you

repay me. You've no gratitude, no loyalty. . . how dare you speak
to me you sanctimonious little bitch.

(ibid.: 91)

In her Preface to the published play, producer Rona Laurie points out
how the play 'challenges the social conscience of the audience' (ibid.: 5–7).
It condemns, through Helen, a bourgeois and Victorian attitude toward
the poor, and in particular toward single, unmarried mothers. The
physical stage space is interior and claustrophobic: Laurie's suggestion
is that a small cramped stage can only enhance the mood of the play.
Helen Allistair is a product of her own greed and socio-political beliefs, left
over from the days of the Empire. Her bitterness is largely the cause of her
exploitation of others, usually women of a lower social class, but the
bitterness is disguised as philanthropy. What Rayman is clearly expressing
in her play is the complete contradiction in women's inherent social roles
as mothers, in a society that cannot cater ideologically or economically for
the requirements of its so-called moral culture. The women take the law
into their own hands when Vivianne, who did not want to be a mother in
the first place, offers Christina, who has been told that she is unable to
have any more children, her child for adoption.

Rayman's play received mixed reviews. One critic claimed the title was
nothing but a euphemism for 'unmarried mothers' and that as such it was
a play about a 'sad sisterhood' awash with unrelieved femininity, neurosis
and hysteria (*Daily Telegraph*, 16 October 1951). Another reviewer, for the
Sunday Times, felt the production to be 'as great an advance on the
Embassy's recent offerings as Neanderthal man was on the anthropoid
ape. It is no doubt founded on fact, and yet seems splendidly improbable'
(*Sunday Times*, 21 October 1951). It is interesting to note that the play was
not as well received in America as in Britain, and that in the film version,
the narrative has been re-worked so that the relationship between
Vivianne and her imprisoned lover is foregrounded. This of course means
that what was originally an all-female cast has become a mixed one.
Because of the direct and overt social critique within the play, emphasising
romance made the narrative more 'acceptable' to a film company and
perhaps a wider film audience.

Women of Twilight in many ways marked a new direction for the
investigation and writing out of experiences of motherhood in plays
written by women for the London stage. From this point onwards there
are more plays where mothers 'refuse' to carry out their mothering role
according to the prerequisites of a dominant ideology. After the 1950s,
one could argue that a number of texts provide images of dissenting

mothers where the normality of the mental state of the mother is not necessarily put into question. Rather, motherhood is presented as far more of a social than a 'natural' role for women.

One of the earliest texts which unashamedly features the refusing mother is Susan Glaspell's *The Verge*. Written and produced almost three decades before *Women of Twilight* brought to bear the social and economic context for the refusing mother, Glaspell's play is important because it makes a primary connection between the desire to create and the lack of desire to mother. For J. Ellen Gainor, the conflict presented in *The Verge* 'evolves' from the heroine Claire's

> feelings of confinement – her desire to break away from the conventions and constraints of 'inside': society, her family, and their definition of her, to move 'out' to a new form and identity without barriers. Her horticultural experiments... mirror her own struggle to control her life and break free from convention.
>
> (Gainor 1989: 83)

For Claire, the cultivating of new hybrids is more important than rearing her own child Elizabeth who has spent the greater part of her youth being brought up by her Aunt Adelaide, Claire's sister, who is 'fitted to rear children' (Glaspell 1987: 74). Claire's energy goes into her work, the creative products of which are more her own than is her child. When Elizabeth arrives home at the end of the first act, she is met with a chilly disregard by her mother:

ELIZABETH: Mother! It's been so long (*she tries to overcome the difficulties and embrace her mother*)
CLAIRE: (*protecting the box she has*) Careful, Elizabeth. We mustn't upset the lice.
ELIZABETH: (*retreating*) Lice?... Oh yes. You take it – them – off plants, don't you?
CLAIRE: I'm putting them on certain plants.
ELIZABETH: (*weakly*) Oh, I thought you took them off.

(ibid.)

Claire and her daughter have very little in common. Claire disapproves of her daughter's good manners and education, finding it very difficult to be maternal or even mildly friendly towards her. Elizabeth, on the other hand, finds it hard to understand why her mother's horticultural ambition does not stretch to improving plant life but is rather focused simply on the *creative act* itself. This provides another insurmountable divide between mother and daughter, and one which highlights not only their ideological differences but those between Claire and the society in which she lives:

ELIZABETH: You know something tells me that this is wrong

CLAIRE: The hymn singing ancestors are turning up.

ELIZABETH: I don't know what you mean by that, mother but . . . well of course you can make fun of me, but something does tell me that this is wrong. To do what – what –

DICK: What God did?

ELIZABETH: Well – yes. Unless you do it to make them better – to do it just to do it – that doesn't seem right to me.

CLAIRE: (*roughly*) 'Right to you!' And that's all you know of adventure – and of anguish. Do you know it is you – world of which you're so true a flower – makes me have to leave? You're there to hold the door shut! Because you're young and of a gayer world, you think I can't see them – those old men? Do you know why you are so sure of yourself? Because you can't *feel*. Can't feel – the limitless – out there – a sea just over the hill. I will not stay with you! (*buries her hands in the earth around the Edge Vine. But suddenly steps back from it as she had from Elizabeth.*) And I will not stay with *you* (*grasps it as we grasp what we would kill, is trying to pull it up. They all step forward in horror*) . . . (*pointing to Elizabeth – and the words come from mighty roots*). To think that object ever moved in my belly and sucked my breast! (*Elizabeth hides her face as if struck.*)

(ibid.: 78–79)

Gainor points out that Claire had maternal feelings toward her baby boy, who died at a young age, and uses a Freudian interpretation to explain the significance of the relationship between a mother and her absent son, that is to say, through the mother/son relationship a woman will be able to 'transfer to her son all of the ambition which she has been obliged to suppress in herself'; as the son has died, Claire feels that she has no child onto which she can transfer her ambition (Gainor 1989: 91). We can see a similarity in the way in which Joan Morgan creates her mother/son narrative in *This was a Woman*. In Glaspell's play, the relationship with the daughter is different, as Elizabeth has come to represent a 'social ideal' of womanhood which frames her in opposition to Claire.

To a great extent, within the confines of an early twentieth-century expressionist text, Claire is written as a 'hysterical' female, although Gainor suggests that she is very much a 'feminist' within what Gainor sees as the locus of a patriarchal culture which relegates women to motherhood as their only creative outlet. When Adelaide is critical of the way in which Claire treats her child, Claire's response is both clear and logical:

ADELAIDE: A mother cannot cast off her own child simply because she does not interest her!

CLAIRE: . . . Why can't she?

ADELAIDE: Because it would be monstrous!

CLAIRE: And why can't she be monstrous – if she has to be?

ADELAIDE: . . . You are really a particularly intelligent, competent person, and it's time for you to call a halt to this nonsense and be the woman you were meant to be!

CLAIRE: . . . Well isn't it about time somebody got loose from that? What I came from made you, so . . .

ADELAIDE: . . . But if you would just get out of yourself and enter into other people's lives . . .

CLAIRE: . . . Then I would be just like you. And we should all be just alike in order to reassure each other that we're all just right. But since you and Harry and Elizabeth and ten million other people bolster each other up, why do you especially need me?

(Glaspell 1987: 79–80)

Thus, despite the fact that Claire is rather a tragic heroine, and has many of the clinical characteristics of the so-called hysterical woman, her logic puts into question the logic of those, especially the women, around her. She has a clear goal, the process and product of which goes against the beliefs, for example, of her daughter and her sister. Claire's behaviour is considered by the other women to be contrary to that expected of a feminine woman, and this is their rationale for critique. Similar to the criticism aimed at Stella in Rose Franken's *Another Language* (1933), for Claire to want something outside of family and marriage, the fact that she wants something either for herself, or to do something that will give her life meaning other than motherhood, is for her to be an 'outsider' and an 'unnatural' woman.

Motherhood is not the main narrative focus in *The Verge*, but Claire's relationship to her role as a mother is used as a device to shape both her character and the central theme of the play. She is both a creator and a destroyer. *The Verge* was both radical and experimental for its day: Glaspell was using popular perceptions of the role of mother as a means of creating a central character whose life choices place her outside the popular and socially acceptable. The strength and intellectual basis of refusal in terms of motherhood was rare in its lack of subtlety, and is not an image of motherhood which is often directly used by women playwrights until the

1950s in Britain. Certainly there are critical exposés of the assumption that women have a either a natural desire to mother or a disposition which makes them 'natural' mothers, and in cases like *Women of Twilight* there is an assertion of society's failure to support mothers living outside a secure family context. There were also a number of plays, such as the extraordinary *Men Should Weep*, where the realities of motherhood as a neverending battle against poverty and exhaustion were dramatised.[9] It is not really until the 1950s, where there is far more experiment in the dramatic form of playwriting, that the 'natural' mother and the symbolism of motherhood itself are directly questioned centre stage.

Anne Jellicoe, one of the few women playwrights to be championed by the new Royal Court in the 1950s, has in common with many of the other women playwrights of the pre-Second World War period the fact that she originally trained as an actress. Thus she came to playwriting from a practical theatre experience rather than a literary background. As Taylor notes, this unquestionably had a significant effect on the form of her writing (Taylor 1993: 21). *The Sport of my Mad Mother*, possibly Jellicoe's most interesting, although by no means her most successful play – it ran at the Royal Court in 1958 for fourteen performances – is an investigation of, among other things, the symbolism of motherhood. Seen by one critic as a 'ballet in words about a crazy world', it is a highly experimental piece which uses non-linear narratives, relying heavily on word and image association, rhythm, music and ritual to carry the plot (*Daily Telegraph*, 26 February 1958). Kenneth Tynan saw the play as belonging to 'that part of the century which produced jazz, rebels without causes, Melanie Klein's post-Freudian discoveries, duels with switch knives and the H-bomb' and the 'mother' of the title, Greta, as the

> gang's symbolic mother... she destroys while she creates, punishes while she rewards: and she can provoke in those from whom she withholds sympathy the same envious destructiveness that Melanie Klein has observed in children from whom the breast has at some crucial moment been withheld.
>
> (*Observer*, 2 March 1958)

Greta is, in fact, as much of a Warrior Woman as she is a mother and this is vital to an understanding of her as a mother archetype in the piece. There is a sinister build-up to her entrance, and when she arrives on stage she does so in disguise. Her hair is 'long, straight and red, falling from her brow like a Japanese lion wig', her face is 'heavily made up and almost dead white' (Jellicoe 1985: 143). Greta is both powerful and humorous, and is juxtaposed to Dean, a 'social researching American... who represents discipline, science and the male principle' (*Manchester Guardian*, 27 February 1958). He tells her that he lives 'off cans and gum' while Greta states that she was 'reared in a cave by a female wallaby. Until . . . seven I ran about on all fours and barked' (Jellicoe 1985: 157). The two represent polarised ideologies: Dean preaches love and care, Greta war and survival. Greta is the gang leader, who gives birth on stage, while one of her accomplices brings on a book entitled *How to Deliver a Baby*, and another tells her that to give birth in public is 'not nice, not customary, not legal' (ibid.: 168).

Taylor's critique of the confused or contradictory quality of the primacy of the mother in another of Jellicoe's plays, *The Rising Generation* (1973), has a resonance for *The Sport of my Mad Mother*. Greta is both violent and nurturing which brings her in line with the 'phallic' mother, a dominant figure in many of the earlier plays discussed. She is also far more directly in a state of refusal, if not towards motherhood itself, then certainly in terms of the level to which she is prepared to accept the 'rules and regulations' of mothering as propounded by the representative of the dominant ideology, Dean. Taylor also makes the point that Jellicoe 'defines motherhood problematically as both destructive and prolific' (Taylor 1993: 22). It is possible to argue, however, that many of the definitions of motherhood as signified through dramatic texts by women present it as problematic. Where Jellicoe differs is in her direct return to a 'primitive' context, and the experimental form of her play. She has, whether consciously or not, made use of the Kleinian assertion of the dysfunctional mother, and in many ways, because of this and the fact that she has used the 'primitive' as a context, the strength of Greta's refusing personality is seemingly undermined.

Both Doris Lessing and Shelagh Delaney created mothers as being first and foremost women, for whom motherhood is only a part of life's choices. Lessing's Myra Bolton, in *Each His Own Wilderness* (Lessing 1959), sells her house in order to change her life and provide her son with the opportunity to travel and see the world, as he refuses to finish his studies. While she sees her life as being only half over, that is to say, there is life beyond child rearing and housekeeping, her son Tony wants to settle down, with a roof over his head, to live in the family home and have a steady job. Myra is concerned with social issues, world politics and the H-bomb, Tony is embroiled in the fantasy of comfy domesticity. Myra is both a mother and a sexual woman; she is politically and intellectually mature and has a need to develop her life beyond mothering and marriage. The fifty-year-old woman who leaves the stage at the end of the play is a far cry from the lace-wearing and bespectacled matriarchs of the earlier plays discussed. Once Myra has finally managed to persuade Tony of the fact that she has sold their home she 'makes a movement as if expanding, or about to take flight' and says,

> MYRA: It occurs to me that for the first time in my life I'm free... for the last twenty-two years my life has been governed by... your needs... my whole life has been governed by your needs. And what for... a little monster of egotism... petty... spiteful little egotist.... There are a lot of things I've wanted to do for a long time, and I haven't done them.... Perhaps I'll take the money and go off... with my needs in a small suitcase... I don't have to shelter under a heap of old bricks like a frightened mouse. I'm going... I've never wanted safety and the walls of respectability – you damned little petty-bourgeois. My God, the irony of it – that we should have given birth to a generation of little office boys... who count their pensions before they're out of school...

> (Lessing 1959: 93–94)

Delaney's *A Taste of Honey* similarly presents a mother who, although from a different class, chooses to 'enjoy life and go about it in her own way' (Delaney 1989: xii). Wandor points out that a mother who herself states, 'Have I ever laid claim to being a proper mother?' breaks yet another taboo in a play which dramatises events in the life of a young woman who is pregnant by a 'coloured naval rating' and whose close friend is a young, 'gay' male (Wandor 1987: 40). The breaking of taboos is part and parcel of a play which deals with working-class life in a theatre world which was still predominantly frequented by the middle classes.

Jo's mother Helen re-marries because the man in question has got 'a wallet full of reasons', and she leaves Jo to look after herself while she goes off on her honeymoon (Delaney 1989: 34). The marriage is over very quickly and Helen returns to help Jo with her soon-to-be-born baby. Helen returns to the familiar surroundings and the familiar role of the mother, not through guilt or a sense of duty, but merely because it is the best option from a limited series of choices.

CONCLUSION

The 1950s saw an emergence of refusing mothers whose social circumstances were presented as offering them very few choices. Although only a couple of the plays mentioned in this last section had particularly long runs on the London stage, they are interesting because of the way in which the mother as a stage persona moves away from the 'natural' into the social. That the refusing mother should be created as an 'outsider' is not particularly surprising, but what is interesting in these cases is the seeming lack of authorial judgement. By the 1950s the mother has been moved away from the extended family unit and, as in the Lessing play, there are positive if limited choices outside life in the family unit to be made. The grand matriarch figure which predominates in the 1930s finds resonance in other plays of the 1950s such as Bagnold's *The Chalk Garden* (which ran in London from April 1956 for 658 performances), but even so, the normality of the middle-class family as a traditional living unit is questioned or at least challenged. Even plays with a more traditional flavour of the middle-class drawing-room drama begin to undermine the sanity and function of the English family and the mother's role within it. Lesley Storm's *Black Chiffon* is a case in point. Here the family unit is shown to be dysfunctional and the mother rather than the child is seen to be at a greater risk in terms of her psychological stability.

A number of the playwrights of the period under examination make direct and explicit use of psychoanalytic theory in their work, albeit in its popularised form. Certainly much of the theoretical discourse is reflected in or correlates with the narrative dynamics of many of the plays. It would appear that the influence of theories on motherhood and mothers is strong in the plays examined, whether they are affirmed or questioned. Equally, the social and economic factors which affect the lived experience of motherhood directly influence the way in which the family and in turn the 'stage mother' is framed. Whether the mother is seen as being a coercive force in the re-enforcement of the dominant ideology of the time, or whether she is presented as a figure who goes against expectations, she is a central character in many of the plays written by women between the wars and into the early 1960s. Where the mother is an over-bearing, power-crazy, controlling force, the context for her behaviour is often presented and examined. Where she uses her position as mother as a means to gain more power within the family unit, again her motives are examined. Arguably the predominance of the 'mother' in plays of the period, is connected to the fact that, for women, it is one of the primary social and 'natural' roles expected of them, and it is often the dynamics and complexity of this expectation which is discoursed, albeit within the parameters of the well-made middle-class play.

6

DRAMATISING HISTORY
The search for national heroines

After the First World War Britain was a nation that found itself lacking the strength of a unified identity, which had been so much a part of the propaganda behind its war effort. It was both in this context and in the context of the recent women's suffrage movement that women playwrights of the inter-war years turned to women from history as a means of creating role models in their plays. They were, to a certain extent, fitting in with a new trend among commercial theatre managements and audiences, yet the using of history as a framework for dramatic narratives appears to have had a specific appeal to women playwrights. In the context of women's social position after the First World War the re-placing of women within British cultural history and women's history in general could be seen as having a specific function. It is interesting that social pressure to return to the home and hearth – traditionally an 'insignificant' environment as far as history is concerned – was met by a renewed interest in key exceptional women from history, whose fame had come from their positions and roles within the public sphere.

From the late 1910s through to the early 1930s the representation or revisioning of history became a popular subject for the British playwright in general. According to Short, the post-First World War 'trend' is seen by most to have begun with John Drinkwater's *Abraham Lincoln* in 1919, although history had been the narrative framework for many dramas beforehand (Short 1942: 113). The history or chronicle play is, at the simplest level, a dramatised chronological record of historical events, where history is used as a framework around which a plot can be structured. As a dramatic form it was popular with both male and female writers, and usually involved the 'reconstruction of a central character' (Pellizzi 1935: 198). Drinkwater, for example, followed *Abraham Lincoln* with *Mary Stuart* (1921), *Oliver Cromwell* (1922) and *Robert E. Lee* (1923). It was often the case, certainly by the late 1920s and into the early 1930s, that the central figure was female, in plays by both men and women. For example, Nurse Cavell, Florence Nightingale, Elizabeth Barrett Browning, the Brontë sisters, Queen Elizabeth, Mary Stuart, Emma Hamilton, Elizabeth of Austria and the pirate Mary Read were all used as central figures in chronicle plays of the inter-war years.

That many of the historical 'facts' were often distorted in order to fit in with the overall through-line of narrative intention caused many critics to make disparaging remarks about the choice of 'history' as a framework for drama. One of the common criticisms was that authors not only showed little concern for the accuracy of facts but that they took great authorial liberties in interpreting any facts they did choose to note; this was a particular criticism of, for example, Morna Stuart's *Traitor's Gate* (1939). If a play showed 'an intelligent writing out of conjecture', then it was considered to be a worthy drama. So, for example, the same critic who states his concern for 'theatrical value' forgives the 'liberties' taken by the author in her interpretation of historical facts, because her play shows that:

> Here is a mind at work. And though the theatre is not a very good thinking-shop and perhaps not essentially concerned with thought at all (emotion being its chief business), it is a great treat to the theatre-goer to encounter intelligence on occasion.
>
> (*Daily Telegraph*, 18 November 1938)

For many critics the attempt to dramatise the biography of an historical character necessitated the problem of over-burdening a dramatic text with fact and plot. Gwen John's *Gloriana*, a chronicle of the life of Elizabeth I, was criticised for the fact that the author was 'too determined to leave nothing without at least a passing reference', thus she was accused of 'creating nothing more than an episodic summary of a reign' (*The Times*, 9 December 1925). Many critics shared this view in essence – that history was not a good starting point for dramatic writing as there were too many problems involved:

> History, when it supplies speculative and imaginative *subjects*, and not simply opportunities for dramatic representation...leads to the...impurity of art...[history plays are] prevailingly non-dramatic [although they] have dramatic elements.
>
> (Pellizzi 1935: 191)

Other critics shared Pellizzi's concern that using history as anything more than an inspiration for dramatic writing produced unnecessarily complicated results. So Gordon Daviot's *Queen of Scots*, which ran at the New theatre in 1934 for 106 performances, was seen by one critic as

> a muddled and puzzling, intricate story... a series of elliptical hints which are rather bewildering.... It would be allowable for these episodes to tell us little history if, in return, they established character and created personalities.
>
> (*Evening News*, 9 June 1934)

Whatever the critical response in terms of the level to which history or chronicle plays were considered to be 'art', they appear to have been popular with both audiences and dramatists alike.

WOMEN PLAYWRIGHTS AND THE CHRONICLE PLAY

Using representations of 'great' historical women as a strategy for replacing women into positions of status within the cultural consciousness is not specific to the inter-war female playwrights, and was a popular strategy for both the suffragist playwrights (see Gardner 1985), and more recent women playwrights of the 1970s and 1980s. Many of the chronicle plays written by women during the inter-war period fail in some ways 'to challenge conventions of stage stereotyping of women' (Bassnett-McGuire 1984: 453). The earlier chronicle plays used exceptional women from royalty or nobility as central figures. Where women playwrights often deviated from presenting the exceptional was in the way in which they theatricalised war as a specific framework for representing women's lives during a 'key' moment in history. In this way certain parallels can be drawn between the significance to the female playwrights in question, of women in history, and the significance of history to feminist historians of the post-1968 years.

> Women's history has come to mean history about women and usually done by women. It began with the necessary task of resurrecting women's hidden experience by focusing on great women in history.... This tendency has... been criticised as being elitist. In response another type of women's history has arisen: revealing ordinary women's lives as part of history.
>
> (London Feminist History Group 1982: 3)

RE-PRESENTING 'HEROINES' AS THE 'WOMAN BEHIND THE MAN'[1]

One of the most pressing concerns for middle-class women after the initial franchise had been granted was the feeling that, as a whole, women had not taken real advantage of their new voting power, that the 'popular' images of women as passive and frivolous had been assimilated by women as representing some kind of 'real' and tenable identity. There appears to have been an active effort to undermine the primacy of this image, certainly by those women who continued with the struggle for women's equality after the First World War: many female dramatists seemingly had this aim in mind when choosing to use the chronicle play as a dramatic form.

Clemence Dane, one of the most prolific playwrights of the inter-war period and beyond, wrote in her social text *The Women's Side* (1926) of how there were women who still evaded 'responsibilities of citizenship by declaring that, "women's sphere is in the home" '.[1] Her complaint was that if these women took no interest and active part in national affairs, then they ran 'the risk of having their private house-keeping threatened by forces – outside of their control' (Dane 1926: iv). For Dane, women needed to leave the required social mores of their foremothers behind them and be prepared to function on as equal a par with men as possible.

> A woman who cannot drive a car, deal with a drunken man, speak in public and run a business and a home is getting to be as much of a rarity as fifty years ago a woman who could not faint when she was proposed to.
>
> (Dane, *Daily Express*, 15 October 1926)

Many women in socially visible positions were encouraging women generally to realise that what had during the nineteenth century been 'unfashionable virtues' in a woman were now a necessary part of being a 'modern woman' – one now needed to be active and assertive. Equally, this promotion of both the historical validity of women and the virtues of the 'modern woman' is closely linked to an investigation of 'Britishness' itself. Thus a re-examination of historical women has a less threatening function within the context of a nation without an integrated sense of its own identity. This may be why so many of the chronicle plays use royal women and women from nobility as subject matter.

Dane's portrayal of Elizabeth I in *Will Shakespeare* (Dane 1961d) appears to have been a conscious attempt to present an image of woman as determined, courageous and yet selfless; one critic felt it to be 'one of the most plausible portraits of Elizabeth, who has frequently been just a "Tudor in a Tantrum" behaving like Alice's Red Queen' (Trewin 1958: 25–29). The play offers a 'fantasy' portrayal of Shakespeare, and it is the women in the play around whom most of his actions revolve. For Elizabeth, her duty to England is of the utmost importance, thus she manipulates her courtiers and subjects only to serve this end. She is both intelligent and rational. The queen gives advice to the men who surround her and when Will informs her that he can no longer write because he has lost the love of Mary Fitton (Dane's 'Dark Lady'), Elizabeth stresses that inspiration comes from one's desire to fulfil one's duty to the nation:

> ELIZABETH: . . . I send my ships where never ships have sailed, to break the barriers and make wide the ways to the after world. Send your ships to the hidden lands of the soul. To break barriers and make plain the ways between Man and Man. Why else were we two born?
>
> (Dane 1961: 138)

Elizabeth is able to work with abstract concepts and ideas. For her, Shakespeare's duty is to write successfully enough to ensure a good return on her own and, therefore the nation's, investment in Henslowe's theatre company. She encourages Mary Fitton to welcome 'romantic advances' from Shakespeare and, when Fitton's relationship with Marlowe has disastrous results, she banishes her: 'Here is a man upon your lap that England needed. . . . Go blunted tool' (ibid.: 130–131).

Elizabeth is an all-powerful matriarch figure, she is neither vain nor fickle and she takes full responsibility for her position within society. Dane uses Elizabeth's psychological make-up in combination with her social position to contrast with that of Shakespeare, who is portrayed as rather an inept character. Thus, although the title suggests that Shakespeare might be the prime mover in this piece, it is Elizabeth, along with the other women, who are shown to be the motivating forces in his life and possibly behind his work. As she later suggests in *The Women's Side* of the Dark Lady, for example, 'Lions don't mate with rabbits. Some equal power, something, not mere beauty, there must have been in her and her kind . . . that gave them their place beside their great men' (Dane 1926: 138). *Will Shakespeare*, a play written in verse, received mixed reviews, although it has been suggested that this was not the only reason for its relatively short run.[2] Dane used an archaic form of language to represent a 'great' woman from history. In turn it is possible to argue that she used this historical figure as a means of promoting a contemporary proposition of a new direction for womanhood. In *Richard of Bordeaux*, produced by and starring

143

John Gielgud, which ran in the West End for over 400 performances from 1933, Gordon Daviot (Elizabeth Mackintosh) created a very different queen. Here, Anne is very clearly written as almost a prototype for a 'woman of the 1930s', she is intelligent, kind, intuitive and loyal. The achievement of her duty to the nation is sublimated in her relationship with her husband.

The relationship between Anne and Richard in *Richard of Bordeaux* resembles what would have been a fashionable ideal of marital partnership among the upper-middle classes at the time of writing. Anne is not English and has been brought up in a country where 'women do not wait to be spoken to before they speak' (Daviot 1966: 36). She is also fashionable to the extent that she 'gives the clergy something to preach about' (ibid.: 34). Thus Anne lives up to expectations of beauty but is also active and critical with her own perceptive ideas on politics and the power of the church:

ANNE: . . . It is only that I think the Church has become too rich, and forgotten its mission. I think that something should be done to make it simpler and kinder.

(ibid.: 37)

Daviot's queen persuades her husband to remain true to his ideals, and she encourages him to learn to laugh and 'play the game', providing rational and constructive advice when all his official advisers fail him. The suggestion, it would seem, is that Richard's public life and decision-making are shaped and nurtured by what goes on in his private life, that this 'great' man worked as part of a male/female, husband/wife team. When Anne dies and the team is no longer his basis of support, he fails.

Daviot's Mary Bohun is drawn in sharp contrast to Anne: she is overly domestic and unwilling or perhaps unable to partake in an active public life. Like the upper-middle-class woman of the late Victorian period, she sees her duty as being confined almost entirely to the private sphere: the most important contribution she can make to the health of the nation is to leave her 'personal touch' visible around the home. The two women represent polarised propositions for womanhood; it would seem that Daviot is suggesting that Anne is a more relevant and necessary model in a society which is working towards re-constructing the national identity simultaneous to promoting a maintenance of peace and stability.

Elsie Shauffler's *Parnell*, produced at the New theatre in November 1936, carries a similar perception of the role of a wife to a great man, although there is a twist in that Katie's 'great' man is not the man she originally married. Despite the fact that the play, because of the implications of its political content, took some time to achieve the approval of the Lord Chamberlain, some critics felt it to be a 'pedestrian chronicle play'. The majority, however, praised the author's ability to create a drama which, although it used history as a framework, contained contemporary characters and a plot line which, because of the romantic emphasis, would appeal to contemporary audiences. More than anything it was seen as a 'love story':

> How far a great love story may survive contemporary events and the passing years is shown by this triumphant play. Sticklers for the dead bones of accuracy may quibble here and there, but the human heart outlives all else.
>
> (*The Times*, 4 November 1936)

Katie O'Shea marries a man with whom she soon discovers she has very little in common. They live apart and he comes to her when he needs money. For him it is a convenient arrangement, but she wants more from a marriage:

> KATIE: ... I'm tired of ... getting up, going to bed, dressing ... hearing the clock tick ... why does anyone marry anyone ... life is blowing by outside and it doesn't touch me.
>
> (Schauffler 1936: 128)

When Willie O'Shea is elected as member of parliament for County Clare, Katie is obliged to organise and host social entertainments for him. She now has to lure the leader of the Irish party, Parnell, to one of their social events. Parnell, who finds all the social pretence of parliamentary work tedious, agrees to come, whereupon he falls immediately in love with Katie. As he puts it: 'A man sees a woman for a moment – and he loves her. Is there any more to be said?' (ibid.: 167).

The play differs little from many others of its kind, where love is idealised and the language used by lovers is contemporised. Nevertheless, Katie, who of course reciprocates the love of this 'great' man, now has a means of escaping the confines of a marriage to a man whom she despises. She puts all her energy into helping Parnell with *his* career and work. Willie invites Parnell to work in his home, and when Katie decides to sue O'Shea for divorce on the grounds of adultery (he has been having numerous extra-marital liaisons), O'Shea uses it as a means of gaining political support. Although popular with neither party nor voter, O'Shea tries to enlist sympathy by saying that his wife and the leader of his party have wronged him; that he has been cuckolded by his boss. O'Shea is even prepared to cause a public scandal for his own mistress, Bridgit, in order to save himself. She points out to him that his accusations are ridiculous and that he should back down or he will completely ruin his own political career.

> BRIDGIT: Willie for once forget about yourself.... You never
> dreamed Kate would talk back. You think now you can manage
> her because you always have. You're wrong.
>
> (ibid.: 197)

Parnell will not defend himself, which Katie realises is political 'suicide'. In the end, neither Gladstone nor Parnell's own followers will support him. Many of his colleagues turn against him, using his unfortunate circumstances as a means of furthering their own political careers. The anti-Irish English members of parliament also use the scandal as an excuse to outlaw the parliamentary acceptance of Home Rule. The strain of all the adverse publicity and the pain of seeing his former friends turning against him causes his early death, but Parnell and Katie's love for each other remains strong until the end. When Katie, in a state of mourning, tells one of his faithful friends that she feels as though she has caused his death, he points out, 'No more than all of us' (ibid.: 238).

Critics clearly saw the play as being specifically a biography of Katie O'Shea rather than of Parnell. For the vast majority this was largely due to the acting of Margaret Rawlings, who both translated and took the lead in the play: 'Her rich, warm personality, her deep, thrilling voice and her power of emotional intensity make her acting of Mrs O'Shea one of the most exciting experiences that the London theatre has seen this year' (*Daily Telegraph*, 5 November 1936). The play was written from the point of view of the female protagonist who, in most other contexts, would have been perceived as a philanderer. In *Parnell* the implication is that we should not condemn the woman who has deserted her husband and sought divorce, as she has done so first for 'real' love, and second in order that she might use her skills and intelligence to help her new partner achieve his aims. These aims could be seen as personal, but Parnell has a national rather than a personal mission. As such he is set up in contrast to Willie O'Shea for whom personal interests are of the utmost importance. Therefore Katie is 'forgiven', because ultimately she chooses the national over the personal.

HEROINES WITH A MISSION

The idea of women 'working for the nation' runs through the narratives, often subtextually, of many of the chronicle plays by women of the inter-war period. When romance goes hand in hand with the journey to fulfilment of duty, then the heroines are fulfilled. If not, as in the case of Mary in Daviot's *Queen of Scots*, then the relationship between romance and duty is contrasted, with one being shown as detrimental to the achievement of the other (Daviot 1934).

Mary Stuart had been a popular subject for dramatisation in the nineteenth century, although from almost all perspectives she was seen as a woman vulnerable to the need for romance and primarily male approval. One reviewer of *Queen of Scots* suggested that,

> To Mr Drinkwater she was an idealist in love who got the wrong sort of lover every time; in *The Borderer*, the romantic drama which Fred Terry and Miss Julia Nielson made and kept familiar, she was an even sweeter idealist; and in the present play she is a woman too weak or rather too much at the mercy of capriciously feminine nature to cope with the perpetual plots and treasons of jealous and uncouth lords.
>
> *(The Times, 9 June 1934)*

Here, however, Daviot presents the history as a battle not only of the sexes but of a 'male' set of knowledge and rules against those which could be considered to be 'female'. Mary's aim is to find a way of taking what she considers to be rightfully hers, that is to say, the throne. Both beautiful and vain, she is also determined and wily. Her fatal flaw is that although she knows what she wants, she is ignorant of the rules and mores which line the pathway to the fulfilment of her goals. Mary, when battling to possess the throne in what is effectively a country of strangers, is unaware of the ambition which drives her own courtiers, an ambition which runs counter to her own. One of her advisers informs her that 'cuteness', as opposed to brain power, will get her what she wants. Her beauty is no weapon in this 'battle': it proves to be a hindrance. For her courtiers the priority is to find her a husband as soon a possible:

> MORTON: Then perhaps we'd have a King and Queen who were really King... and Queen.
>
> (Daviot 1934: 417)

Yet, for Mary, romance comes second to her desire for the throne. As she says,

> Oh Love! Some thing to pass a summer's afternoon. With kingdoms to play with what should a queen do with love?
>
> (ibid.: 381)

Mary grants Bothwell a pardon in order to secure his support, but when she discovers that he has been plotting against her she sends him to France. Beforehand she has also delayed her coronation in order to right the mistake which she has made in marrying Darnley. All of this is carried out contrary to the wishes of her advisers. For Mary, the struggle for the throne is as much a struggle with the men around her as it is with Elizabeth I. Her brother's hold on her is broken only to send her into the clutches of her ambitious self-interested courtiers. Ultimately Mary's failing is her naivety and inability to understand the rules of the political arena in which she is manoeuvring. Daviot paints her as a tragic figure who, but for her own sometimes overt vanity and lack of guile, fails to attain her goal.

Daviot constantly juxtaposes Mary's beauty with her intelligence but also with her naivety. In Helen Jerome's *Charlotte Corday*, with its context of the French Revolution, set immediately before and after the murder of Jean-Paul Marat, Corday could not have been drawn in greater contrast. Romance cannot intercede in the fate of this character who has, without doubt, been written as a 'pure' heroine, one whose 'duty' comes before all else. Rather like Elizabeth in *Will Shakespeare*, romance is not allowed to get in the way of duty to 'nation'. Jerome's lesser characters make constant references to information about the heroine's upbringing, personality and motives. Charlotte is drawn as very self-reflective, constantly re-positioning herself in a way which makes her aim easier to achieve. Just as with Katie O'Shea, she has a constant companion at home in her aunt, Madame de Bretteville, who acts as a confidante. Madame de Bretteville worries that Charlotte has a handicap because she is too bright, well read and determined.

> Voltaire! Plutarch! Corneille . . . Rousseau (*shakes her head dubiously*). Always pouring over such stuff! A fine way to get a husband. . . . What's more important for a woman . . . a young gallant round the corner. . . . That's the only thing that makes a woman happy.
>
> (Jerome 1937: 2–3)

For her aunt, intelligence is detrimental to an achievement of *femininity*. In such a way Charlotte's obsessional hatred for Marat is also seen by her aunt as being 'unnatural' in a woman. One of Charlotte's friends describes the way in which one of their school masters felt that Charlotte was 'pre-destined'. Thus the author juxtaposes descriptions of Charlotte's beauty with those which praise her intelligence and point to the rarity of such determination in a woman.

For Charlotte, Marat is 'the germ that must be destroyed'; she has no accomplices and takes orders from no one (ibid.: 24). During the final court scene, not even the most pessimistic of accusers can believe her single-minded courage. Jerome ironically detracts from the power of this character by portraying her as some kind of myth-inspired woman who lives in a 'secret world'; Charlotte sees herself as an instrument of some greater meta-human power. However, the subtext is based upon promoting an ideology which suggests that the personal is subservient to the greater needs of the nation, arguably pre-empting the narrative line of Charles Morgan's *The Flashing Stream*, where heroism is purely altruistic. Characters are compelled by fate to serve their country rather than their own needs, as Morgan suggests:

> This singleness of mind . . . resembles, in the confused landscape of experience, a 'flashing stream', fierce and unswerving as the zeal of saints, to which the few who see it commit themselves absolutely. They are called fanatics.
>
> (C. Morgan 1938: 7)

Although Corday never actually describes herself as a fanatic she speaks as one, and certainly matches Marat in her determination. When asked why she killed Marat she replies simply and with a sense of great calm:

> CHARLOTTE: To prevent civil war . . . I killed one man to save a hundred thousand . . . the resolution to put private interests aside and to sacrifice myself for my country. . . . One would have to feel such a thing oneself (*smiles*) . . . I see that you are reluctant to offer a mere woman the shade of the great Marat. Nevertheless, I . . . alone . . . conceived and executed the plan (*murmurs of reluctant admiration*)
>
> (Jerome 1937: 114–115)

Her determination of character and clarity of both goal and action are matched only by Marat:

> MARAT: . . . You can't expect obedience from the weak unless you show them a master! . . . My ferocity is necessary . . . I have been crucified, let *them* be. The race must agonise to be regenerated . . . mass extermination, before we can clean up France. . . . Extinguish the public debt by paying the creditors with national bonds.
>
> (ibid.: 75–79)

It is interesting to note the similarity of ideology between Marat and Hitler's National Socialist party who, at the time of writing, had a stronghold in Germany, and whose actions and political ideology would not have been unfamiliar to theatre audiences of the day. This is not to suggest that the play foregrounds politics over personality, as it clearly does not; rather, that Jerome chose her historical subject, a national heroine, with an acute recognition, perhaps, of the growth in the direction of a section of European political ideology towards fascism. The play validates the possibility of the existence of an active heroine, who can achieve her aim or, perhaps more romantically, achieve her destiny on equal terms with her male counterpart. Equally it would appear that the intention behind the play was to re-formulate in the public mind some kind of knowledge of the role of a woman at a particular key point in history. Gordon Daviot's *The Laughing Woman* encompasses a similar intention.

WOMEN, CREATIVITY AND HISTORY

In the final scene of Daviot's *The Laughing Woman*, a play based loosely on the relationship between the sculptor Gaudier and the philosopher Sophie Brzeska, the female protagonist Frik (Brzeska) is seen by the audience, although barely recognisable, sheltering from the weather in a museum.[3] As a party of schoolgirls passes her by, one of them notices a sculpture by the now dead artist, Réné (Gaudier), of 'The Laughing Woman'. The sculpture is of Frik as a younger woman, and as the schoolgirl stares at it she says thoughtfully, 'I wish they had said who *she* was' (Daviot 1935: 470). After the early death of her sculptor companion – like the real-life character he is drawn from, Réné is among the early victims of the First World War – Frik is unable to continue with her work, and sees her life as no longer worth living. Réné's art survives him, but her creative work is incomplete. To the outside world the statue of a nameless woman is all that remains of Frik's youth; she leaves no great creative work to posterity.

The play is as much concerned with the relationship between creativity and gender as it is with a romantic history. Frik is written in contrast to Hazel, who has fewer choices and is tied to the carrying out of domestic duties for her father. A writer, with a veritable working knowledge of art history, Hazel is usually only introduced in relation to her more famous father. With no income of her own she has to oversee her father's domestic affairs, which means that she does not have enough time to devote to writing and thus cannot earn a living from it. Hazel is caught in a vicious circle of middle-class domestic servitude to her father. Frik, by comparison, has numerous choices; she has an income of her own which means that she can live both comfortably and with enough time to write her book on philosophy. Yet she actively chooses to live with Réné, whose desire for a bohemian lifestyle goes against her own bourgeois love of home comforts. The two are not lovers. As Réné says: 'To the others you are a woman... but to me you are a person... another person like myself' (Daviot 1935: 468). Frik, some years his senior, an intelligent woman, fluent in five languages, chooses to put his needs before her own, despite her companion's advice to the contrary. Towards the end of the play he even suggests that she might have written her book had it not been for the time and energy which she invested in his work. While he rises to fame with the help of a rich patroness, of whom Frik has become visibly jealous, Frik moves more and more into the supportive role. They come to London under the pretence of being brother and sister, yet her role is much more that of a mother.

One reviewer saw the play as 'a study of genius' (*Evening Star*, 9 April 1934) while others saw it as a 'presentation of the modern temperament' (*Manchester Post*, 9 April 1934). Again, to the modern eye, it is more a study of the relationship between the sexes and, specifically, the psychology of a particular generation of women. To some extent Daviot is questioning women's role in the historical process: Frik has choices and those she takes effectively maintain a situation where her own creative work will remain hidden from history. Daviot stresses the difference in the power relationship between men and women as much as she points to the difference in the way in which men and women see themselves as artists. Frik actively chooses to sacrifice her work for that of a man, who feels himself perfectly able to look after his own domestic needs. As such, Frik's need for a domestic role and for what boils down to male approval is the biggest hindrance between herself and the goals which she claims she wants to achieve.

Clemence Dane's *Wild Decembers* to some extent uses a similar perspective in the dramatising of the life of Charlotte Brontë. Originally commissioned by Katherine Cornell and entitled *How Clear She Shines*, the play opened in London at the Apollo in May 1933, running for fifty performances. The Brontës were for some reason fashionable subject matter for dramatists at this particular point – as Trewin put it, 'the Brontës took London this year' – and Dane's play, 'second in the field' to Alfred Sangster's *The Brontës*, was soon followed by John Davison's *The Brontës of Haworth Parsonage* (Trewin 1960: 55).

The three Brontë sisters are characterised as extremely hard working, intelligent and humble women, and their dedication to work is contrasted with their brother's lack of dedication. Dane accentuates the dichotomy between Charlotte as a romantic heroine and Charlotte as a writer and businesswoman, who fights for the opportunity to write and to educate herself. When she returns to Belgium as a teacher rather than a pupil, her former tutor, Heger, no longer finds himself able to pursue a scholarly friendship with her; in his eyes she is now an adult woman and as such should spend her spare time among the other women for whom he admits to having no intellectual respect. For Charlotte, having to associate herself with 'manly' rationality during working hours, and with 'feminine' activities during her free time, is hypocrisy. The idea that Charlotte may have been in love with her former tutor is later suggested, but emphasis is put upon the fact that her aim was to maintain and nurture what she had considered to be a deep and intellectual friendship, with someone who just happened to be a man. As she herself says: 'Does the beggar love the hand that feeds it? . . . I do not ask the full banquet, beauty and love . . . but a crust, a crumb of friendship' (Dane 1961c: 228).

For Dane, romance is only present in Heger's imagination. When in later years he writes to Charlotte asking her to write to him at his university address, as his wife disapproves of the fact that they correspond with each other, Charlotte quickly writes back that she had no idea that there was anything to be disapproving of and that she would certainly not wish to write to him behind his wife's back. She then states that she will therefore no longer communicate with him.

Dane foregrounds the ideological context in which the Brontës wrote: she implies that they actively worked against a cultural ideal of femininity by writing for the public at all. She is also very careful to contrast them with their brother who, although far better educated, is incompetent and lacks determination. Arguably the author's intention in *Wild Decembers* is not simply to re-tell the history of Charlotte and her sisters; rather, she makes a conscious effort to use history as a means of questioning the cultural position of women in her own time.

Many other theatrical images of creative women from history found their way onto the London stage during the inter-war years. A number of these were portrayals of actresses such as the London Repertory Company's *Nell Gwynne* (sic.) at the Regent theatre in 1927 and Naomi Royde-Smith's *Mrs Siddons*, with Sybil Thorndike in the lead, at the Apollo theatre in 1933. The latter had a very short run; some critics felt it to be written in such a way as to be only of interest to those working in theatre. One reviewer commented that all the author had achieved was to impress upon the audience that not only did Mrs Siddons obtrude 'her private affairs upon the public ear . . . [but also] . . . relentlessly . . . obtruded her theatrical life upon the family ear' (*The Times*, 29 November 1933). The play focuses almost entirely on the turgid domestic details of Mrs

Siddons's life and the inter-relationship between the public actress and the private woman. Despite her insistence that she would like to 'leave it all – be no more Sarah Siddons the actress, but just the wife and mother I am never allowed to be for more than a few days at a time', she spends most of her time concerned with learning her lines and managing her career (Royde-Smith 1931: 5). The private plot centres around her relationship with Thomas Lawrence, a painter and suitor to both her daughters, who eventually reveals his secret and unbending love for Sarah herself. Ultimately, as a play, *Mrs Siddons* is simply a re-vamping of history, albeit the history of 'a blinded woman of great genius, warm affection and pardonable vanity; at times an august, at others a richly comic creature, but, at the end, sincere and with a true and dignified pathos' (ibid.).

The use of historical women as a filter through which to examine contemporary women's present cultural position was not unique to British playwrights. The American Susan Glaspell's Pulitzer prize-winning *Alison's House* is a complex play which also deals with the relationship between the private and public working life of a female artist.[4] Based on the life of Emily Dickinson (who Paglia has recently described as being 'a virtuoso of sadomasochistic surrealism . . . she finds metaphors among the mechanical and domestic arts – blacksmithing, carpentry, cooking and sewing' (Paglia 1992: 264), the play is set at the dawn of the new century). Alison Stanhope (Emily Dickinson) has been dead for eighteen years, and so never appears, a fact which a number of the critics found difficult to accept. Pellizzi states that one of the most important things about Glaspell was the fact that she helped Eugene O'Neill to gain recognition, and he provides a rather peculiar commentary on *Alison's House:* 'comedies such as *Alison's House* . . . which portray familiar surroundings and psychological problems with certain penetration' (Pellizzi 1935: 252). It is difficult to understand why Pellizzi should have perceived the play as a comedy, nor is the play any more dependent on psychological analysis than it is on an analysis of social or ideological factors. Glaspell does not reveal a poet such as the one which Paglia describes, rather she slowly reveals the rather repressed personality of the dead poetess through the perceptions and memories of Alison Stanhope's relatives.

Alison's house is a kind of bell jar out of which only John Stanhope's youngest daughter, Elsa, has managed to escape. Elsa followed her emotions and disgraced the family by eloping with an older, married man, risking social isolation and disapproval for the sake of love. This is by way of contrast to her Aunt Alison, who years before sacrificed her feelings for a man in order to maintain the family reputation. The context of the play is that all the family have been brought together for the occasion of selling Alison's house. At the close of the play Alison's secret love poems are found, the extraordinary quality of which Elsa recognises at once. John Stanhope wants to protect the memory of his dead sister and so refuses to let the poems be published, as he makes clear when he says: 'she does not have to show her heart to the world. . . . My sister who loved to the utmost and denied because it was right' (Glaspell 1930: 664–667). John is torn between the desire to keep the memory of Alison alive through her work, and protect an idealised image of the family. Elsa, however, understands the significance of the poems, and in turn the sacrifice which her aunt made, but which she herself was unable to make. For Elsa it is vital that the poems are made available to the public, because of the passion and honesty which they contain:

> The story she never told, she has written it . . . the love that never died, the loneliness, the anguish and beauty of her love . . . looking into her heart. . . . It was death for her. . . but she made it into life eternal.

> (ibid.: 662–663)

Despite the protestations of Stanhope's niece Louise, who is prim and moralistic and has never forgiven Elsa for eloping into such a socially unacceptable alliance, the decision is made to publish the poems. Alison's life has materialised for the audience through the thoughts and actions of the other characters, and there are echoes of her sorrow and joy throughout the play. It is almost as if the women do for Alison that which she could not do for herself. The two 'family' women, Elsa and Stanhope's secretary Ann, choose freedom, one from the ties of moralism and family secretiveness and the other, Ann, from her long-standing entanglement with the Stanhope family itself. The implication is that they have been inspired by the memory of Alison to break with the ties of a family structure in which their needs are subservient to the rules which bind and the moral code which the idealised notion of 'family' imposes on its members.

Joan Temple's *Charles and Mary* shares the same frameworking of the family in terms of the confinement which it entails for women. The first signs the audience has of Mary's 'madness' in Act One are presented as being caused by the fact that although she is working at home to keep the family coffers in order, she also has to service the needs of her invalid parents. The demands which they constantly make on her as she tries to do her work cause her temper to rise as she realises that her assistant can't follow simple orders. Mary's mother gives her no sympathy and the family demands drive Mary to the point where she lets out: '(*jumping to her feet and stamping her foot, as she regards them all like an animal at bay*): Give me a little peace! I – I insist that you give me a little peace!' (Temple 1930: 24).

The prerogative of duty to family runs as a current through many of the history or chronicle plays written by women during the inter-war years. Whether 'family' is represented by 'nation', as in *Will Shakespeare*, or arguably 'nation' is represented by some idea of genius, a woman's duty is to serve the genius's needs and therefore the betterment of the nation and the 'family of nation'. Where the 'genius' of woman herself is the subject, then the position of fragmentation caused by a need to fulfil both a 'female' role and a traditionally 'male' role is placed at the centre of the narrative. The idea that genius and, at times, the creative act itself is associated with maleness, was accepted within the cultural context in which many of these women were writing (see Battersby 1989: 35–60). In *The Women's Side* Dane acknowledges the argument that traditionally a notion of 'genius' has been associated with a 'male' trait. However, she suggests that 'genius in women is not absent, but working with different tools, expressing itself in a totally different medium'; thus absence is merely framed by the process and method by which presence is defined (Dane 1926: 125–126). On some levels this adumbrates the position taken later by feminist theorists like Linda Nochlin, who posits that rather than attempt to answer the question, 'why have there been no great women artists?', we should look at the underlying assumption behind the question itself (Nochlin 1994: 148). Dane suggests that we should look at those who surround the 'artist' and investigate the relationship not only between the artist and model, but also the artist and she [sic] who provides and nurtures the working environment.

It is possible to argue that, at this point in the history of women playwrights, the choosing of these historical subjects was a deliberate strategy aimed at either re-inventing or re-instating women as an important component of cultural development. In order to do so, a merging of two contrary projections of woman takes place. The 'new woman', who is active, intelligent and patriotic, with her own ambitions and a 'modern' perception of her role in the world, is transposed onto elements of a late nineteenth-century popular image of the feminine woman – supportive, nurturing, altruistic and so on. Women of this post-suffrage generation had to search for acceptable role models in a cultural context where, first, the whole question of what it *meant* to be a woman prevailed and, second, the economic climate caused women's social and work-roles to change rapidly from decade to decade. The theatre for which these women playwrights were writing was largely middle and upper-class, and this is, to an extent, reflected in the chronicle subjects which they chose. Equally, there had been a tradition of historical plays in the nineteenth century, and one only has to turn to the popularity of the historical novel and the frequent use of 'exceptional' women from history as subject matter for early girls' books and comics to see that historically based narratives had a strong cultural appeal. Although, as Bassnett-McGuire points out, the choosing of a central figure for stage representation from the ruling classes is not the stuff of radical theatre, at the time women playwrights in the main, it would seem, were not concerned with the structure of theatre and the class which it served, but more that they should feature more positively and actively within it (Bassnett-McGuire 1984: 453). The trend for chronicle plays served them twofold: first, 'the woman question' was very much on people's minds, and second, 'the form of the chronicle play lent itself to possibilities of re-positioning women in cultural history. . . in other words, to reveal women's role in history and to give women a sense of a tradition of which they were and are a part' (Griffin and Aston 1991: 7–8).

WAR AS A HISTORICAL MOMENT – WHAT DID YOU DO DURING THE WAR MOTHER?

> We have proved in two wars that we can pull our weight, just as in peace-time we have always proved it when we were allowed the opportunity. . . . Give us after the war that continued opportunity to be paid according to the value of our labour and let our taxes be adjusted to our human needs and actual responsibilities without regard to the accident of sex.
>
> (Clemence Dane, *Daily Herald*, 1941)

British women suffered from a particularly ambiguous relationship to the two world wars. With regard to the loss of loved ones and the loss of domestic and emotional security, women experienced a great sense of devastation. But in terms of status they became the main thrust of the workforce labouring for the war effort on the home front. Their introduction *en masse* into the workforce during both wars in many ways gave women an opportunity for a new-found independence. Even though actual work opportunities were withdrawn after 1918 and 1945, within a short span of time two generations of women had experienced – and would remember – the transformation of their role within society. Yet it is only recently that women's war work has received anything other than a superficial examination. Although at first glance the notion of history and war appear only loosely linked, when we look at war as a key historical moment which inevitably creates social change as well as unrest, it is possible to see parallels between women playwrights' examinations of women's relationship to history and their depictions of women living in wartime. Frequently there is a focus on the relationship between women, nation and family and war is seen as enhancing this relationship. Similarly, the theatricalisation of women's lives during wartime mostly looks at life on the home front, but again there appears to have been a conscious desire to place this experience inside a framework of historical development.

After the brief closing of London theatres in 1939, various theatrical entertainments continued to go into production. While the Windmill and others produced revues and light entertainments aimed at attracting the transient London theatre audience, other West End theatres continued with programmes of well-made plays of the kind that had grown in popularity and number between the wars. Outside London, an entirely new audience was being sought: ENSA ran a full national and international programme of entertainments for the troops, and other organisations such as the Army Bureau of Current Affairs (ABCA) made use of drama for propaganda and the education of soldiers. Bridget Boland, for example, was part of a small creative team (under the direction of Michael Macowan) which wrote short plays illustrating a war theme or issue which would in turn be presented in both theatre and non-theatre spaces by a company of professional actors, all of whom were serving soldiers. Many of the performances contained improvised scenes and the scripts often had clearly educative and propagandist intentions, with titles such as *What Are We Fighting For?* and *Where Do We Go From Here?* (Willis 1991: 37).

Very little drama during the 1939–1945 conflict questioned the ethics of war itself. This is perhaps as much a reflection of the theatre and those who worked within it as it is of a nationalistic trend during wartime in British culture and society. In 1939 Auriol Lee, the prolific director of inter-war West End hits, was heard declaring at a Hollywood party that 'history will reveal Hitler as the greatest man of the last one hundred years' and that 'Germany deserved Czechoslovakia'. Challenged on her comments, she declared that she didn't like to 'talk politics'. A few months after this report by a gossip columnist for the *Daily Mirror*, the journalist apologised, claiming that his sources were incorrect and that in fact Lee had never made such statements (*Daily Mirror,* January/April 1939). Enid Bagnold, one of the few women playwrights of the era whose work has to some extent been re-evaluated, is also known to have had early sympathies with Hitler's ideas (Sebba 1986: 114–115). During a visit to Germany in 1933 Bagnold made observations about Hitler and his regime as representing a 'vital movement onwards to something'. She wrote to a colleague that she was 'so sick of the dreary socialist–communists, growling, carping and doing nothing' (ibid.).

These two examples of ideological stance are somewhat extreme and were later seen as naive by the artists themselves. The right-wing leanings of a number of women playwrights whose work is examined here are arguably reflected in the lack of detailed political analysis in their plays which deal with war experiences. Within these dramas the idea of war was often romanticised as an accepted state of affairs, the control of which was beyond the powers of the ordinary man or woman. One could contribute to victory by joyfully managing as best one could within the given domestic circumstances. In opposition, however, many of the dramas present a world which, although it remains largely located within the domestic sphere, necessitates a subversion of power relations and the gendered distribution of labour. Thus one could argue that underlying the theatrical representation of the seemingly ordinary daily life of women coping in wartime Britain, there was a desire to validate women's extraordinary and visible contribution towards the war effort. Many of the plays foreground a transgression of normalised roles for women.

> The importance of women was played down, I'm sure. Yet, how would they have managed the anti-aircraft batteries? It was all women on these.... The barrage balloons? Women kept those going up. There was a tremendous number of women in communications. Nurses on ships.... Everybody taking part in the war effort was important.
>
> (Nicholson 1995: 212–228)

Few commercial plays addressed this revolution as directly as the cinema did; but for the largely middle-class women who were writing for the West End theatres, the contemporary war experiences of the middle- and lower-middle-class women left at home had both theatrical viability for the West End managements and appeal for what would have been predominantly female audiences. Needless to say, plays by women over the period under discussion can only loosely be grouped together in terms of dramatic location and narrative through-line, but there do appear to be two very clear polarities: namely, those which outline everyday women's experience on the home front, in the back parlour as it were, and those which place women somewhere near the front line.

IN THE AFTERMATH OF THE GREAT WAR

The use of the First World War as a setting for drama in the London commercial theatres was uncommon. Certainly R. C. Sherriff was among the first to do so in *Journey's End*, which was produced in 1928. However, for a number of the early women playwrights of the immediate post-First World War period, the effects of war on the family, home, and in turn on the way in which women's identity had been shaped, formed an important component in a number of plays. The Second World War was different, somehow less taboo as a subject, and a number of women dramatists took advantage of the war and post-war environment as a context for dramatic plot. As most of the plots centre on women's domestic, professional and emotional experiences during wartime, these plays position women's experience within key historical moments. As such they are not history plays, but rather plays which either directly or indirectly examine a moment in history, through examining the way in which the events of that historical moment influence women's everyday lives.

Fryn Tennyson-Jesse and Harold Harwood's *Billeted*, described as 'a war play that has only just enough to do with war to make it amusing and not enough to make it serious' (*Tatler*, 5 September 1917), uses war as a setting for a reconciliation of marriage and the blooming of romance (Tennyson-Jesse and Harwood 1918). Betty Tarradine and her friend are the two protagonists living in a country manor house in which two army officers have been billeted. One of the army officers happens to be Betty Tarradine's estranged and erstwhile unreliable husband, yet she pretends not to know his real identity for most of the play, preferring to assess his seeming personality change from a distance. She has to economise because of the war, and is under constant threat of losing her cook to the 'mewnitions everyone's talking about' (ibid.: 50). Although the context of war is important, the play is essentially a comedy of manners, without any real critique of war as such. It is, however, a clear attempt to appeal to an audience which may well have been predominantly female by dramatising the changes which the war enforced on the lives of upper-middle-class women.

Thirteen years later *Mrs Fischer's War*, adapted from Henrietta Leslie's novel by herself and Joan Temple, took a much more serious look at the consequences of war for one woman.[5] Mrs Fischer is married to a German who has lived in England for many years, never bothering to become naturalised. On a family holiday in Germany his previously repressed feelings of loyalty to his country of birth inspire him to leave his family and volunteer to fight in the German army. His son, on returning home, joins the British army. Mrs Fischer is bereft not only of her husband and son, but as a 'German' by marriage she becomes a social outcast in England. She tries to reconcile husband and son but, because of her relatively powerless position is at first unable to do so. Mrs Fischer's attempts to re-unite the men in her life finally reach fruition, although both have been embittered and wounded by war. Ivor Brown's view of the play was that it was 'unequal in execution, but above the normal in ambition, and its production is a courageous assertion of faith in the existence of an audience who will face the less glamorous aspects of battle, the war behind the war, where spite and loneliness are doing the work of spiritual attrition' (*Observer*, 11 July 1931).

There were a number of plays, such as G. B. Stern's *The Man Who Pays the Piper*, where war is significant as the event which creates a fatherless family, leaving a young generation of women to take control of family affairs; their mothers are of the pre-war generation and as such unused to managing money and so on. There were very few plays which actually used women's war work as a central subject, just as plays by men which presented the realism of the experience of the First World War did not make their mark in the London theatres until the late 1920s. Before this point, although there were novels and other literary forms on the subject available to the public, it would seem that the experience of war was too close for it to be acceptably reconstructed live on stage.

Muriel Box's *Angels of War*, written in 1935, unashamedly exposes the hardship experienced by women working in the Army Auxiliary Corps in France at the close of the First World War.[6] It is a remarkable play which views war through women's experiences, written at a point when conflict in Europe began to seem imminent again, which may be one reason why it was never taken up by West End managements. Here, Edna Clarke, the new arrival to the headquarters (an old cottage behind British lines), tells her colleagues that her mother was thrilled when the order came through for her to go to France to join the corps. Their descriptions of life behind the lines soon whip Edna, or 'Nobby' as they have re-named her, into a patriotic fury:

SALOME: Britain's brave daughters!
MOANER: Brave! And I'm sick with fear every time I take out my bus!
VIC: I know. Terrified at every pot-hole in case you shake up some poor devil inside with his legs half off.
COCKY: Ploughing through blinding snow

SALOME: Or a bombing raid on a moonlight night

SKINNY: Noble work!

JO: Cleaning lavatories!

MOANER: Swilling out your ambulance – blood and filth, till you vomit at the sight of the muck.

VIC: Britain's brave and beautiful daughters . . .

SALOME: Doing their bits, bless 'em.

COCKY: Keep the old flag flying! [*Nobby, who has been standing in a strained attitude, suddenly bursts out*]

NOBBY: Stop it! Stop it! [*They are all suddenly silent, surprised at her outburst*]

NOBBY: . . . You don't really feel like that – you couldn't. I suppose you think it funny to say these things in front of me just to make me scared. . . . It won't have any effect. I'm proud of being British – I'm proud to do my bit . . . If you don't like being here, why don't you go home?

MOANER: I'll tell you. Because we're afraid of being pointed at and told we showed the white feather and ran away. We don't go on because we like it. We'd go home to-morrow if we could – but it would only be more misery than this. There's a nice position for you – afraid to stay and afraid to go home. That's war!

(Box 1935: 25–26)

The women are as brutal to each other as their commander is to them. The atmosphere of loyalty and friendship is fragile, broken frequently by loss of temper and patience which itself is caused by lack of sleep and food. The author undermines any possibility that an audience could go away after having seen the play with a romanticised ideal of life in the WAAC. *Angels of War* shows women who are at one and the same time infantilised, having to live under archaic and authoritarian regulations which are imposed at the will of the officers, and yet idealised as 'Britain's beautiful daughters'. By the end of the play 'Nobby' is no longer naive and gushing with patriotic enthusiasm. Those women who have survived ('Cocky' is killed on the road the night before the cease-fire is announced) feel that they have made a great sacrifice in giving up 'all they wanted out of life' to win the war. The play ends with a number of the women stating that they have 'fought' in a 'war to end all wars', that they have ruined their chances of marriage, but that the next generation will look after their needs, otherwise they will have 'been through it all for nothing' (ibid.: 74). Box shares the clarity of analysis expressed by Fryn Tennyson-

Jesse in her final descriptions of her impressions of the WAAC women, where she says,

> I saw them not as unthinking 'sporting' young things, who were having a great adventure, but as girls who were steadily sticking to their jobs, often without enjoyment save that of the knowledge of good work well done.... Even if they did not marry all would be well, because they would have had their adventure.
>
> (Tennyson-Jesse 1918: 94–96)

With the hindsight of some seventeen years of history, and the potential of the dramatic form within which to create an image of the experiences of these women at work, Box's play foregrounds the severe and exhausting conditions in which these women worked with far more impact. The play might also be seen as a warning against the potentiality of the forthcoming war. In *Angels of War* the women are not 'Roses of No Man's Land', as in the popular image which became an efficient aspect of wartime propaganda (Ouditt 1994: 10); rather, they suffer from fear, hunger and exhaustion, which creates rude and defeminised women – not angelic ladies.

DOMESTIC LIFE AND THE SECOND WORLD WAR

In Mary Hayley Bell's *Men in Shadow*, the action of which takes place in a barn loft behind enemy lines in France, there is only one female character (Bell 1943). Chérie, a tall 'large-boned French woman' of about sixty, speaks very little and only in French. She brings the fugitive British soldiers food and nurses them back to health before they find return routes home. *Men in Shadow* is essentially a play about a world in which men live and fight. Chérie is a constant reference to an idealised role for women, the provider and loyal nurturer, yet she is no romantic heroine, rather a member of the resistance forces. It is unusual for any of the plays of this period not to have a 'romantic' element as a stereotyped role for a woman – but Bell forgoes using this stereotype in her attempt to represent the 'truth' of war.

The plot of Esther McCracken's *No Medals* (McCracken 1947) which ran in the West End from 1944 for 740 performances and was, in 1948, made into a film directed by Roy Baker and re-titled *The Weaker Sex*, moves gradually toward a romantic dénouement, and as such the protagonist Martha Dacre could be considered to be a 'romantic heroine'. Described rather discerningly by one reviewer as a play which throws light on the everyday life of 'a good housewife gallantly struggling with the all too familiar shortages and emergencies of wartime', the setting is purely domestic (*The Times*, 5 October 1944). Martha, played to great acclaim by Fay Compton, has two strange men billeted in her home and takes care of their requirements as well as those of her married daughter, younger daughter, sister and so on. The play has a tremendous energy, the stage constantly fills and then empties of bodies, only to be filled again as soon as the heroine tries to take a rest. She frequently decides that she's had enough of housekeeping:

> MARTHA: ...I've suddenly grown sick of being an unpaid nanny, messenger-boy, house-keeper, and general servant (*she turns back to the ironing board*). I realised it the other day as I was persuading myself and my family for the five hundredth time that potatoes were both delicious and nourishing, while an egg was no longer either of those things.
>
> (McCracken 1947: 36)

But the rhythm and requirements of the everyday domestic comings and goings soon make her return with relentless dedication to her 'duties'. Martha, though, wants something more useful and fulfilling to do for the war effort. She tells her sister that if she gets called up she will go, even if it means her family going into digs. When her sister, who has few family responsibilities, asks her why she didn't sign up for a 'proper' job when the war broke out, Martha replies that her conscience told her not to go, though her inclination was to leave the family duties behind her, as she says earlier on to one of her billeted men, Geoffrey:

> MARTHA: It's deadly! Oh, you can't think how I long...to sweep through the seas protecting the convoys, or to sweep through the skies protecting England...and all I can do is sweep through the flues once a week....I'm a – a frustrated heroine, that's what I am...have you never thought that with all the big, exciting things that are going on all around me, it's pretty soul destroying to have the achieving of a couple of indifferent oranges the big moment of the year? There are times when I could weep.
>
> (ibid.: 43–44)

Martha's sister Harriet's work in a war office administrative unit 'isn't a hundred jobs in one and all of them dull' (ibid.: 53). Harriet doesn't work alone but, rather, has all her 'underlings' to order about. Martha is under no illusion about the validity of her own work. She yearns for something which would provide some kind of public recognition of her worth, yet she laughs at Geoffrey when he lovingly says, 'Someday someone will write a real appreciation of mothers in wartime' (ibid.: 87). By the end of the play

Geoffrey has proposed, and Martha is glad to know the 'luxury of being comforted for once instead of always having to do the comforting' (ibid.: 95).

Critics were scathing about both the subject and context of *No Medals*, largely finding it 'comfortable' and 'trivial', and the fact that it was a 'domestic comedy' only went to fuel the argument that McCracken was not a 'serious playwright'. Yet the play is a serious attempt to entice audiences, albeit middle- and upper-class audiences, through using an integrated context of war and a vision of women's experience within it.

A central thematic manoeuvre in many of the plays aforementioned is the transposition of what would have been considered as traditionally female roles into a male context, that is to say, war. Similarly many of the playwrights explore what happens when male roles are taken over by women once the men are at war. This is certainly the case in *The Years Between* where, during her husband's absence on war duties, Diana Wentworth takes his place as MP for Arlsea and learns how to do the job with more ruthless efficiency than he had ever achieved.

The play's heroine Diana Wentworth is transformed from a 'quiet and subdued thirty-five-year-old mother and wife' into what her returned husband describes as

> One of those managing, restless women, always writing letters, going to meetings arguing about ridiculous questions, having interminable conversations on the telephone, and it's no use pretending that patriotism has driven you to it. It's become your life. You are that sort of woman.
>
> (Du Maurier 1994: 373)

Whereas Michael Wentworth's experiences of secret duties behind enemy lines have made him lose sight of his previously held conviction that the war was 'a crusade, a fight for good against evil', Diana's new role as an MP has given her an opportunity to air her nationalistic and in many ways pro-war beliefs, as she reveals during the preparation of her speech for a division of the Girl's Army Training Corps:

> To those of you who are about to enter one of the services, I would say a special word. . . . Nothing will matter to you now but your duty to your country. . . you will put aside all thought of personal selfishness or individuality, and become one small unit in a magnificent army of women, the great army that is helping in so large a measure to win this war. The girls of today are the women, and the mothers of tomorrow. Much of the responsibility for the peace of the world will rest upon your shoulders. We none of us want

to return to the dreary, slack, go-as-you-please Britain that existed
before the war; but side by side with our men folk . . . we shall build a
saner, stronger Britain, where slackness and inefficiency will not be
tolerated: where everyone will work for the community, and our
children shall be brought up to service, duty and obedience to the
State.

(ibid.: 370–371)

The war literally creates a situation where husband and wife change roles.
Michael returns to find that his wife has taken his political place. The
support which Diana once gave him in his parliamentary work is now
given to her by their neighbour Richard, with whom she has fallen in love.
Michael's critique of Diana's changed personality, his unhappiness with
the cold hard edge which her responsibilities have brought out in her,
contribute toward her decision to change the ending of her speech
significantly: 'We hope to build a wiser, happier Britain, where our
children and ourselves shall grow in courage, faith and understanding'
(ibid.: 397).

The play closes with the ending of the war and a number of separa-
tions: Diana and Richard part company as they both come to the
conclusion that her duty lies with her husband, with whom she will have
to negotiate their new emotional divide. Michael reverses his original
decision to stay at home and re-acquaint himself with his family and
accepts a government job assisting with the re-building of Europe after the
war. The play does, however, end with the re-uniting of mother and child,
watched over by the faithful family nanny. Diana accepts that the war has
changed everything she loves, but is resigned to the fact. At the close of the
play the audience is left with the sense that Diana, physically and
emotionally divided from her husband and thus effectively a single
working mother, will play an important role in the re-building of Britain.

Although Du Maurier's play is by no means experimental, there is no
traditional romantic happy ending. The romance of war is presented as
nothing more than an illusion once the war is over. Diana's leanings
toward moral re-armament are just about reversed but there is an overall
imperative to sacrifice one's own wishes to the greater good of the nation.
There is a narrative focus on the impersonal within the war context: not
just in the sense that Diana Wentworth's situation may well have been a
dramatised account of many women's experiences during the war, but in
the sense that individual choice is inevitably ruled by national need. Du
Maurier makes use of a physical cycle – the separation and re-uniting of
families – as a means of representing a woman's, and perhaps in turn a

nation's, experience of war. *The Years Between* ran at the Wyndham's theatre from January 1945 until June 1946, thus sustaining its appeal for a London audience which would have changed radically during its production run. The wartime audience arguably had a much closer link to the immediate post-war audience than one might at first assume. Plays such as *No Medals* and *The Years Between* may well have held such large appeal for wartime audiences because they discoursed the here and now of life during war, without any pretence at metaphor or, certainly in the case of the McCracken play, philosophy. The war is fought on home ground, with the women in a situation where everyday life becomes somehow accentuated, or gender-roles are reversed, but only as part of a service to the nation.

Bringing 'romance' into the scenario somehow normalises the tragedy of war, making easier the depiction of a world in which, although life is full of hardship, everyone must battle on and do their best to make sure that all, family and nation, survive the trauma. In *The Same Sky* (Mitchell 1951), written by the actress Yvonne Mitchell and first produced in 1951, the setting is the East End of London in the early 1940s. The protagonist, Esther, is in love with a soldier by whom she later conceives a child. She is from an orthodox Jewish family, he is not. When she insists on continuing their relationship, her father refuses to talk to her; to let his daughter marry a gentile would be to sanction her withdrawal from God. Her mother negotiates between father and daughter. 'Momma' tries to persuade her daughter that Sammy would be a better match, but Esther insists, and so the tension of the war between her and her father grows. Mitchell exposes the racial mistrust both from Jew to gentile and vice versa, and somehow the context of the war both accentuates the differences of the races and yet ultimately brings them together. The family all draw around to support her when her fiancé Jeff is killed on active service, and she is left bearing his child. Her mother talks frantically to Esther, who is in a state of near-suicide:

> MOMMA: ... Not any more for my sake I ask you to live, but for your own sake and for the baby. Live how you will Esther; let the baby be what you will, teach him to be like his father. Yes ... I will understand: only live, mine little one. Momma wants you to live for your life not for her. ... Jeff too will want you to live. To give life to his baby. Part of him will live too in his child. We will love the baby Esther. We will love too the part that is his father. ... Give momma a chance to love the baby Esther. Forgive.
>
> (ibid.: 304)

Even her father rallies around when he sees what pain his daughter is in, suggesting that they talk to Jeff's mother about what should be done. The war has separated and eventually united both family and races.

WOMEN AND WAR – OUTSIDE THE HOME

Bridget Boland's *The Cockpit* (Boland 1949) uses character types rather than in-depth personalities to examine racial difference and the dehumanising effects of war for those left without a nation in the aftermath. The play is unusual in its complete refusal to romanticise war or the people who are caught within its grip. Boland was one of the few playwrights, male or female, to discourse the effects of the Second World War outside the domestic family unit, although the nature of everyday domestic life is transposed onto the behaviour of her characters in their real theatrical setting. Boland was also one of the few women playwrights making use of the form of the 'well-made play' to experiment with theatrical space. For *The Cockpit* the environment beyond the stage and the whole theatre auditorium becomes a 'provincial theatre in Germany in May, 1945'. The play is a treatment of the fate of a group of 'Displaced Persons' left 'crawling about the cockpit of Europe after Hitler's defeat . . . and what they felt and thought about each other and the British way of handling them and their problems'. The *dramatis personae* run the gamut, in terms of the female characters, from Rebecca, a Polish Jewess, to a Russian housewife, to a French communist resistance fighter who was a pianist in the pre-war years. The displaced persons are forced to stay in the theatre when plague is diagnosed. Boland thoroughly re-creates the confusion and squalor of the war on stage and in and around the audience. As theatre *The Cockpit* is vibrant and energetic, and although there is much action, the piece is without a single protagonist. Women are shown to pitch in – both mothers and the single women; they are as aggressive as the male characters, who are no less prone to fear. The suggestion is that the consequences of war do not differentiate between the sexes.

Both *The Same Sky* and *The Cockpit* met with some success among London theatre-goers, even though they were plays where the audience were asked to look back in time to a war which many were already trying to forget. The portrayal of war in Martha Gellhorn and Virginia Cowles's *Love Goes to Press*, a romantic farce set in a press camp on the Italian front, met with consternation and disapproval when the play transferred to America. The American critics felt that the authors had displayed 'strange human ethics' and 'incredible human callousness'.[7] London audiences and critics reacted differently, enjoying the comic irreverence which the authors applied to the depiction of life in a foreign press camp during the war. As one reviewer wrote, 'out of the turmoil of life in a press camp where battle is as bitter as anything at the front, they have fashioned a comedy of tremendous pace' (*Daily Mail*, 18 June 1946).

The play centres around two American women war correspondents, Jane Mason and Annabelle Jones, who have come to the camp as part of their work detail. They are very 'feminine' in the traditional sense, but there is no doubt that work comes before all else, and we are immediately struck by the speed and efficiency with which they get their work done, by comparison to the male correspondents who fight over the use of the typewriter and bicker with each other. Hank describes the women:

> HANK: Let me warn you , Leonard. Don't be deceived by Miss Mason. She and her pal Miss Jones sail around looking like *Vogue* illustrations and they get all the stories before you've even heard of them. Some of our colleagues have a low opinion of those girls just because of that little trait.
>
> (Gellhorn and Cowles 1995: 15)

For Jane and Annabelle, the battle is not so much with the enemy forces as it is with the false chivalry of their camp commanders and fellow male journalists. Both women are aware that they are treated differently because of their gender, but they deal with it with insight and humour.

> ANNABELLE: If I'm told once more I can't do something because I'm a woman . . .
>
> JANE: (*Reciting*) What if you got wounded, Miss Jones? All the forces on land, sea and air would stop fighting the war and take care of you. Not good for the war effort.
>
> ANNABELLE: And considering the number of times we couldn't even get out of a car when a shelling started because the men pinned us down with their elbows while they stepped over us. It makes me sick with rage. Darling, your hair's wonderful cut short like that.
>
> JANE: Do you like it? It started in the desert, about Alamein it must have been. I couldn't get any water to wash it . . .
>
> (ibid.: 27)

At any given opportunity, the authors make use of Jane and Annabelle's femininity by juxtaposing it with the risk-taking nature of their work, and 'because their womanhood is something that they have never been allowed to forget, they have great fun flaunting it'.[8] Both women manage to over-ride orders by making use of friendships with officers of higher rank, but we are asked to view this in the context of Annabelle's estranged husband Roger, who happens to be at the camp. Roger had, in the past, found ways of 'scooping' stories before his wife could get to them, usually by putting obstacles in her way – if the women live on an 'every man for himself' basis, it is because they have learnt the habit from their men.

Gellhorn has stated that she and Cowles, both experienced war correspondents, wrote the play as a joke and as a way of making money; that it bears no resemblance to the reality of camp life (ibid.: i). What is interesting about the play, however, is that war is used as a background for another war, the 'battle of the sexes'. The women are not only up against the way in which they are viewed as individuals, but also the way in which women in general are perceived. Jane eventually passes up the offer of marriage to Philip because of his description of his mother and sister living in quiet domestic bliss in Yorkshire. The idea of a life of fishing, shooting and horse riding, with a few village teas thrown in, does not excite her. Instead she goes off with Annabelle to Burma, to the 'forgotten army' and 'Leeches, jungle sores, heat, fever, terrible casualties' (ibid.: 142). Even though at the very close of the play Philip receives orders to go to Burma himself, Jane has already left. The women create a woman's world inside that of men: we follow their perspective throughout a play in which women are shown to be often torn between the conflicts of the personal and the professional.

CONCLUSION

The women playwrights who wrote using the chronicle format during the inter-war years did not do so in a vacuum. They were writing at a point in the history of the women's movement where the momentum and shape of pressure for political change in terms of gender-roles changed and fragmented. These women seemingly tuned into a social and cultural interest in debates around 'the woman question', which in turn had been influenced by women's experiences during the First World War. Second, the playwrights were influenced by the filtering into popular culture of 'new psychology', which in itself often centralised women and both the complexities and the defining of *femininity* itself. The chronicle play contained a workable theatrical formula used by both male and female playwrights, and provided an opportunity to re-vision history in a way which had relevance and appeal to the largely middle- and upper-class theatre audiences and especially the female audiences of the time.

Alison Light's theory of a renewed conservatism in women's writing after the 1914–1918 war has relevance to examinations of the earlier plays looked at in this chapter:

> something happened to middle-class femininity after the Great War which sees it taking on what had formerly been regarded as distinctly masculine qualities: in particular the ethics of a code of self-control and a language of reticence whose many tones can be picked out in the writing and also in the construction of writing selves in the period.... The concept of British nationality can be seen as pre-eminently masculine before the First World War... and while Englishwomen could be the Guardians of their race, their Englishness as primarily wives and mothers, derived from the men in their lives... their work during the First World War... and their acquisition of citizenship... suggests a new level of State recognition and of national inclusion.
>
> (Light 1991: 210–211)

For women this situation ultimately meant that they were being assimilated into an essentially imperialist national identity, and this is reflected in many of the chronicle plays and 'war' plays by women of the time. However, there are very few plays where ideals of nation are not entwined with questions about the nature of femininity and women's role within the family. Another factor which needs to be taken into account is that many of the reviewers saw the writing of plays about historical women as vehicles for actresses: it is important to assert the significance of this in terms of a history of women's involvement in the development of theatre. While many of the female protagonists in the plays in question promote an ideal of duty to the nation, they also create a discourse around women's roles and women's experience as written by women for a public arena, that is, the theatre. It would be interesting to compare portrayals of women/heroines in chronicle plays by women with those of men at the time. I would suggest that there may be a marked difference in relation to the significance of discourse around notions of femininity.

The female protagonists in the chronicle plays were often 'exceptional' women from history – albeit that their stories were told in such a way as to somehow parallel the lives of 'modern' ordinary women. Women playwrights who made use of war as an historical event which produced very specific living conditions for women, on the other hand, used ordinary women in exceptional situations as a framework for dramatic narrative. The women playwrights who used the two world wars as a background for their well-made plays saw that a social and cultural interest in debates around both war and women's experience of war, integrated with 'the woman question' itself. Thus the female protagonists in war plays were often found fighting similar domestic battles to those of peacetime. For those left to fight the war on the home front, working for unity and the fulfilment of duty to the nation were accepted as the vital domestic and public contribution toward the war effort itself. Moreover, in plays where war, as a significant moment in history, is used as a setting, the idea of 'working for the nation' often appears as a central theme. The focus is on women's lives during times of war; the battlefield is on the home front. In the later plays which use the Second World War as a context, 'nation' is less confused with family. There is far more confusion between which roles to prioritise, that of head of family or joining the public workforce. Ideals of masculinity and femininity are also less confused, although often, as in *Love Goes to Press,* the battle of the sexes becomes the lens through which war is seen. Equally, women are often still shown to be torn between the personal and the political, and the private and the professional.

As a whole the plays theatricalise both history and war as having a different significance, both on a practical and emotional level, for each of the sexes. Clearly, even for those on the front line of battle, war was a vastly different experience for women, where their traditional feminine roles are highlighted even though the boundaries of femininity are changed. A number of the plays were commercially very successful, although most are largely forgotten. Equally, there is a sense that the women who wrote them knew exactly for whom they were writing and understood both the importance and the commercial viability of realistic depictions of contemporary women's experience during wartime.

7

SPINSTERS AND WIDOWS
Women without men

> The economic slump, the revolt against reason, the resurgence of military values, the cult of the cradle and...the preoccupation with physical modesty – these are the chief forces which cause the pendulum of emancipation to swing backwards...reaction follows progress.
>
> (Holtby 1934: 158–168)

The levels of social antagonism towards single women, and especially 'spinsters', which had already begun to rise before the 1914–1918 war carried on doing so through the war into the 1920s and 1930s. Pre-First World War sentiment that the spinster was 'a barren sister... shamefaced, bloodless and boneless... seen as converting her desperate disappointment and frustration at being cheated of a man and motherhood after being reared to expect such things' were not dissimilar to sentiments espoused after the war (Jeffreys 1985: 95). Changes in attitude, influenced by the fact that First World War losses imposed a limitation on the numbers of available unmarried men, weren't often voiced. During the inter-war years about a third of the women who had not married by the age of twenty-nine remained unmarried (Lewis 1984: 4). The post-First World War spinster was counted among the supposedly 'two million superfluous women' and some recent historians and literary critics suggest that 'speculations on the future prospects' of the unmarried women 'became a national pastime' (Joannou 1995: 79). As far as some contemporary social theorists were concerned, spinsters were 'bitter or sub-normal women with thwarted or deficient passions' and thus spinsters were often castigated for their moral standards, 'prudery' or old-fashioned perceptions of the world and their role within it (ibid.: 81). The inter-war spinster was often ridiculed or seen as a threat: if the spinster was seen as a 'man-hater', who disapproved of male behaviour, she was accused of being a moralist whose ideological stance represented a threat to the development of the nation. We should remember that this is also the era when 'female frigidity' became a popularised and misused clinical label for women who chose either not to get married or not to have children – or simply for women who chose not to have a sexual relationship with a man. The 'feminine ideal' was a woman who sought marriage and homemaking, not one who actively chose to stay single or have sexual relations outside marriage.

For Winifred Holtby, the writer, novelist and critic, 'the legend of the frustrated spinster is one of the most formidable social influences of the modern world' (Holtby 1934: 125). Her lifelong friend and companion, Vera Brittain, in her biography of Holtby, portrayed her as a woman without bitterness who never felt at a disadvantage being a woman, and one who 'brought to the service of women ideas which were positive and constructive' (Brittain 1940: 134). In her social tract, *Women in a Changing Civilisation* (1934), Holtby analysed the social position of her female contemporaries both in relation to their pioneering foremothers and in relation to the social and political issues contemporary to her own age; she was concerned that the scapegoating popular image of the spinster had very little to do with the lived experience of single women.

The social code of the late 1920s and early 1930s, with its emphasis on child rearing and marriage, meant that women who either chose not to get married, or chose marriage after a career, were not provided for socially or economically. Holtby was concerned with the problems which arose merely from the use of the term or label of 'spinster' (previously the term had always been associated with virginity). Clearly 'spinster' as a social label did not account for the fact that many women were choosing to have sexual relations with men outside marriage, nor did it account for the rising numbers of women widowed by the war, or women who had children outside marriage. Holtby stressed that as the supposedly 'ideal' feminine woman was married, with children and with a healthy sexual life within her marriage, certain political voices felt justified in decrying single women as a 'distressing type'; yet no such attitude was applied to single men. Later critics, such as Beauman, state that during the 1930s attitudes to single women were 'somewhat kinder' (Beauman 1983: 62), but this pays little regard to the effects of what Holtby, among others, saw as a direct correlation between the rising tide of fascism with its accompanying ideology, and the belief that the 'manless thirties' were causing a social problem. In the popular press the spinster and the single woman were seen as economic problems, despite the fact that most of them supported themselves financially. The perception, generally speaking, was that if a single woman supported herself by working, a possible place of employment for a man was being taken by a woman. In addition, at a point in

173

history where fecundity was 'revered as a patriotic virtue', Holtby was very clear that the position of single women, whatever their sexual orientation or marital history, was precarious in a fluctuating economy where the position of women generally was dependent on frequent changes in 'popular' perceptions of what a woman's 'proper' role should be (Holtby 1934: 166).

In terms of the women playwrights creating roles for actresses at this time, the general attitude toward single women is reflected, but where the popular press actively attack spinsters, the playwrights merely present them as character types. In plays where 'family' as a social unit is emphasised, the single woman was often placed in juxtaposition to the married woman. Again, though, this was more to do with an attempt to present a rounded vision of middle-class women's lives than it was a conscious effort to place one against the other as good and bad women. During the 1920s and 1930s widowed women are often the focus of the dramatic narrative, albeit that the play worked toward the eventual re-marriage of the woman in question. Here, the social reality of war widows is used as a plot device, such as in *Billeted* or Joan Temple's *The Widow's Cruise* (Temple 1926) where Francesca is re-acquainted with her husband who had disappeared during the First World War. Certainly, the play-wrights appear to have categorised single women into types, the least 'thought out' being the spinster. In plays of the period, the spinster was often, although not always, virginal, naive or simply judgemental, thus becoming a comic figure or ideological device.

THE SPINSTER

The spinster as a stage character made frequent appearances in many of the plays examined in this book. A few examples are looked at here as a means of indicating the typical, or most frequent context in which she appeared. Spinsters were often depicted in the form of sharp-minded businesswomen, typically dressed in pince-nez or tweeds, such as Miss Mutchison in Aimée and Philip Stuart's successful *Her Shop* or Miss Leith in Rosamond Lehmann's haunting *No More Music* (Lehmann 1939). At times the spinster is cold and disapproving of the morals of the younger generation, as in *Escape Me Never*, Margaret Kennedy's play which ran at the St Martin's theatre for 232 performances from late 1933. Here the spinsters are given no name other than one which represents their marital status. They are given a limited appearance while trying to ascertain who is the mysterious father of Gemma's child:

SECOND SPINSTER: How is the wee baby?

SPINSTER: We just couldn't work out, my sister and I, which was the lucky man. But now (*archly*) I think I can guess.

GEMMA: The lucky man?

SPINSTER: Your husband... the baby's father...

GEMMA: (*Taking Caryl's hand as well as Sebastian's.*) They are both my husband. But they are not the father of my child. (*The Spinster is speechless. She escapes into the hotel.*)

(Kennedy 1934: 44)

However, the spinster figure was just as frequently a 'barrel of fun', ready to try any new adventure and with great admiration for the new ways of the younger generation. This is certainly the case with Miss Mayne in Dodie Smith's highly successful first play, *Autumn Crocus* (Smith 1931), played in the original production by Muriel Aked, a popular comedy actress of the time.

Another common usage of the spinster as a character 'type' was as a confidante to the female protagonist, but here she was more likely to be a 'maiden' or widowed aunt of some close relative, as in *Sixteen*, or Mme de Bretteville in Helen Jerome's *Charlotte Corday*. Again, the role of confidante could work just as easily against the agenda of the main characters as it did in its favour. For example in Dane's first play, *Bill of Divorcement* (later made into a film starring the young Katherine Hepburn), Miss Fairfield is a remnant from a bygone age (Dane 1961b). She is disillusioned by the fact that her nephew's wife Margaret should seek divorce, and even less happy about the fact that she is considering re-marriage. For Miss Fairfield, Margaret's liaison with Gray Meredith is immoral, as is the way in which she has raised her daughter, Sydney (Hepburn). Sydney, as far as her great aunt is concerned, is far too strong minded and determined for a respectable young woman. Sydney's desire for a career is, in Miss Fairfield's eyes, a signifier of the typical selfish thoughtlessness of young women which has brought about the downfall of the nation. Thus what connects these various spinster characters is the fact that they are often used as 'fill in' to the main plot for moments of comic relief or as a means of opposing one ideology with another. They share with many representations of single, working women, a defined series of characteristics, but are rarely the centre of narrative focus.

SINGLE WOMEN AT WORK: THE LONELY SECRETARY

In Britain, especially during the inter-war period, where areas of employment were limited for women, the vocation of secretary was at one and the same time sought and reviled. Pay was low and prospects were limited, but for single women it was a respectable job. In plays of the period the secretary is often a hovering background presence in the middle-class professional family. Devoted to her work, with very little life outside it, she is often naive and lonely and almost always has romantic intentions toward her employer. Elsie, in Dodie Smith's *Call it a Day*, which ran at the Globe for 509 performances, is a case in point.

Elsie, devoted secretary of Hilton – a London accountant, who is waiting for his last client of the day to arrive – suggests that if they were to work late as she 'loves her work', he will 'feel clear' the next day. He likes the suggestion and offers to drive her home after they have finished working. Hilton then gets caught up with a late client who, much to Elsie's consternation, has taken it upon herself to re-arrange the office flowers. The time spent with the glamorous female client undermines Elsie's perceived closeness with Mr Hilton who, as he is running late, withdraws his offer of a lift home and tells Elsie to take a taxi with money from petty cash instead. Her response is a pastiche of the forlorn and rejected woman:

(*Elsie looks after him, disconsolate. . . . For a moment she looks at the ravished bowl of scillas. Suddenly she gives a little gulp of tears and takes out her handkerchief. She goes out of the room, repressing her tears with a sniff.*)

(Smith 1936: 249–250)

Miss Trimmerback and Miss Watts, two secretaries in the American playwright and society figure Claire Boothe-Luce's *The Women*, appear in the second act, where they are sent by Mr Haines to his home in order to sort out final divorce arrangements:

MISS TRIMMERBACK: . . . Is he going to marry her?

MISS WATTS: I don't butt into his private affairs . . .

MISS TRIMMERBACK: . . . She's lucky . . . I wish I could get a man to foot my bills . . . a lot of independence you have on a woman's wages. I'd chuck it like that for a decent or an indecent home.

MISS WATTS: The office. That's my home.

MISS TRIMMERBACK: . . . I see. The office wife?

MISS WATTS: (*defiantly*) He could get along better without Mrs

Haines or Allen than he could without me... I relieve him of a thousand foolish details. I remind him of... his good opinion of himself. I never cry and I don't nag. I guess I am the office-wife.... He'll never divorce me!

MISS TRIMMERBACK: Why you're in love with him...

MISS WATTS: What if I am? I'd rather work for him than marry the kind of dumb cluck *I* could get (*almost tearful*) – just because he's a man.

(Boothe-Luce 1937: 602)

They get a cold reception from his wife who, against the advice of her friends, has forced her husband into admitting his adulterous behaviour with Crystal Allen and is suing him for divorce. Despite her sad realisation that her love for her boss will never be reciprocated, Miss Watts carries out her duties with a flourish, pointing out to Mrs Haines that 'there are always tag ends to a divorce... you know how Mr Haines hates to be bothered with inconsequential details' (ibid.: 604).

These two secretaries are caricatures in a play full of exaggerated stereotypes of women. Booth-Luce was writing about people she knew, the rich, bored women of New York in the late 1930s. As such, *The Women*, which successfully transferred to the London stage where it ran at the Lyric for 155 performances, is a fairly thinly disguised attack on the moral values and social behaviour of both these women and the world in which they lived; a world of women whose lives are controlled by their obsession with pleasing men and reaching some unattainable level of femininity. The two secretaries are among the few working women in the play and the social message behind their words has a resonance with the social reality of their age.

In both *Dear Octopus* and *Family Affairs* the family secretary is used as a means of opposing the 'bad' woman with the virtuous woman. Both Fenny in the former and Margaret in the latter play are devoted to the family unit. Both are outsiders – a fact which provides an alternative, an outsider's view of the family. Through work, however, they have been integrated into the family unit. In *Family Affairs* Lady Madehurst encourages her son to see Margaret as a potential wife who is loyal and kind. More than this, she is a preferable alternative to his girlfriend who has already been married and wants to take Harvey away from the family enclave. Margaret is the 'innocent', who ultimately shares the same values and beliefs around the sanctity of the family as Lady Madehurst.

In Dodie Smith's *Dear Octopus* – the play by which Smith is most remembered (see Grove 1996) – the family secretary Grace Fenning is 'a slender woman of twenty-nine, unobtrusively pretty with a pleasant, unaffected manner. She wears old tweeds' (Smith 1966: 283), and has virtually become an honorary family member. Fenny (Fenning) is loved by all; she helps the domestic servants and plays with the children as well as coping admirably with all her secretarial duties. When others complain about the amount of work they are expected to do, Fenny is unremittingly loyal to her employers. She is central to the plot, and eventually comes to represent the future of the family unit. When the eldest son, Nicholas, a witty and charming director of an advertising firm, finds himself sitting chatting with her at the grand family celebration around which the play is centred, he tells her that she is 'a very sweet person ... you look about fourteen', and then puts her hand against his cheek, and remarks, 'that poor little hand – just like a little nutmeg grater' (ibid.: 316). After the party his sister reprimands him for 'leading Fenny on', and during their next encounter Nicholas criticises Fenny for the way in which she behaved at the party. Later, when he discovers that Fenny is considering a marriage proposal from a local chicken farmer, Nicholas becomes angry and tells her that she is 'cheap'. In true Dodie Smith style, the play has a happy ending when Nicholas realises that his anger was caused by nothing other than jealousy and that, in truth, he is madly in love with Fenny. He proposes to her and she reveals her feelings towards him by refusing:

FENNY: (*recoiling*) No! Oh, how could you? I can't help loving you.
I'm not ashamed of it. It's been my secret happiness for years.
But to say that to me when ... it's meaningless ... pity can be very humiliating...

NICHOLAS: ... men don't propose out of pity... I really love you Fenny... all that matters now is if you'll take me on.

(ibid.: 380–382)

Fenny has the same love and loyalty for the family – the 'dear octopus' of the title – as if she were related by blood. But she is an outsider who has been absorbed by the fictional upper-middle-class family at a point in British history when life as it was known was again on the edge of change – with war once more on the horizon and memories of the way in which the First World War had both directly and indirectly heralded a change in the structure of the wealthy British family. Thus the outsider provides future structure and security for a traditionally closed social unit, the foundations of which are beginning to crumble.

In Elizabeth Baker's *Miss Robinson* the respectability of an upper-middle-class English family is shown to be a facade through the actions of the honest and morally upright family secretary.[1] Here we find an unusual focus upon the secretary as a stage character, whereby she is the nucleus of the narrative. Angela Robinson, a 'charming young person, quick in movement, bright in manner, well but quietly dressed', is loyal secretary to Walter Vintage MP. She is dedicated to her work and in awe of the class of family for which she works. Angela is shy about letting her employers know of her affections for Arden, a man from her own class. He has fewer delusions about the grandeur of the ruling classes and tells her to make sure that she does not allow herself to be exploited by them:

ARDEN: ... But look here, Angy, take a tip from a – a pal. Don't make yourself cheap with these people. Don't be a slave to them. You women spoil the people you work for. Don't you do it.

(Baker 1920: 20)

Walter Vintage is concerned that his valuable secretary should not become sexually exploited by his overly amorous son:

VINTAGE: What has he been doing?

MRS VINTAGE: He? Well I don't suppose he was entirely to blame –

VINTAGE: On the contrary, I dare say he was.

MRS VINTAGE: I came into the room unexpectedly today and saw them standing very close together – they were obviously very intimate.... Of course they jumped apart...

VINTAGE: You mean Horace did?

MRS VINTAGE: ... I dare say she has encouraged him a little. Of course she is a nice, respectable girl...

VINTAGE: A fact of which Horace must be made aware...

MRS VINTAGE: But I think she's flattered, and very naturally, by Horace's attentions. That's why I want you to speak to him. I don't want her to have her head turned. She comes of decent, quiet people –

VINTAGE: Poor but honest.... But I don't see that Miss Robinson's family concerns us. It's the girl herself... I should have thought that Horace would have got used to her good looks – the confounded little ass!

(ibid.: 31)

Angela Robinson witnesses the revelation of a family scandal, and quietly leaves the room in an attempt to be tactful and remain unnoticed. Walter Vintage, we discover, was married to a woman previously; the original wife, we are told by a dying servant, is still alive and is legally still Vintage's 'real' wife. When the family rally around Vintage to discuss what they can do to alleviate any possibility of his bigamy being discovered, it is Miss Robinson who holds the key to maintaining the family secret. She is trusted, but there are implications that, because she is not from the Vintage's social class, she will have no real loyalty to the family over such a grave matter. Vintage's solution is that Horace should ask Miss Robinson to marry him. Lister, the elder brother, is shocked at such a suggestion, his concern being purely for his own social position: 'And what will Sir Eustace and Lady Agatha say when they know brother has married the typewriter?' (ibid.: 60).

References to class origins increase as the plot develops. For the Vintage family, there is no question but that a young woman, with a family from Kennington and a father who is a clerk, should be delighted to marry into the 'superior classes'. For Horace, Miss Robinson is an 'obedient little girl'; for Ivy, Miss Robinson's sister, the Vintage family are very tolerant and 'awfully decent' as most 'people in their position, if anybody in the family wanted to marry the typist, would cut up frightfully' (ibid.: 80).

Miss Robinson dresses up for dinner so that she looks the part, but she suspects that something strange is going on; Mrs Vintage and her friends give her discerning looks and she somehow doesn't 'feel right'. When Miss Robinson tells her mother that the Vintages don't seem to show their feelings, Mrs Robinson points out that 'it's just something in their manner... they're different from us' (ibid.: 89). Eventually Miss Robinson finds out that the real reason Horace proposed to her was in order that she keep the family secret quiet. When in turn she tells Horace that she can no longer consider marrying him, the family cannot believe their ears. They were convinced that she must have known all along that they would never let their son marry into a lower class, unless there had been a very good reason. Miss Robinson cannot believe that she has been so stupid and ultimately sees her unhappiness as being her punishment for putting the knowledge of Vintage's previous marriage out of her mind, as she says to them:

MISS R: Why didn't you trust me?... I knew all along that I was wrong to come into your life... when there was this wicked thing in it – but I was so proud to think you wished it.... I never imagined you were doing it to – bribe – me.... And I was so pleased to think that I might live among such people and... have all you have.

(ibid.: 111)

Miss Robinson's admiration for the Vintages and their class is effectively destroyed. She says to her friend Arden that it was pride which made her want to be 'one of them'.

In *Miss Robinson* Baker highlights the unworkability of an integration between an unmarried secretary from the suburban lower-middle classes and a man from the upper-middle classes. In this sense the play picks up on what Trewin saw as a typically Edwardian theme, that of marriage between the classes (Trewin 1976: 102), but with the feminist twist expected of a writer who had early associations with the suffrage move-ment (see Stowell 1992). The implication is primarily that the classes don't mix, that each has different moral codes and standards. Rather than marriage to Miss Robinson representing some exchange of property, it represents an affirmation of the moral code and values of the ruling class by the [new] suburban class – the collapse of the wedding plans puts the possibility of this affirmation into question. Simultaneous to accentuating class differences Baker posits the question of whether or not it may be better to stay single (although it is Arden who takes Miss Robinson away from the Vintage household) and respect the validity of your own position than become absorbed into a class which changes the moral code according to its own needs. It is interesting to note here Baker's own autobiographical affinities with Angela Robinson, for she too had been in the secretarial profession and had also come from a lower-middle class family. Within the Vintage household, Miss Robinson is consciously identified with the *outside*, and it is only her position as secretary which brings her recognition within the family. Family honour is too important to risk revelation by an *outsider*. By the end of the play the first wife has died and so, when Miss Robinson leaves, there are few regrets for the Vintages who take no responsibility for the way in which they have maltreated her. For Vintage, 'It is all most satisfactory – except that I want a new secretary'; the implication being that life goes on, and that there are plenty more available secretaries, just like Miss Robinson. Baker is critical not so much of the new suburban class as she is of the moral hypocrisy of the upper-middle classes, a 'vintage' class represented by the Vintage family. If she is critical of the suburban class, it is because of their adherence to a false consciousness, which becomes apparent in the awe with which Miss Robinson and her family initially hold the Vintage family. Her critique is displayed through a character who is a single woman, from the suburban classes, working to support herself – and it is she who is presented as being morally upright and honest.

SINGLE WOMEN AND SEXUALITY

There are a few plays where the fact that a woman has chosen to remain unmarried is placed positively within a context where marriage is seen as part and parcel of an unchallenging or unadventurous middle-class or suburban life.[2] Here, the heroine is shown to want from life something other than conventional marriage. Occasionally, the implication is that her desire to be independent is evidence of her naivety; more often, though, this desire is shown to signify her lack of adherence to what was considered as 'normal' female sexuality. Rosamund Lehmann's Hilda, in *No More Music*, is a case in point. Here, the virginal Hilda, spending a vacation with her aunt on a holiday island, takes time out from her academic studies in order to make a real-life study of Jan and Miriam. The young couple have caused a stir as no one is really sure of their marital status. By all accounts they are 'bohemians', and the fact that Jan seems able to do whatever he likes with his time holds a fascination for Hilda, who spends a great deal of her time with her head 'stuck in a book'. Hilda feels that Jan can do whatever he likes because he is male, whereas she sees herself as neither male nor female. Lehmann deliberately contrasts Hilda with Miriam, who is in many respects an 'ideal' of femininity, even though Miriam and Jan are not married:

> HILDA: ... I like sort of concentrating on something. A ... sort of problem.
> MIRIAM: Do you? I hate it. Puzzles and acrostics and things make me feel faint. Once Jan tried to teach me chess and I really felt faint. We had to stop.
> HILDA: (*laughing*) Did you honestly? I used to play chess with my father. I loved it. ... Of course I really like reading best ...
> MIRIAM: ... what I really like best is doing nothing.
>
> (Lehmann 1939: 37)

Miriam loves cooking and socialising, while Hilda prefers the social isolation which a life of study involves. To her aunt's dismay, Hilda prefers to teach herself German than concentrate on searching for a husband. Hilda's fascination with Jan turns into a melancholic love. The fact that he sees her as amusing, in her capacity as a 'terribly earnest English virgin', serves to build up her feelings of rejection and, ultimately, she commits suicide. Lehmann's juxtaposition of Miriam's so-called femininity with Hilda's supposed lack of traditionally feminine qualities is clearly used as a means of positioning Hilda in a world where she cannot find a satisfactory locus as an adult woman. The result is that Hilda is a single woman and an outsider, even among people who are themselves essentially outsiders.

In Susan Glaspell's *Bernice* – the original London production opened the season at the new Gate theatre in 1925 – the unmarried woman is again the outsider who, because of the close nature of her friendship with the deceased heroine, is able to make perceptive comments about the relationship between the deceased woman and her philandering husband. Glaspell uses Margaret to comment on the existence and nature of gender inequalities within marriage. Bernice's father calls for Margaret, who has some involvement with both unions and business, when Bernice dies in mysterious circumstances. Bernice's husband Craig, a writer who has spent much of his time away from the marital home, arrives only to be confronted by Margaret, who has always despised Craig for his adulterous and selfish behaviour toward her closest friend:

CRAIG: ... did you ever feel that you didn't really get *to* Bernice?
MARGARET: ... So far as I had power. She never held me back. Life broke through her – a life deeper than anything that could happen to her.
CRAIG: ... something you couldn't destroy. A life in her deeper than anything that could be done to her. That – makes a difference.... I never *had* Bernice.
MARGARET: ... Beneath what you 'had' was a life too full, too rich to be had? I should think that would flow over your life and give it beauty.
CRAIG: I suppose a man's feeling is different... he has to feel that he has the power to reshape.

(Glaspell 1924: 10)

Margaret discovers that Bernice committed suicide, and although at first she finds this 'unnatural' death hard to understand, she finally comes to appreciate that this was the only way her friend could find of avenging herself against her husband. To confront him with his behaviour would have been to 'give in' to his desire to 'possess' her. Here the author appears to be condoning the close nature of women's friendship as a means of survival in a world controlled by men; Bernice's final words were a call to her friend, for she whispered '...Margaret...' with her dying breath. The fact that Margaret is self-defined, active in her work and single is presented as positive in the context of this play.

In Lillian Hellman's *The Children's Hour* the friendship between two women services the realisation of both their ambitions to found and run their own school.[3] Martha Dobie and Karen Wright have invested their energy, time, financial security and emotions in the running of their small school. Martha's aunt, Lily Mortar, an out-of-work actress who has no income of her own, is employed as a teacher. When Martha discovers that her aunt has no real interest in or competence at her job, she decides to use the last of her savings to send the aunt on a trip around the world. Her gesture is met with anger and an argument ensues where the aunt accuses her of being ungrateful and casts aspersions about the 'unnatural' closeness of Martha's friendship with Karen. She accuses Martha of being jealous of Karen's relationship with her fiancé Joe:

> MRS MORTAR: I should have known by this time that the wise thing is to stay out of your way when he's in the house. . . . Every time that man comes into the house you have a fit . . . you're jealous . . . it's unnatural . . . you'd better get a beau of your own – a woman of your age . . .

(Hellman 1971: 17–18)

Mary, one of the schoolchildren, hears the argument and uses the information as ammunition in order to get out of being disciplined for her bad behaviour. Events then snowball, the effect of which is that parents withdraw their children from the school, the aunt disappears and Martha and Karen present a libel suit to clear their names of the accusation of illicit lesbianism and save the reputation of their school. Act Three shows the two women depressed and penniless after their libel suit has failed. When confronted, Joe tells Karen that their relationship can never be the same; he has never been comfortable about the close nature of her friendship with Martha. Thus the man who originally supported their work, and was proud of the way in which these two women had founded and run their school, withdraws his respect and falls in line with the 'outside' social puritanism which has brought their downfall. In the closing scenes of the play Martha commits suicide after having told Karen that she has felt 'more' for her than was perhaps 'acceptable' and Mary admits to her treacherous dishonesty.

Hellman has been criticised by recent feminists for the negative portrayal of lesbianism in *The Children's Hour*. However, this play is not simply a polemic for or against lesbianism. Hellman is dealing with false morality, using the framework of a friendship between two single women. Martha's state of spinsterhood works directly against her in a social structure that is determined to maintain fixed criteria for the way in which women should live their lives. With the exclusion of Karen, those females who succeed or at least survive by the dénouement are essentially passive, and use immoral behaviour as a way of promoting morality. As Mary Broe has pointed out:

> Just as meta-theatrics permits moral disguise...so too does it become a metaphor for other forms of playing in *The Children's Hour.* Even structurally the play proves deceptive...the truth-revealing scenes are interrupted so that the continuous action of dramatic unravelling and revelations are missing from the play. By such sleight of structure, Hellman shifts the focus from blackmail, extortion, and lesbianism (more dramatic subjects) to the quiet business of re-defining a moral capacity....Hellman suggests complex new moral possibilities for passivity by giving a dramatically central role to the indirect revelations of Lily Mortar. At the same time she mocks the theatrics of social passivity by linking it with moral disguise.

> (Broe 1981: 31)

Both Karen and Martha choose to be part of an institutionalised family, that is, the school, rather than be married. They prioritise career over family and marriage; Joe is, however, clear that Karen will spend less time and energy on the school once they are married. To some extent the issue of lesbianism is used as a device to indicate a social attitude to women who make the choice to remain independent. Banned in Britain a year before the banning of *The Children's Hour,* Aimée and Philip Stuart's *Love of Women* is a play with a similar theme.[4] In a number of the reviews the play was seen as dealing with an 'old conflict in a new play' (*Daily Telegraph,* 2 June 1935) – the 'old conflict' being between a single life and creativity or marriage and children.

In *Love of Women,* Vere and Brigit have fled the city and *men,* to write plays together. After five years of hard work in their Sussex cottage, they produce a hit which brings them into the public eye. The younger of the two, Brigit, becomes engaged to a young Harley Street doctor, and is criticised by Vere who thinks that her time would be spent more fruitfully in the writing of plays than producing a family with John. Their Sussex neighbours also begin to gossip about the nature of the relationship between Vere and Brigit because they are now in the public eye. Brigit's mother informs her that she can gain just as many 'important triumphs' on the amateur tennis court as she could otherwise in a career as a playwright. Vere and John have a vehement argument in the final act where he suggests that 'by cutting out sex Vere will render sterile not merely her life but that of her muse also' (ibid.). One critic saw the third act as centring on the 'case for marriage versus artistic celibacy' (*Observer,* 9

June 1935). The main debate is as much about spinsterhood and creativity as it is about the need to be celibate if one is a woman artist. For Vere, to write plays is to serve the nation artistically, whereas for those around her, to be a mother is the right way for a woman to serve her nation. The thematic focus of the play reflects the social reality of the way in which single women who chose not to get married, and therefore came under the category of spinster, were viewed. Clearly during the 1920s and 1930s spinsterhood was associated with sterility both sexually and creatively. (Note the way in which John connects the Muse with sexuality.)

Thus pre-First World War attitudes to spinsters had carried forward to the inter-war period. For many social theorists and sexologists during the inter-war period, the fact that a woman was intentionally single and desired economic and personal independence indicated that there was indeed something 'wrong' with her, that in fact she wasn't a 'natural' woman:

> I would even say that after twenty-five, the woman who has neither husband nor lover and is not un-vitalised and sexually deficient, is suffering mentally and bodily – often without knowing why she suffers: nervous, irritated, anaemic, always tired, or ruthlessly fussing over trifles: or else she has other consolations, which make her so-called chastity a pernicious sham.
>
> (Rowbotham 1977: 101)

THE GREAT BRITISH WIDOW: THE RHYTHM OF DOMESTIC LIFE

The locus for the vast majority of plays examined in this book is that of the domestic environment, where women are in control of the action and of the organisation and administration of life. In terms of plays by women the widow is a key character; during the 1920s and 1930s she was more likely to be a businesswoman, the honourable breadwinner in a family made fatherless by the war – being at the head of a fatherless family puts her into the position of having to be 'just like a man' and provide economic stability for the family. During the 1940s dramatised widows, and especially war widows, were more likely to be situated within the home, where their devotion to domestic life is a signifier of 'Britishness': they are presented as being anything but a burden to the nation and, at times, as the foundation upon which the nation is built. One of the main lines of argument in Naomi Mitchison's *The Home* (Mitchison 1934), a social tract comparing historical and modern perceptions of 'the home', is that in

Britain no other social institution had changed so speedily as the home during the early twentieth century. For her, the factors which made the English home 'secure' disappeared after the 1914–1918 war. Similarly, the two world wars were seen by the women playwrights in question to have caused irreversible change to women's position within the family and the home. The widowed female protagonists of the 1920s and 1930s administer and nurture the family from an economic stance. The widows in plays of the 1940s return to home management, but this is presented in terms of its value to the nation, rather than as a direct comment on their femininity. It is the widows in plays by women of the 1940s and 1950s who finance and manage the family home, and the style and rhythm of their systems of management are often at the core of the text.

In Enid Bagnold's *Lottie Dundass,* for example, Mrs Dundass is a 'square, middle-aged calm woman' who, having mothered seven children, is effectively widowed as her husband is serving a life sentence in Broadmoor asylum.[5] She tells her daughter, who wants to have a career in theatre but can't because of her unstable medical condition, that she must be brave:

> Where's your courage? *I've* had courage, I've *got* it, where's yours? How'd you think I've brought you all up after what happened to me?
>
> (Bagnold 1944: 17)

It is not being a widow which bothers Mrs Dundass, but rather the fact that her daughter is idle and day-dreams, something which she cannot afford to do. Lottie, Mrs Dundass tells us, wears her out with her idleness. It is the mother who continually balances child care with taking on extra work to make the housekeeping last the week and patiently looks after Lottie, when she has her 'attacks'. The whole play moves to the rhythm of domestic life with short moments of calm punctuating the constant doing of domestic duties.

Similarly in McCracken's *No Medals,* the energy of domestic life is what sets the pace of the play. There are constant references to domestic activity; the play opens with one of the younger daughters re-laying the fire while her sister brings in the dinner-wagon full of cutlery and dishes and lays the table for the many characters who are living in Martha Dacre's home. At one point, one of the lodgers is vacuuming with a loaf of bread under his arm and continues to chat with the potential home help, Mrs Gaye, with the vacuum cleaner still running. This is a home run by a widow during wartime where mealtimes are staggered to deal with the different working hours of those who form Martha's household.

Virtually each time that Martha is in conversation with other characters, she is simultaneously carrying out some household duty. Every few sentences are accompanied by domestic actions:

> (*She starts clearing the large plates, knives, etc. from the table to the trolley*)
> (. . . *Putting all the serviettes to the end of the table*) (. . . *clearing the small plates and pieces of toast*) (. . . *she puts the cups on the bottom end of the trolley*)
> (. . . *packs the milk jug, basin, hot water jug and bread knife on the top end of the trolley*) (. . . *Martha has now put the butter and marmalade dishes on the sideboard, and now takes the teapot below the table to the end of the trolley*)
> (. . . *picking up a plate from the table and holding it as she talks*) (. . . *During the above line Martha takes the sauce bottle to the sideboard . . .*)
>
> (McCracken 1947: 25–26)

As soon as Martha has finished making sandwiches, sewing, preserving plums or tomatoes, she switches on the iron, still in conversation, usually with someone who wants her to do them a favour of some sort. When Harriet suggests that she take a rest, Martha points out that running the home is a twenty-four hour job; with little if any help, her domestic lifestyle does not allow for breaks.

> HARRIET: You're letting things get on top of you. What are you doing today?
>
> MARTHA: I'm going to make marmalade – when I've finished these and washed up – out of two orange skins, some lemon essence, some damp sugar that's gone into a hard lump, and a great deal of faith. . . . After that I'm going to queue up hopefully for plums. And when I come back I'm doing my Penny-a-Week Red Cross Fund, and in between times preparing an evening meal of two sorts – for my family of five, not to mention lunch for myself and Paul – besides dusting and sweeping and making all the male beds, booking your hair appointment and collecting Monica's chop from the butcher's.
>
> (ibid.: 36)

The pace of domestic life is the foundation rhythm of the play, and the only thing which alters the pace for Martha is news about the family's safety or the possibility of change promised by the offer of marriage made by Geoffrey – one of her billeted civilians. Equally, the action of domestic life is centre stage and accompanies most of the unravelling of the plot and the action of the play. The heroine is effectively a champion of housework and the running of the home. Whether or not the play provides a positive portrayal of women's lives, the author's attempt to validate domestic action is clear. Thus single or widowed women have the same domestic responsibilities as women supported by men during wartime.

Making public, via theatricalisation, the machinations of domestic life was not new to the London stage by the 1940s, and it would appear that it had come to be expected of plays written by women. The centring of action around domestic action and domestic life appears to have been very specific to the early 1940s. *No Medals* clearly appealed to audiences because of its direct connection with women's experience of home life during wartime, and for the fact that the narrative provides a proposition that somehow war can be 'romantic' or at least romance can be found during times of war. Aimée Stuart's *Jeannie*, which, as with her later plays, was written without her husband, opens in a spotless but small kitchen-cum-living room, scullery and wash-house in a grey village in Scotland.[6] Romance and domesticity are brought together during the final scenes where Jeannie is offered relief from drudgery by the introduction of domestic appliances into her life.

WIDOWS AND WOMEN WITHOUT HUSBANDS: ECONOMIC CHOICES

Jeannie's life is one of extreme hardship and poverty, her list of domestic duties for an old father who refuses to allow her to go out to the cinema and is too mean to let her take their dirty linen to the laundry, seems inexhaustible. One of Jeannie's friends calls her father a 'mean old skunk', and tells her that she is treated as little more than a servant:

JEANNIE: (*shocked*) A servant, me?

MRS WHITELAW: It's what you are now. Only you don't get paid for it. You could get a pound a week and an evening off and every second Sunday and a whole day a month. *And* you could refuse the sheets.

JEANNIE: It sounds like Paradise.

MRS WHITELAW: I don't know about Paradise. But it'd be a darn sight better than this.

(Stuart 1940: 18)

When her father dies, after some deliberation Jeannie decides to go on holiday with the two hundred pounds he has left her. En route to Vienna she meets Stanley, a widowed father of two sons, who is on his way to the Vienna exhibitions with his new domestic appliance inventions. They spend a little time together and he tells her where he is staying in Vienna, in case she should need assistance. Later they meet in the hotel and she tells him a little of her history:

> JEANNIE: I never got going out and about. First I was my mother's companion. I liked that fine. While she was alive I never needed anyone else. She needed me, too. She'd a thin time with Father. When I think of him having all that money put by and her having to scrape and save! She never had anything. He never even gave her a civil word.
>
> (Stuart 1940: 71)

Jeannie and Stanley part company and she then meets the Count, on whom she lavishes money when he takes her out for the evening. They then become engaged! By the end of Act Two, he tells her that they must live on her fortune until his 'rents come through'. When she tells him that her 'fortunes' total two hundred pounds, which has now been spent, he slinks off and in Act Three we find her housekeeping in a private flat in Glasgow. There is nothing here which resembles 'Paradise'; her wages amount to ten shillings a week and her employer has no intention of wasting money by sending laundry 'out'. Miraculously, Stanley comes to visit her and although he feels that being a servant is a 'more natural job for a girl than a shop or an office', they chat for a while and he eventually persuades her to marry him, promising her that he will 'throw in a washing machine and... a fool-proof oven as well' (Stuart 1940: 156–157).

Seen by a number of critics as 'a Cinderella play' *Jeannie* is pure domestic comedy (*Sunday Times*, 6 February 1940 and *Daily Telegraph*, 4 April 1940). Stuart does, however, appear to stress the limitations of Jeannie's choices as a single woman, with no family money and little education. The romance of spending an evening with a Viennese Count who then proposes is, of course, depleted by the fact that he has no money and cannot promise her a better life than she already has. Her fantasy of being a paid housekeeper is destroyed when in practice she realises that her employer, a lower-middle-class woman with delusions of grandeur, is as much of a spendthrift as her father was. Stanley, although kind and well meaning, offers her a continuation of domestic life. He is not as romantic a proposition as the Count may have been, but at least he can provide for her, he is not 'after her money' and offers her the bonus of domestic appliances which will make her domestic married life less treacherous.

In Dane's *Cousin Muriel*, the economic choices for Muriel Meilhac are limited once her husband has died. Played to great acclaim by Edith Evans, Muriel is housekeeper for her relative, a distinguished surgeon, Sir Hubert Sylvester. She has organised his household and brought up his daughter Dinah, who has fallen in love with her son Richard. When Richard comes home from America to join up for the impending war, he and Dinah decide to get married. Sylvester will not allow the liaison because he is certain that Richard has been borrowing money via loans which Sylvester has made to Muriel. We then discover that Muriel has been forging Sylvester's cheques at the bank so, for example, each time he writes a housekeeping cheque for eight pounds, she cashes a cheque for eighty.

Muriel's husband was fond of spending money and her own need for spending contributed to his final downfall. She is from a well-to-do background, and although widowhood left her with few economic choices, she house-kept for various rich families in order to keep herself and her son financially secure over the years. Muriel had always felt that, for the quality of work she produced for Sylvester, she ought to have been paid more, and she used the housekeeping money to buy herself the clothing which she considered suitable for a woman of her class. When eventually confronted by Sylvester she tells him everything but without any sense of remorse or feeling that she would do things differently given another chance.

Muriel rises, shuts the piano, takes up the bag, puts the money into it, shakes herself together like a bird preening, and comes across to the centre of the room, takes a cigarette and silently asks him for a light . . . she lights her own cigarette, then settles herself in the easy chair.

MURIEL: So you've found me out at last! I used to wish some-
    times that you'd be more suspicious. But that was after I fell out
    of love with you . . . all this. . . . You've a lovely home – as Alice
    would say. Dinah's my doing, too. She was impossible when I
    came. I've done a lot for you. . . . (*furiously*) You're a baby, Hubert!
    You and your knighthood – when you just gathered up the house
    and everything in it and dumped it on my lap – well, I was
    touched. Any woman would be. . . . A shabby run to seed
    establishment, with your servants ruling the roost and your
    patients dropping off – that was in 1933. And by 1937 – the
    honours list. . . . Well, then I began to look round, and I saw that
    I'd wasted a lot of time. . . . I suddenly discovered that I enjoyed
    spending money on myself . . . money is the only thing that never
    lets you down. I began to think about my old age. . . . I wanted to
    save and I wanted to spend. . . . It was exhausting, this ever
    present need for money, this ever present need to spend it. So I
    did all sorts of things . . . I used to take a premium when I got a

girl a good position . . . I bought my first shares for a rise . . . anyway, if you take off what you ought to have paid me in salary,
you're only down about five hundred. . . . I get so bored. At least
the war will give me something better to do than waste my good
brains on the lot of you. . . . I'm quick, and clever, and strong. So
why shouldn't I take what I want? You can do it if you're a
millionaire: you can do it if you're a nation; then why shouldn't I
do it? . . . I'm *too* sane . . . completely logical.

(Dane 1940: 99–101)

The ending of the original production was changed so that Muriel's recent
thieving episode from a London department store is squared with the
management, at which point Sylvester gives her fifty pounds and packs
her off to America. Audiences were, it would seem, unhappy with an
ending which left the narrative 'hanging in the air', in a play which is full of
radio interjections which give constant narrative references to the
impending war.

Muriel makes choices within a limited range of options, and her calm
rationale for her behaviour does not invite negative judgement of those
choices. As one critic pointed out, the frequent radio announcement of
progress in the path toward war make her actions seem harmless
(*Manchester Guardian*, 9 March 1940). As a widow, Muriel justifies her
dishonesty by pointing out that she can only maintain the standard of
living to which she had become accustomed within marriage, through
dishonest behaviour outside marriage.

Muriel develops a sense of survival and behaves accordingly. The
single-minded precision of her survival technique has resonance with the
behaviour of other single and widowed women in plays by women of the
era. Often these stage characters are written in the context of the domestic
comedy, but this should not automatically detract from the serious nature
of the narrative subtext. This is not to say that the women playwrights
were necessarily consciously attempting to reflect the economic and social
problems which faced single and widowed women. Spinsters, for example, were almost always represented as adjuncts to other more 'marriage-
able' women. It is possible, however, to argue that the frequency with
which these women arise as characters in the drama is a reflection of the
fact that they had become a problematised social phenomenon. The
women playwrights in question rarely turned this social phenomenon into
the issue at the root of their drama. They were not, it would seem,
concerned with arguing for an improvement in the spinster's social and
economic situation. Rather, they tended to capitalise upon spinster and

widow figures, in full knowledge that they held interest for contemporary theatre audiences and so made appealing theatrical material. Unlike mothers, working women and historical figures, the spinster in particular was rarely taken on board as a character who might throw general light on the female condition of the time. The women playwrights appeared to see her as interesting but marginal, and this ideological position is reflected in the way in which she is treated within the drama.

8

POSTSCRIPT

During the 1950s there were a number of plays where the lives of single working-class women and mothers were foregrounded. These were, however, few and far between. The West End was still largely occupied by plays which were dominated by the concerns of the middle and ruling classes. Shelagh Delaney was one of the few playwrights who brought the experiences of a new generation and a new class to the stage. In *A Taste of Honey* Helen's life as a single mother, living by the rules of survival, is echoed in the events which affect her daughter Jo. By the end of the play Jo is pregnant by a coloured naval rating and has befriended a gay man, with whom she has developed a platonic and nurturing relationship. Even though Delaney expresses very clearly the fact that the generations to which Helen and Jo belong are very different, she is clear that, as single women, their lives are susceptible to the same social judgement and economic constraints. The ideal family unit, so promoted by the middle classes, is for Delaney an imagined ideal which bears little relation to the lived experience of working-class women who have no financially secure family unit from which to operate. In *A Taste of Honey* 'family' denotes a fragmented and ever-changing series of relationships between people who are not necessarily related by blood. Gone are the matriarchal figures, ever supportive and altruistic; gone are the easy solutions to financial or emotional problems which held together the middle-class family, especially in plays written by women during the inter-war years. For Delaney, the working-class family, and especially working-class women, live in an entirely different world, with different emotional bonds and laws of survival.

In *The Lion in Love* (Delaney 1977) Kit is an alcoholic mother still living with Frank, her husband who has had numerous affairs with other women. Kit has no emotional support from her husband, nor does she have any illusions about her role as mother:

KIT: Is it worth it, I often wonder. You suffer bringing kids into the
world, you wear yourself out keeping one end full and the other
end dry, and as soon as they're able they're off and away. Out of
sight, out of mind.

(Delaney 1961: 19)

Kit stays with her husband for lack of inspiration or means to leave him.
As a result of this, and of the insistent poverty which Frank's vocation as a
street-corner salesman maintains, Kit spends her life on an angry pathway from one drink to the next. Nell is a prostitute who continues to 'work'
for Kit's son Andy. Andy promises Nell that one day he will be able to stop
being her pimp when he gets a few good gigs for his stage act, in which she
will partner him. By the end of the play, Nell has discovered that Andy is
not the showbiz star she imagined him to be. She stops speaking to him,
but the implication is that she will continue to work as his prostitute, as
Andy's grandfather points out to him:

JESSE: She'll start talking soon enough.... Some women will
have any sort of man rather than no man at all.

(ibid.: 101)

Nora has been having a long-standing affair with Frank. She has a little
money of her own and offers to help him leave Kit; her plan is that they
will buy a small business in the country. But Frank can't make a decision,
and when he does he hasn't the courage to follow it through. Again, there
is no implication that Nora will not go on waiting for him. Kit's daughter
Peg asks her mother what she would say if Peg told her that she was going
to follow her boyfriend to London.

PEG: What would you say if I went with him?
KIT: It's your life. You ruin it your own way.
PEG: All right. Ta'ra.

(ibid.: 97)

Here, the maternal concern so dominant in other plays examined has
no place. Peg's decision is not based on any real process of consideration, either by herself or by her family: as far as they are concerned,
she can do what she likes. There appears to be an acceptance of the
inconsistency of aspirations and lived experience. The rules of family
life are not set in this world – each person lives according to their own
needs and the family is not a closed unit: Nora is as much a part of the
family as is Kit; Banner emigrates to Australia in hope of finding a new
and better life; Peg leaves home with a man she hardly knows; and Kit

195

ends the play with the line, 'Ah!... it's a bugger of a life, by Jesus' (ibid.: 104).

The Lion in Love, less liked by critics than *A Taste of Honey*, heralds a new class of woman playwright who shows a stronger desire to experiment with form as well as content. Delaney combines a 'modified realism' with traceable elements of the domestic comedy exploited by the women playwrights who preceded her.

> Miss Delaney has a wonderful ear and she can really create out of cliché and the small coin of kitchen comedy and Northern Music Hall exchanges, a pathos of bathos which it is not absurd to call Chekhovian, because to a Russian audience much of the charm of Chekhov consists exactly in the overtones given to strings of banalities of the order of 'It never rains but it pours'.
>
> (*Guardian*, 30 December 1960)

The Lion in Love is as much a play about the human condition as it is about the female condition, although interestingly it is the women, in the main, who take action in order to fulfil their desire for a 'different' kind of life to the one which is on offer. Along with Jellicoe, Delaney was one of the few women playwrights of the period in question to experiment with form. Although a number of critics saw the play as 'reproducing the naturalism of everyday life', the style, form and content have very little in common with the three-act well-made play much used by the earlier women playwrights of the period (Hall 1981: 214).

In some ways Delaney opened out the field for women playwrights, and certainly her work has more in common with women playwrights of the 1970s and 1980s than it does with playwrights like Clemence Dane or Esther McCracken. However, there are narrative threads in her work which relate to the work of earlier women playwrights, if only by the fact that she subverts them. Certainly, in *A Taste of Honey*, the social and economic conditions under which women make choices about their lives are foregrounded. Like many of the other women playwrights whose work has been examined in this book, Delaney focuses on the way in which women create a means of survival in a culture which does not provide for those women who fall outside a definition of the 'ideal' feminine woman. Similarly, women playwrights often became household names during the years which span from the end of the First World War into the early 1960s – even though living so much in the public eye as a writer of hit commercial plays or even as a journalist or social commentator, as many of the women playwrights were, would not have been considered as 'ideal feminine' behaviour.

This book has been an attempt to explore some of the issues around a small proportion of these playwrights' work. Even though they were a force to be reckoned with, many were not treated seriously as writers by the critics of their day, nor has their work thus far been integrated into a history of twentieth-century British theatre. When critics and journalists interviewed women playwrights, comments on how these women wrote while stirring porridge and feeding their babies dominated the pages of the popular press more than genuine appraisals of these women's worth as as artists. The playwrights were rarely treated as skilled craftswomen, in tune with the theatre, society and women's lives. Yet it is exactly these sensibilities which these women must have possessed in order to create such successful plays. By taking away the imposition of a closed feminist framework of analysis and contextualising the work of these West End women in terms of theatre and history, this book has, I hope, gone some way towards a re-evaluation of what has until recently been an invisible but highly significant contribution made by women, to both the history of plays on the London stage and a continuum of women writing for the theatre.

APPENDIX

Table of plays by women on the London stage 1917–1959

Play	Author	Theatre	Dates	No. of perfs
1917–1919				
Sheila	G. Sowerby	St. James'	7.6.17/ 28.6.17	19
Their Mothers	Evelyn Glover	Globe	26.6.17	1
Billeted	F.Tennyson-Jesse and H.M. Harwood	Royalty	21.8.17/ 23.3.18	240
Wild Heather	Dorothy Brandon	Strand	25.10.17/ 5.1.18	79
Yvette's Dilemma	Juliette Mylo	Court	7.2.18	1
Pauv'Yvette	Juliette Mylo	Court	7.2.18	1
Paulina	Marion McCarthy	Court	7.2.18	1
Signs of the Times	Mrs D.F.C. Harding	Court	7.2.18	1
Rosmary	Elsie Fogerty	Court	11.3.18/ 14.3.18	4 mat.
Mrs Riggles Makes a Match	Elsie Fogerty	Court	15.3.18	1 mat.
Betty at Bay	Jessie Porter	Strand	9.4.18/ 18.5.18	53
The Last Match	Georgina Hamilton	Wyndham's	2.4.18	1
Dawkins	Mrs Greenaway	Shaftesbury	19.4.18	1 mat.
Princess Suri Sama	Erica Beale	Shaftesbury	19.4.18	1 mat.
Lot 79	Rida J. Young	Queen's	20.4.18/ 4.5.18	17
Soldier Boy	Rida J. Young and Edgar Wallace	Apollo	26.6.18/ 22.3.19	374
The Chinese Puzzle	Marian Bower	New	11.7.18/ 11.7.19	415
The Great Moment	Gwen Lally	St James'	3.12.18	1
Time to Wake Up	Evelyn Glover	New	11.4.19	2
The Honourable Gertrude	'Henry Seton' Vera Beringer	Court	13.5.19	1

198

APPENDIX

Play	Author	Theatre	Dates	No. of perfs
1919–1920				
The Altar of Liberty	Marion Bower and Leon M. Lion	New	13.5.19	1
The Storm	Odette Tcherning	Ambassadors	5.6.19/ 12.6.19	2 mat.
His Little Widows	Rida J. Young	Wyndham's	16.6.19/ 21.8.19	172
		Garrick	4.8.19/ 1.11.19	
Riding for a Fall	Mrs Hardy	Court	14.7.19	1 mat.
Dr James Barry	Oldga Racster and Jessica Grove	St James'	22.7.19	1 mat.
Little Women (adpt.)	Marion de Forest	New	10.11.19/ 13.12.19	35
The Young Person in Pink	Gertrude Jennings	Prince of Wales'	10.2.20	1 mat.
		Haymarket	29.3.20/ 17.4.20	208
The Young Visitors (adpt. from Daisy Ashford 1919)	Mrs George Norman and Margaret MacKenzie	Court	24.2.20/ 24.5.20	104
The Magnet	'Gaston Gervex' (Mrs Montague Fowler)	Ambassadors	20.2.20	1 mat.
According to the Evidence	Mrs D. F. C. Harding and Bibsie Leveux	Ambassadors	26.3.20	1 mat.
The Polar Post	Hon. Mary Augusta Pakington	Ambassadors	24.2.20	1 mat.
The Higher Court	Margaret M. Young	Strand	11.4.20	1
Husbands for All	Gertrude Jennings	Little	6.5.20/ 22.5.20	18
Why Marry?	Jesse Lynch Williams	Comedy	12.5.20/ 5.6.20	29
For Husbands Only	G.B. Stern and Mrs D.F.C. Harding	Ambassadors	4.6.20	1 mat.
The Moon Went Behind a Cloud	Ursula Keene	Ambassadors	4.6.20	1 mat.
The Advocate	Beatrice Heron-Maxwell	Criterion	7.6.20	1 mat.
The Lonely Wife	Nita Faydon	Comedy	5.7.20	1 mat.
The Lonely Lady	Nita Faydon	Duke of York's	24.1.21/ 5.2.21	16
Brown Sugar	Lady Arthur Lever	Duke of York's/ Garrick	7.7.20/ 9.2.21	265
Daughters of Eve	'Rita' (Mrs D. Humphreys)	St James'	13.7.20	1 mat.

Play	Author	Theatre	Dates	No. of perfs
1920–1921				
Precilla and the Profligate	Laura Wildig	Duke of York's	13.10.20/ 14.12.20	64
The Fair and the Brave	Cicely Hamilton	Kingsway	29.10.20	1 mat.
Love Tokens	May Aldington	Queen's	29.10.20	1 mat.
Adoption	Xenia Lowinsky	Ambassadors	16.12.20	1 mat.
For Her Sake	Marion Crofton	Ambassadors	16.12.20	1 mat.
Where the Rainbow Ends	Mrs Clifford Mills	Apollo	23.12.20/ 22.1.21	26 mat.
		Apollo	22.12.21/ 28.1.22	36
Daniel	Sybil Harris	St James'	15.1.21/ 26.2.21	45
The Five Wishes	Laura Leycester	Ambassadors	27.1.21	1 mat.
No Winkles	Olive Greenaway	Savoy	11.2.21	1 mat.
Kynaston's Wife	Winifred Dolan	Shaftesbury	28.2.21	1 mat.
Bill of Divorcement	Clemence Dane	St Martin's	14.3.21/ 4.3.22	402
Nightie Night	Martha Stanley and Adelaide Mathews	Queen's	22.3.21/ 23.4.21	73
The Chemist	Blanche Weiner	Little	20.3.21/ 25.6.21	104
Love Among the Paintpots	Gertrude Jennings	Aldwych	30.4.21/ 2.7.21	73
Reggie Reforms	Irene Bubna and Edgar Camille	Everyman	2.5.21/ 7.5.21	7
The Blast	Irene Bubna and Edgar Camille	Everyman	2.5.21/ 7.5.21	7
The Goat	Dorothy Massingham	Kingsway	27.5.21	1 mat.
Tipperary	Honor M. Pulley	Kingsway	27.5.21	1 mat.
Mother of Pearl	Gertrude Jennings	Winter Garden	30.5.21	1 mat.
Rising of the Moon	Lady Gregory	Court	10.6.21	1 mat.
The Cinema Lady	Nancy and Jean Rioux	Royalty	14.6.21/ 16.6.21	4
The Toast	Irene Bubna and Edgar Camille	Everyman	2.5.21/ 7.5.21	7
Who Pays	Margaret Pedler	Comedy	26.6.21	1
The Doctor of Dreams (Freudian c 3a)	'Michael Orme' (Alix Augusta Grein)	Prince of Wales'	13.7.21	1 mat.
The Legion of Honour	Baroness Emmusea Orczy	Aldwych	24.8.21/ 10.9.21	21
The Hotel Mouse	Fryn Tennyson-Jesse and Harold Harwood	Queen's	6.10.21/ 5.11.21	36

Play	Author	Theatre	Dates	No. of perfs
1921–1922				
The Child in Flanders	Cicely Hamilton	Lyric	7.11.21	1 mat.
Wolf! Wolf!	Mrs Leo Myers	Palace	15.11.21	1
Virginia	Mrs Clifford Mills	Palace	15.11.21	1
Pierrot's Wellcome	Constance Smedley (Mrs Armfield)	Palace	15.11.21	1
Will Shakespeare	Clemence Dane	St Martin's	17.11.21/ 7.1.22	62
Clothes and the Woman	'George Pabton' (Emily Morse Symonds)	Ambassadors	7.12.21/ 28.1.22	66
Me and My Diary	Gertrude Jennings	Strand	19.1.22/ 18.2.22	37
Money Doesn't Matter	'George Pabton' (Emily Morse Symonds)	Aldwych	21.1.22/ 11.3.22	46
Lady Larcombe's Lapse	Mrs Jessie Porter	Kingsway	15.2.22	1
Some Detective	Harvey J. Higgins and Harriet Ford	Empire	16.7.21/ 6.8.21	25
The Cone of Beyond	Kay Horniman and Ruby Miller	Garrick	9.8.21/ 14.1.22	192
Araminta Arrives	K. Smith and Dorothy Brandon	Comedy	11.10.21/ 12.11.21	39
Enter Madam	Gilda Varesi and Dolly Bynre	Royalty	15.2.22/ 1.4.22	53
The Rise of Silas Lapham	Lillian Keal Sabine	Lyric	20.2.22/ 24.2.22	2
Me and My Diary	Gertrude Jennings	Aldwych	22.2.22/ 11.3.22	22
In Nelson's Days	Mrs Clifford Mills	Shaftesbury	11.3.22/ 14.3.22	3
Elegant Edward	Gertrude Jennings and C. Boulton	Palace	17.3.22	1 mat.
Hyacinth Halvey	Lady Augusta Gregory	Ambassadors Aldwych	18.3.22 7.4.22	24
Nightie Night	M. M. Stanley and Adelaide Matthews	Shaftesbury	18.3.22/ 1.4.22	17
When Eyes Are Opened	Mrs St. Clair Stobart	Kingsway	24.3.22	1 mat.
Slings and Arrows	Betty Bower	Kingsway	24.3.22	1 mat.
Pride and Prejudice	Eileen H. A. Squire and J. C. Squire	Palace	24.3.22	1 mat.
Washed Ashore	Dorothy Massingham	Kingsway	2.4.22	1 mat.
The Girl and the City	Beatrice Mayor	Kingsway	2.4.22	1 mat.

Play	Author	Theatre	Dates	No. of perfs
1922–1923				
Thirty Minutes in a Street	Beatrice Mayor	Kingsway	2.4.22	1 mat.
The Bat	Mary Roberts Rinehart and Avery Hopwood	St James'	21.1.22/ 4.11.22	327
Lass O'Laughter	Edith Carter and Nan Marriott-Watson	Queen's	29.4.22/ 12.8.22	121
Life's A Game	'Michael Orme'	Kingsway	18.5.22/ 26.5.22	6 mat.
The Green Cord	Marion Bower and A. L. Ellis	Royalty	2.6.22/ 16.9.22	122
Quarantine	F. Tennyson-Jesse	Comedy	6.6.22/ 2.9.22	102
The Stop-Gap	Florence N. M. Atack	Aldwych	7.6.22	1
Elegant Edward	Gertrude Jennings and C. Boulton	Daly's	9.6.22	1 mat.
The Way of an Eagle	Ethel M. Dell	Adelphi	20.6.22/ 30.9.22	150
Concerning Mary Dewhirst	Florence Marriot-Watson and Grace Edwin	Savoy	28.6.22	1 mat.
Suppressed Desires	George Cram Cook and Susan Glaspell	Everyman	17.7.22/ 22.2.22	7
Secrets	May Edgington and Rudolf Besier	Comedy	7.9.22/ 28.7.23	373
The Scandal (adpt. of M. Bataille, 'Le Scandale' 1909)	Lady Bell (Mrs Hugh Bell)	New	19.9.22 25.11.27	77
Little Lovers	Esme Wynne-Tyson	Aldwych	22.10.22	1
Biffy	Vera Beringer ('Henry Seton') and William Ray	Garrick	28.11.22/ 3.2.23	91
When Knights Were Bold	Harriet Jay ('Charles Marlow')	Court	26.12.22/ 27.1.23	31
Via Crucis (adpt. Hugo V. Hofmannstal, 'Jedermann' 1911)	Hon Sybil Amherst and Dr C. E. Wheeler	Garrick	5.2.23/ 22.2.23	21
Good Gracious! Annabelle	Claire Beecher Kummer	Duke of York's	14.2.23/ 27.2.23	15
Lavender Ladies	Daisy Fisher	Strand	25.2.23	1
The Alternative	Lucy Wilson and Adrian Alington	Everyman	12.3.23/ 24.3.23	14
The Inevitable	Isabel Jay	St James'	21.3.23/ 16.6.23	101

Play	Author	Theatre	Dates	No. of perfs
1923–1924				
Beltane Night	Vera Beringer 'Henry Seton'	Aldwych	23.3.23	1
Isabel, Edward and Anne	Gertrude Jennings	Haymarket	31.3.23/ 16.6.23	101
The First Stile	Elsie Hayes	Kingsway	24.4.23	1
The Voice Outside	Gertrude Jennings	Globe	28.4.23/ 16.6.23	58
South Wind	Isabel C. Tippett and N. Douglas	Kingsway	29.4.23/ 30.4.23	2
The Outsider	Dorothy Brandon	St James	31.5.23/ 1.9.23	107
The Proof	Phyllis Birkett	Vaudeville	21.5.23	1 mat.
Come Through a Cranford Door	Irene Ross and Frank Lind	New	10.7.23	1 mat.
The Young Person in Pink	Gertrude Jennings	Adelphi	13.7.23/ 25.8.23	98
Tancred (from Disraeli's novel of 1847)	Edith Millbank	Kingsway	16.7.23/ 28.7.23	14
Trust Emily	May Edington	Criterion	10.10.23/ 27.10.23	21
Fledglings	Marguerite Rea	St Martin's	1.11.23/ 14.11.23	6 mat.
Our Ostriches	Dr Marie Stopes	Court	14.11.23/ 2.2.24	91
The Morals of Vanda	Hazel May Marshall	Everyman	29.11.23/ 15.12.23	18
The Rising Generation	Wyn Weaver and Laura Leycester	Shaftesbury	3.12.23/ 5.4.24	235
When Knights were Bold	Harriet Jay ('Charles Marlow')	Criterion	17.12.23/ 16.2.24	105
The Painted Lady	Vera Beringer	Everyman	12.1.24/ 19.1.24	8
Outcasts	May Creagh-Henry	Strand	13.1.24	1 mat.
The Stepmother	Githa Sowerby	New	13.1.24	1
The Immortal Hour	Fiona Macleod and Rutland Broughton	Regent	28.1.24/ 17.5.24	127
The Way Things Happen	Clemence Dane	Ambassadors	2.2.24/ 29.3.27	65
Not In Our Stars (adpt. M. Maurice's Nov. 1923)	Dorothy Massingham	Wyndham's	4.2.24/ 5.4.24	72
The Fairy Tale	May Edgington	Apollo	6.2.24/ 1.3.24	28

Play	Author	Theatre	Dates	No. of perfs
1924–1925				
Monsieur Beaucaire	Booth Tarkington and Mrs E. G. Sutherland	Strand	23.2.24/ 22.3.24	101
		Prince of Wales	24.3.24/ 17.5.24	
Her Market Price	Frances Nordstrom	Lyceum	17.4.24/ 24.5.24	51
By Chance	Lady Violet Greville	Daly's	5.5.24	1 mat.
Before Sunset	Nan Marriott-Watson	Aldwych	20.5.24	1 mat.
Two Women and a Telephone	Rica Bromley-Taylor	Aldwych	25.5.24	1
Wife to a Famous Man (adpt. G. M. Sierra's 'La Muier Del Herde')	Mr and Mrs H. Granville-Barker	Aldwych	25.5.24	1
In The Next Room	Eleanor Robson and Harriet Ford	St Martin's	6.6.24/ 29.11.24	202
The Rat: The Story of an Apache	('David L'Estrange') Constance Collier and Ivor Novello	Prince of Wales'	9.6.24/ 13.9.24	282
Punchinello	Laura Wildig	Court	22.6.24	1
Tiger Cats	Mrs J. T. Grein ('Michael Orme')	Savoy	26.6.24/ 17.7.24	7 mat.
The Pleasure Garden	Beatrice Mayor	Regent	29.6.24/ 30.6.24	2 mat.
Waiting for the Bus	Gertrude Jennings	St Martin's	10.7.24	1 mat.
A Surplus Man	Sylvia Earl	Court	21.7.24	1 mat.
Tiger Cats	Mrs J.T. Grein	Garrick	11.8.24/ 13.9.24	116
The Claimant	Mrs M. F. Watts	Queen's	11.9.24/ 18.10.24	44
It Happened in Ardoran	Ann Stephenson and A. MacBeth	Court	19.10.24	1
The Pelican	F. Tennyson-Jesse and H. Harwood	Ambassadors	20.10.24/ 7.3.25	243
Bartons Folly	Gladys Parrish	Court	14.12.24	1
When Knights Were Bold	Harriet Jay ('C. Marlow')	Fortune	15.12.24/ 31.1.25	79
Just Married	Adelaide Matthews and Anne Nichols	Comedy/ Queen's	15.12.24 19.12.25	423
Pollyanna (adpt. Eleanor Porter's nov. 1913)	Catherine Chisholm Cushing	St James'	18.12.24/ 3.1.25	24
The Outsider	Dorothy Brandon	Regent	22.12.24/ 24.1.25	7

Play	Author	Theatre	Dates	No. of perfs
1925				
The Fairway (adpt. of Jacques Deva's 'Une Fiable Femme')	Noel Scott and Auriol Lee	New	4.1.25	1
The Fairway	Auriol Lee	New	4.1.25	1
Meddlers	Agnes Platt and Norman Pugh	St James'	6.1.25/ 10.1.25	6
Camilla States Her Case	Mrs R. Golding Bright ('George Egerton')	Globe	7.1.25/ 14.2.25	45
Me and My Diary	Gertrude Jennings	Garrick	12.1.25/ 17.1.25	45
Cats Claws	Gertrude Jennings	New	20.1.25	1 mat.
It Happened in Ardoran	Ann Stephenson and A. Macbeth	Everyman	24.12.25/ 7.3.25	13
Anyhouse	F. Tennyson-Jesse	Ambassadors	12.3.25/ 28.3.25	20
Persevering Pat	Lynne Doyle	Little	13.3.25/ 4.4.25	27
The Painted Swan	Elizabeth Bibesco	Everyman	16.3.25/ 4.4.25	21
The Verge	Susan Glaspell	Regent	29.3.25/ 7.4.25	3
The Sign in the Sun	Vere Sullivan	Regent	3.5.25	1
Sun-Up	Lula Vollmer	Vaudeville	4.5.25/ 22.8.25	233
		Lyric	24.8.25/ 21.11.25	
The Swallow	Viola Tree	Everyman	6.5.25/ 9.5.25	5
Educating a Husband	Edith Carter	Regent	11.5.25/ 16.5.25	8
Five Birds in a Cage	Gertrude Jennings	Haymarket	21.5.25/ 6.6.25	21
Nerves	Ann Stephenson	Court	15.6.25	1 mat.
Dear Ann	Elizabeth Fagan	Aldwych	23.6.25	1 mat.
Lavender Ladies	Daisy Fisher	Comedy	29.7.25/ 21.11.25	156
The Man From Hong-Kong	Mrs Clifford Mills	Queen's	3.6.25/ 22.8.25	24
Fires Divine	Rosaline Rossomer	Scala	15.9.25/ 3.10.25	7
The Moon and Sixpence (from Maugham's novel, 1919)	Edith Ellis	New	24.8.25 28.11.25	75

Play	Author	Theatre	Dates	No. of perfs
1925–1926				
That Which Counts	'Shirland Quin' (Enid Gest)	Duke of York's	4.10.25	1
The Rising of the Moon	Lady Augusta Gregory	Royalty	17.10.25/ 17.11.25	26
The Old Adam	Cicely Hamilton	Kingsway	17.11.25/ 16.1.26	67
Gloriana	Gwen John	Little	8.12.25/ 23.12.25	19
The Godless	Karen Bramson	Wyndham's	15.12.25/ 17.12.25	2 mat.
The Child in Flanders	Cicely Hamilton	Old Vic	21.12.25/ 8.1.26	6
Baby Mine	Margaret Mayo	Apollo	23.12.25/ 7.1.26	10
Inheritors	Susan Glaspell	Everyman	28.12.25/ 10.1.26	21
The Man Who Was Thursday	Mrs C.Chesterton and R. Neale	Everyman	20.1.26/ 30.1.26	12
Blind Alley	Dorothy Brandon	Playhouse	27.1.26/ 6.2.26	13
The Widow's Cruise	Joan Temple	Ambassadors	3.3.26/ 8.5.26	81
Ashes	Vera, Countess Cathcart	Prince of Wales'	15.3.26/ 20.3.26	9
The Rescue Party	Phyllis Morris	Regent	28.3.26	1
Enchantress	K. Bramson and A. Augusta Grein	Garrick	7.4.26/ 24.4.26	21
The Cat's Cradle	Aimée and Philip Stuart	Criterion	8.4.26/ 21.8.26	156
Temptation	Gladys Hastings Walton	New Oxford	19.4.26/ 24.4.26	13
The Rescue Party	Phyllis Morris	Comedy	26.4.26/ 12.6.26	56
The Great Lover	L. Ditrichstein, Fanny and F. Hatton	Shaftesbury	30.04.26/ 5.6.26	42
Distinguished Villa	Kate O'Brien	Aldwych	2.5.26	1
The Song	Adela Maddison	Court	3.5.26	1 mat.
Intimate Enemies	Zenia Lowinsky and N. McKinnel	Savoy	17.5.26/ 29.5.26	15
As We Are	Gertrude and M. J. Landa	Scala	27.5.26	1
Billeted	F. Tennyson-Jesse and H. Harwood	Royalty	31.5.26/ 26.6.26	32
Granite	Clemence Dane	Ambassadors	15.6.26/ 7.8.26	62

Play	Author	Theatre	Dates	No. of perfs
1926–1927				
Down Hill	(Constance Collier and Ivor Novello) 'David L'Estrange'	Queen's/ Princes	16.6.26/ 4.9.26	94
Jiggs in Clover	Margaret Coulan	Regent	21.6.26	1
The Twin	Vere Sullivan and G. Brenchley	Everyman	29.6.26/ 10.7.26	4
Cock o' the Roost	Rida Johnson Young	Garrick	2.7.26/ 17.7.26	18
Distinguished Villa	Kate O'Brien	Little	12.7.26/ 4.9.26	12
A Balcony	Naomi Royde-Smith	Everyman	25.8.26/ 4.9.26	12
Virginia's Husband	Florence Kilpatrick	Comedy	6.9.26/ 2.10.26	31
The Whole Town's Talking	Anita Loos and John Emerson	Strand	7.9.26/ 18.12.26	118
The Constant Nymph	Margaret Kennedy	New	14.8.26/ 13.8.27	387
The Edge O' Beyond	Ruby Miller and Roy Horman	Regent	23.10.26/ 29.10.26	12
Shavings	Pauline Phelps and Marion Shorts	Apollo	1.11.26/ 20.11.26	24
Yellow Sands	Eden and Adelaide Philpotts	Haymarket	3.11.26/ 25.2.28	612
It Is Expedient	Lady Kathleen Curzon-Herrick	Royalty	14.11.26	1
Aspidistras	Joan Temple	Strand	5.12.26	1
Christmas Eve	Rose Fyleman	Old Vic	20.12.26/ 1.1.27	9
When Knights Were Bold	Harriet Jay 'Charles Marlow'	Scala	22.12.26/ 15.1.27	42
Daddy Long Legs	Jean Webster	Regent	27.12.26/ 7.1.27	22
Nobody's Daughter	George Paston 'E. M. Symonds'	Regent	8.1.27/ 14.1.27	12
The Square Peg	Mildred Hodson	Everyman	18.1.27/ 5.2.27	20
The Bat	Mary R. Rinehart and A. Hopwood	Regent	29.1.27/ 4.2.27	12
En Pension	Mrs Cyril Scott	Globe	30.1.27	1
The Rat	David L'Estrange (Constance Collier and I. Novello)	Prince of Wales'	12.2.27/ 26.3.27	49
No Gentleman	Aimée and Philip Stuart	St Martin's	8.3.27/ 23.4.27	58

APPENDIX

Play	Author	Theatre	Dates	No. of perfs
1927				
Angela	Lady Florence Evelyn Bell	Prince's	14.3.27	1
A Hen Upon a Steeple	Joan Temple	Globe	23.3.27/ 23.4.27	37
Bert's Girl	Elizabeth Baker	Court	30.3.27/ 16.4.27	20
Abie's Irish Rose	Anne Nichols	Apollo	11.4.27/ 30.7.27	128
Lolotte	Betha N. Graham	New	6.5.27	1 mat.
Ishmael	Elizabeth Southwart	Strand	15.5.27	1
The Bridge	Kate O'Brien	Arts	31.5.27	1
Meet the Wife	Lynn Starling	St Martin's	1.6.27/ 10.9.27	117
Wild-Cat Hetty	Florence A. Kilpatrick	Savoy	20.6.27/ 16.7.27	31
Nevertheless	Sylvia Blennerhasseti	Arts	5.7.27/ 8.7.27	4
Streaks of Light	Grace Frank	Arts	10.7.27/ 12.7.27	3
Samson and Delilah	'Michael Orme'	Arts	17.7.27/ 18.7.27	2
The Village	Vere Sullivan	Globe	18.7.27/ 6.8.27	24
The Cage	Joan Temple	Savoy	22.7.27/ 20.8.27	34
Cautious Campbell	Brenda Girvan and Monica Cosens	Royalty	26.7.27/ 13.8.27	22
Billeted	F. Tennyson-Jesse and H. Harwood	Regent	3.9.27/ 11.9.27	12
I'll Give You a Ring	Audrey and G. Carten	Globe	25.9.27	1
Scrapped	Alma Brosnan	Arts	23.9.27/ 27.9.27	5
A Wife in the House	Inglis Allen	Globe	25.9.27	1
The Lady-in-Law	Bertha Murrey	Wyndham's	29.9.27/ 12.11.27	54
The Outsider	Dorothy Brandon	Regent	15.10.27/ 21.10.27	6
At Number Fifteen	Alma Brosnan	Garrick	16.10.27	1
The King Decrees	Constance Smedley	Kingsway	21.10.27	1 mat.
The Seventh Devil	Constance Smedley and Max Armfield	Kingsway	21.10.27	1 mat.

Play	Author	Theatre	Dates	No. of perfs
1927–1928				
The Kingdom of God (adpt. of G. M. Sierra's 'El Reino de Dios' 1916)	Mr and Mrs H. Granville-Baker	Strand	26.10.27/ 3.12.27	47
Woman's Honour	Susan Glaspell	Arts	27.10.27/ 28.10.27	2
Nipper	Susannah Nicholson	Regent	4.11.27/ 11.11.27	13
The Peaceful Thief	Audrey Lucas	Arts	6.11.27/ 7.11.27	2
He Who Gets Slapped	Gertrude Schurhoff and B Jackson	Everyman	8.11.27/ 10.12.27	34
His Grace	Maie B Bacon	Globe	27.11.27	1
A Wife in the House	Inglis Allen	His Majesty's	12.12.27	1
The Caveman	Daisy Fisher and Harold Simpson	Savoy	12.12.27/ 17.12.27	8
Out Flat	Mrs H. Musgrave	Regent	17.12.27/ 23.12.27	6
Whispering Wires	Kate L. McLaurin	Apollo	19.12.27/ 14.1.27	37
Caged	Mrs Henry Germaine Mainwaring	Arts	21.12.27	1 mat.
The Young Visitors	Margaret MacKenzie and Mrs George Norman	Strand	10.1.28	1
Discounted Peter	Marguerite Groswald	Arts	14.1.28/ 18.1.28	4
Jordan	Margaret Kennedy	Strand	22.1.28	1
Sauce for the Gander	Norma Mitchell and R. Medcraft	Lyric	30.1.28/ 21.3.28	72
London Pride	Gladys Unger and A. Neil Lyons	Drury Lane	8.3.28	1 mat.
Tinker, Tailor	Phyllis Morriss	Royalty	8.3.28/ 10.3.28	4
The Way	Constance Malleson	Arts	25.3.28 / 26.3.28	2
Gentleman Prefer Blonds	Anita Loos (Nou) and John Emerson	Prince of Wales'	2.4.28/ 12.5.28	48
The Trail of You	Vere Bennet	Queen's	15.4.28	1
Come With Me	Margaret Kennedy and Basil Dean	New	19.4.28/ 23.6.28	76
For Better, For Worse	May Edgington	Arts	5.5.28/ 8.5.28	4

Play	Author	Theatre	Dates	No. of perfs
1928				
After Death	Virginia and Frank Vernon	Little	14.5.28/ 2.6.28	23
The Many They Buried	Karen Bramson	Ambassadors	6.6.28/ 16.6.28	12
Holding Out The Apple	Betty Wynne-Bower	Globe	16.6.28/ 30.6.28	17
Prejudice	Mercedes of Acosta	Arts	17.6.28/ 19.6.28	3
Chance	Mary Fox-Davies	Strand	17.6.28	1
The Comic Arts	Susan Glaspell and N. Matson	Strand	24.6.28/ 14.7.28	1
Samson and the Phillistines	'Michael Orme'	Little	26.6.28	22
My Lady's Mill	Eden and Adelaide Phillpotts	Lyric	2.7.28/ 14.7.28	16
The Chinese Puzzle	Marian Bower and Leon M. Lion	Regent	7.7.28/ 13.7.28	12
Contraband	Marion W. Fawcett and N. Doon	Prince's	27.7.28/ 18.7.28	26
Her Cardboard Lover	Valerie Wyngate and P.G. Wodehouse	Lyric	21.8.28/ 19.1.29	173
Yellowsands	Eden and Adelaide Philpotts	Court	10.9.28/ 28.9.28	24
The Constant Nymph	M. Kennedy and Basil Dean	Garrick	27.9.28/ 10.11.28	58
Deadlock	May Edgington	Comedy	8.10.28/ 20.10.28	15
The 100th Chance (adpt. of her nov. 1917)	Ethel M. Dell	Regent	20.10.28/ 26.10.28	12
The Workhouse Ward	Lady Augusta Gregory	Arts	25.10.28/ 28.10.28	4
Richmond Park	Gertrude Jennings	Arts	5.11.28	1 mat.
Clara Gibbings	Aimée and Philip Stuart	Vaudeville	19.11.28/ 21.1.29	64
The Pelican	F. Tennyson-Jesse and H. Harwood	Regent	1.12.28/ 7.12.28	12
Adam's Opera	Clemence Dane	Old Vic	3.12.28/ 5.1.29	20
Out She Goes	Lillian Trimble-Bradley	Criterion	11.12.28/ 2.2.29	62
These Pretty Things	Gertrude Jennings	Garrick	14.12.28	1 mat.
Ag and Bert	Mabel Constanduros and Michael Hogan	Arts	16.12.28/ 18.12.28	3

Play	Author	Theatre	Dates	No. of perfs
1928–1929				
The Wallflower	Audrey Scott	Arts	28.12.28/ 30.12.28	3
The Chinese Bungalow	Marion Osmond and James Corbet	Duke of York's	9.1.29/ 13.4.29	109
Byron	Alicia Ramsey	Lyric	22.1.29/ 2.2.29	14
Her Shop	Aimée and Philip Stuart	Criterion	7.2.29/ 4.5.29	99
Fame	Audrey Carten and W. Carten	St James'	20.2.29/ 25.5.29	108
Mafro, Darling	Naomi Royde-Smith	Queen's	25.2.29/ 2.3.29	8
Red Rust	Virginia and Frank Vernon	Little	28.2.29/ 16.2.29	20
The Borderer	Madge Howard and L. Gordon	Strand	28.2.29/ 23.3.29	28
The Pleasure Garden	Beatrice Mayor	Everyman	8.3.29/ 23.3.29	17
The Iron Law	Aimée Scott	Court	10.3.29	1
The Mayor	Adelaide Philpotts	Royalty	11.3.29/ 23.3.29	16
Porgy	Dorothy and D. Heyward	His Majesty's	10.4.29/ 1.6.29	61
The Way of an Eagle	Ethel M. Dell	Regent	13.4.29/ 19.4.29	12
Daniel Deronda	Lily Tobias and Lydia Lewisohn	Palace	14.4.29	1
Requital	Molly Kerr	Everyman	23.4.29/ 4.5.29	15
Mariners	Clemence Dane	Wyndham's	29.4.29/ 25.5.29	32
The Matriarch	G.B. Stern	Royalty	8.5.29/ 23.11.29	229
The Black Ace	Dorothy Brandon and N. Farso	Globe	9.5.29/ 18.5.29	10
Notoriety	Mrs Martha Myers and E. Page	Garrick	12.5.29	1
Why Drag in Marriage?	Audrey Scott	Strand	31.5.29/ 22.6.29	26
Let's Leave it at That	Jeanne De Casalis and Colin Clive	Queen's	10.6.29/ 15.6.29	8
In the Next Room	Eleanor Robson and Harriet Ford	Regent	15.6.29/ 21.6.29	12
Tower of Babel	Karen Branson	Strand	7.7.29	1

Play	Author	Theatre	Dates	No. of perfs
1929–1930				
Bill of Divorcement	Clemence Dane	St Martin's	9.7.29/ 7.9.29	70
The Tower	Mary Pakington	Everyman	15.7.29/ 20.7.29	7
These Pretty Things	Gertrude Jennings	Arts	21.7.29/ 22.7.29	2
		Garrick	6.8.29/ 28.9.29	62
Sun-up	Lula Vollmer	Little	13.8.29/ 7.9.29	30
Scraps	Gertrude Jennings	Garrick	31.8.29/ 28.9.29	33
Yesterday's Harvest	Gladys St John Coe	Apollo	11.9.29/ 5.10.29	29
The Constant Nymph	Margaret Kennedy	Regent	14.9.29/ 20.9.29	12
Secrets	B. Bessier and May Edgington	Comedy	16.9.29/ 23.11.29	79
Happy Families	Audrey Carten and Waveney Carten and J. Ross	Garrick	1.10.29/ 26.10.29	30
The Mother	Olive Lethbridge	Globe	29.11.29	1 mat.
The Helping Hand	Gertrude Jennings	Prince of Wales'	3.12.29	1 mat.
The Workhouse Ward	Lady Augusta Gregory	Haymarket	4.12.29/ 21.12.29	22
The Love Game	Mrs C.A. Chesterton and Ralph Neale	Regent	14.2.29/ 21.12.29	14
A Warm Corner	Arthur Wimperis Lauri Wylie	Prince's	24.12.29/ 19.7.30	238
Nine Till Six	Aimée and Philip Stuart	Arts	22.1.30/ 26.1.31	259
Charles and Mary	Joan Temple	Everyman	4.2.30/ 22.2.30	58
		Globe	28.2.30/ 29.3.30	
Frankenstein	Peggy Webbling	Little	10.2.30/ 12.4.30	72
Oxford Preserved	Helen Simpson	Haymarket	25.2.30	1 mat.
At The Gate	Susan Richmond	Court	11.3.20	1 mat.
Bill of Divorcement	Clemence Dane	Regent	29.3.30/ 4.4.30	12
Fourth Floor Heaven	Kathleen Hewitt	Everyman	7.4.30/ 12.4.30	8
The Door	Ruth Landa	Daly's	8.4.30	1 mat.

Play	Author	Theatre	Dates	No. of perfs
1930–1931				
Debonair	G.B. Stern and Frank Vosper	Lyric	23.4.30/ 24.5.30	37
Our Ostriches	Marie C. Stopes	Royalty	7.5.30/ 31.5.30	29
The Ugly Duchess	Vera Beringer	Arts	15.5.30/ 25.5.30	15
How to Be Healthy Though Married	F. Tennyson-Jesse and H. Harwood	Strand	25.5.30	1
The Last Chapter	Edith and Ed Ellis	New	27.5.30/ 28.6.30	38
The Searcher	Velona Pilcher	Grafton	29.5.30/ 14.6.30	19
Moloch (anti-war play)	John and Winifred Carter	Strand	29.5.30/ 7.6.30	12
Let Us Be Gay	Rachel Crothers	Lyric	18.8.30/ 13.12.30	136
The Bond	Muriel Stuart	Everyman	19.8.30/ 30.8.30	13
Her First Affair	Merrill Rogers and F. Jackson	Kingsway	11.9.30/ 14.10.30	160
		Duke of York's	15.10.30/ 1.1.31	
The Outsider	Dorothy Brandon	Apollo	30.10.30/ 29.11.31	66
Cheri	Una Lady Troubridge	Prince of Wales'	26.10.30/ 27.10.30	2
The Quaker	Mary L. Pendred	Royalty	10.11.30	1 mat.
Wooden Shoe	Beatrix Thomson	Kingsway	13.11.30/ 13.12.30	36
Getting George Married	Florence Kilpatrick	Everyman	26.11.30/ 6.12.30	12
Southeast and Southwest	Vera Berigner	Hippodrome	18.12.30	1 mat.
To See Ourselves	E. M. Delafield	Ambassadors	11.12.30/ 25.4.31	154
The Borrowed Life	Gladys Parrish	Prince of Wales'	14.12.30/ 15.12.30	2
The Pelican	F. Tennyson-Jesse and H. Harwood	Playhouse	7.2.31/ 10.4.31	72
Supply and Demand	Aimée and Philip Stuart	Haymarket	9.2.31/ 28.2.31	23
The Man Who Pays the Piper	G. B. Stern	St Martin's	10.2.31/ 14.2.31	6
Sentence of Death	Gladys St John Loe	Strand	22.2.31	1

Play	Author	Theatre	Dates	No. of perfs
1931				
The Widower	June Boland	Everyman	27.2.31/ 6.3.31	2
The Gaol Gate	Augusta Gregory	Arts	15.3.31	1
Love At First Sight	Una O'Connor	Arts	15.3.31	1
Strange Adventure of a Maiden Lady	Rosalind Wade	Arts	15.3.31	1
Autumn Crocus	'C L Anthony' (Dodie Smith)	Lyric	6.4.31/ 23.1.32	371
		Savoy	1.2.32/ 27.2.32	
Black Coffee	Agatha Christie	St Martin's	9.4.31/ 2.5.31	67
		Little	11.5.31/ 13.6.31	
Fowl Play	Nancy Price and John Thirlwell	Fortune	12.4.31/ 19.4.31	3
The Quarrel	Dorothea Moore	Fortune	12.4.31/ 19.4.31	2
Nine Till Six	Aimée and Philip Stuart	Regent	2.5.31/ 8.5.31	12
Don't Tell England	Mary Dunn	Arts	3.5.31	1
Zipp	Mary Dunn	Arts	3.5.31	1
Tiger Cats	'Michael Orme'	Royalty	27.5.31/ 13.6.31	22
I Want	Constance Holme	Grafton	11.6.31/ 27.6.31	20
Episode	Rosalind Wade	Everyman	21.6.31	1
Sea Fever (adpt. M. Pagnol *Marius* 1929)	Auriol Lee and J.Van Druten	New	30.6.31	1
The Love Game	Mrs C. Chesterton and Ralph Neale	Prince of Wales'	6.7.31/ 29.8.31	64
Mrs Fisher's War	Joan Temple and Henrietta Leslie	Ambassadors	9.7.31/ 11.7.31	4
The Life Machine	Sophie Treadwell	Arts	15.7.31/ 19.7.31	6
Apron Strings	Dorrance Davis	Vaudeville	17.7.31/ 12.9.31	65
Black Magic	Nester Sawyer	Royalty	17.8.31/ 26.9.31	48
Take Two From One	Mr and Mrs H. Granville Barker	Haymarket	16.9.31/ 21.11.31	77
Jane Eyre	Phillis Birkett	Kingsway	24.9.31/ 31.10.31	20

Play	Author	Theatre	Dates	No. of perfs
1931–1932				
Forty Love	Esme Wynne-Tyson	Grafton	12.10.31/ 13.10.31	2
The Dyer's Hand	Gwen John	Everyman	29.10.31	1
Make Up Your Mind	Xenia Lowinsky	Criterion	5.11.31/ 14.11.31	12
Miss Rose's Girl	Lillian Trimble Bradley	Garrick	8.11.31	1
A Hunting We Will Go	Phyllis Morris	Savoy	8.11.31	1
Other Gates	Bertha Graham	Grafton	15.11.31/ 16.11.31	2
Little Catherine	Virginia and Frank Vernon	Phoenix	18.11.31/ 12.12.31	29
The Home Front	Diana and Bruce Hamilton	Grafton	29.11.31/ 30.11.31	2
Britannia of Billingsgate	Christine Jope-Slade and Sewell Stokes	St Martin's	30.11.31/ 12.12.31	34
The Wolves or Tanner's Close of the Crimes of Burke and Hare	Gladys Hastings Walton	New	17.12.31/ 16.1.32	20
Her Shop	Aimée and Philip Stuart	Regent	19.12.31/ 24.12.31	10
The Rising Generation	Wyn Weaver and Laura Leycester	Regent	7.1.32/ 21.1.32	12
The Life Machine	Sophie Treadwell	Regent	9.1.32/ 15.1.32	12
Trifles	Susan Glaspell	Duchess	25.1.32/ 6.2.32	18
Fire	Ernita Lascelles	Fortune	2.3.32/ 12.3.12	12
Security	Esme Wynne-Tyson	Savoy	13.3.32	1
Caravan	Cicely Hamilton	Queen's	6.4.32/ 9.4.32	5
Yellow Sands	Eden and Adelaide Philpotts	Regent	16.4.32/ 22.4.32	12
The Kingdom of God	Mr and Mrs H. Granville Barker	Westminster	1.6.32/ 2.7.32	37
Richard of Bordeaux	Gordon Daviot	New	26.6.32/ 3.7.32	2
The Matriarch	G. B. Stern	Regent	3.9.32/ 9.9.32	12
Many Women	Florida Pier	Arts	28.9.32/ 2.10.32	5
Behind The Scenes	Billie Hill	Shaftesbury	2.10.32	1

Play	Author	Theatre	Dates	No. of perfs
1932–1933				
Please Don't Be Nervous	Anne Stephenson	Shaftesbury	2.10.32	1
Children in Uniform (adpt. by Barbara Burnham)	Christa Winslow	Duchess	7.10.32/ 27.5.33	263
Alison's House	Susan Glaspell	Little	11.10.32/ 29.10.32	23
Service	Dodie Smith	Wyndham's	12.10.32/ 18.3.33	199
Quartette or Quartet	Lucy Leven	Everyman	24.10.32/ 12.11.32	18
Once A Husband	Margot Neville	Haymarket	26.10.32/ 3.12.32	45
Money For Jam	Madge and Alwyn Bolton	Shaftesbury	30.10.32	1
Tonight or Never	Frederic and Fanny Hatton	Duke of York's	10.11.32/ 26.11.32	20
The Romantic Young Lady	Mr and Mrs Granville Barker	Fortune	25.11.32/ 29.11.32	2 mat.
Poet's Licence	Christine Hahlo	Grafton	27.11.32	1
Tomorrow Never Comes	Angela Green and Nora Nicholson	St Martin's	29.11.32	1
Another Language	Rose Franken	Lyric	1.12.32/ 4.2.33	77
Earthquake in Surrey	Lilian Arnold	Phoenix	4.12.32	1
Silver Wedding	Ruby M. Ayres	Arts	14.12.32	1
Fool's Music	Winifred Howe	Grafton	18.12.32	1
Buckie's Bears	Erica Fay (Marie Stopes)	Garrick	19.12.32/ 14.1.33	24
Alice Thomas and Jane (adpt. from E. Bagnold)	Vera Beringer	Westminster	20.12.32/ 21.1.33	29 mat.
Alice in Wonderland	Nancy Price	Little	21.12.32/ 28.1.33	62
Suppressed Desires	Susan Glaspell	Arts	8.1.33	1
Dinner at Eight	G. Kaufman and Edna Ferber	Palace	6.1.33/ 15.7.33	216
Richard of Bordeaux	Gordon Daviot	New	2.2.33/ 24.3.34	463
Steel Harvest	Ruth Landa	Cambridge	5.2.33	1

Play	Author	Theatre	Dates	No. of perfs
1933				
The Lake	Dorothy Massingham	Arts	1.3.33/ 5.3.33	6
		Piccadilly	15.3.33/ 27.5.33	213
		Westminster	29.5.33/ 16.9.33	
The Lonely Road	Mrs J.T. Grein ('Michael Orme')	Arts	21.3.33	1
The Soldier and the Gentleman	Dorothy Massingham	Vaudeville	19.4.33/ 29.4.33	13
When Ladies Meet	Rachel Crothers	Lyric	26.4.33/ 29.7.33	108
The Blue Gate	Vera Gordon	Grafton	20.4.33	1
Clear All Wires	Bella and Sam Spewak	Piccadilly	30.4.33	1
The Day I Forgot	Elsie Schauffler	Globe	12.5.33/ 13.5.33	3
Love for Sale	Beatrix Thamon	St Martin's	14.5.33	1
Whether Pigs Have Wings	Marjory Whyte	Grafton	21.5.33/ 23.5.33	2
The Poet's Secret	Virginia and Frank Vernon	Ambassadors	25.5.33/ 1.6.33	12
Wild Decembers	Clemence Dane	Apollo	26.5.33/ 8.7.33	50
The Mask	F. Tennyson-Jesse and H. Harwood	Everyman	1.6.33/ 5.6.33	6
What Happened Then	Lillian Trimble-Bradley	Fortune Kingsway Garrick	11.9.33/ 16.9.33 3.11.33	59
The House of Jealousy	Betty Wynne Bower	Fortune	18.9.33/ 29.9.33	7
Jewish Madonna	Vera Gordon	Comedy	24.9.33	1
Disharmony	Nora De Worms and Stanley Ford	Fortune	25.9.33/ 30.9.33	7
Singing Gold	Clare Richards	Grafton	8.10.33	1
So Good! So Kind!	Nesta Sawyer	Playhouse	9.10.33/ 21.10.33	16
The Lady From Alfaqueque	Mr and Mrs H. Granville Barker	Westminster	8.11.33/ 9.12.33	37
Unnatural Scene	Kathleen Davey	Grafton	12.11.33	1
The Tudor Wench	Elswyth Thane	Alhambra	16.11.33/ 16.12.33	36
Mrs Siddons	Naomi Royde Smith	Apollo	28.11.33	1 mat.
Escape Me Never	Margaret Kennedy	Apollo	8.12.33/ 12.4.34	232

Play	Author	Theatre	Dates	No. of perfs
1933–1934				
What Happened to George	Vera Berringer	Wyndham's	21.12.33/ 20.1.34	40
Daddy Long Legs	Jean Webster	Victoria Palace	26.12.33/ 20.1.34	46
The Queen Who Kept Her Head	Winifred Carter	Kingsway	20.2.34/ 10.3.34	22
Private Room	Naomi Royde Smith	Westminster	23.2.34/ 29.4.34	67
Fog Over Dybern	Esther Frenen	Grafton	4.3.34/ 5.3.34	2
Jane and Genius	Elizabeth Drew	Royalty	6.3.34/ 10.3.34	7
The Emergency	Bertha N. Graham	Grafton	11.3.34/ 12.3.34	2
Poor Old Bill	Nella Nagra	Grafton	11.3.34/ 12.3.34	2
Double Door	E. McFadden	Globe	23.3.34/ 12.4.34	60
		Strand	21.3.34/ 21.4.34	
Flowery Walk	Joan Temple	Piccadilly	25.3.34	1
Sixteen	Aimée and Philip Stuart	Criterion	4.4.34/ 15.9.34	188
The Laughing Woman	Gordon Daviot	New	7.4.34/ 12.5.34	41
The Eagle's Nest	Mabel Greenwood	Comedy	29.4.34	1
The Lawyer and the Roses	Ruth Collin Allen	Arts	6.5.34/ 7.5.34	2
Touchwood	Dodie Smith	Haymarket	16.5.34/ 17.11.34	213
The Pursuit of Happiness	L. Langern and Armina Marshall	Vaudeville	30.5.34/ 14.7.34	52
Get Out of Your Cage	Mary Plowman	St Martin's	3.6.34	1
Jane Wogan	Florence Howell	St Martin's	3.5.34	1
Ariel	Grace Carlton	Scala	5.6.34	1 mat.
Queen of Scots	Gordon Daviot	New	8.6.34/ 8.9.34	106
Meeting at Night	Marjory Sharp	Globe	14.6.34/ 30.6.34	19
The Nightingale Sings	Nella Nagra	Ambassadors	24.6.34/ 25.6.34	2

Play	Author	Theatre	Dates	No. of perfs
1934–1935				
Family Affairs	Gertrude Jennings	Ambassadors	22.8.34/ 16.3.35	331
		Phoenix	10.6.35/ 22.6.35 18.3.35/ 25.5.35	
Moonlight is Silver	Clemence Dane	Queen's	19.9.34/ 1.12.34	85
Theatre Royal	Edna and George Ferber	Lyric	23.10.34/ 23.3.35	174
The Wise Woman	Lesley Storm	Criterion	1.12.34	12
Young Mr Disraeli	Elswyth Thane	Kingsway	12.11.34/ 1.12.34	61
The Greeks Had a Word For It	Zoë Akins	Duke of York's	22.11.34/ 19.1.35	193
		Cambridge	21.1.35/ 18.5.35	
Three Cornered Moon	Gertrude Tonkonogy	Westminster	26.11.34/ 15.12.34	24
The Luck of the Navy	Mrs Clifford Mills	Playhouse	24.12.34/ 5.1.35	22
Three For Luck	Mabel Constanduros	Westminster	26.12.34/ 5.1.35	16
Tarakin	Martha Steinitz	Kingsway	13.1.35	1
A Boy For the Surgeons	Ada Heather Bigg	Kingsway	20.1.35	1
Susanna	Margaret Haythorne	Kingsway	20.1.35	1
The Box	Dorothy Hewlett	Kingsway	3.2.35	1
The Convict	L. Openshaw and Ethel Dickens	Westminster	4.2.35/ 16.2.35	16
The Rising of The Moon	Lady Gregory	Kingsway	10.2.35	1
The Two Shepherds	Mr and Mrs H. Granville Barker	Old Vic	11.2.35/ 2.3.35	21
The Wise Woman	S. L. Bensusan	Fortune	24.2.35/ 25.2.35	2
Summer's Lease	Winifred Howe	Vaudeville	25.2.35/ 16.3.35	24
Someone At The Door	Dorothy and Campbell Christie	Aldwych	3.3.35	1
		New	29.5.35/ 8.6.35	305
		Comedy	17.6.35/ 29.2.36	
Happy and Glorious	Winifred Walter	Westminster	4.3.35/ 9.3.35	8

Play	Author	Theatre	Dates	No. of perfs
1935–1936				
Family Group	Dorothy and Campbell Christie	Phoenix	31.3.35	1
The Travelling Man	Lady Gregory	Little	7.4.35/ 9.4.35	3
The Workhouse Ward	Lady Gregory	Little	7.4.35/ 9.4.35	3
The King of Rome	Madge Pemberton	Royalty	14.5.35/ 17.5.35	2
Hervey House	Jane Cowle and R. Lawrence	His Majesty's	17.5.35/ 22.6.35	42
The Abbé Provost	Helen Waddell	Arts	19.5.35/ 20.5.35	3
Golden Arrow	Sylvia Thompson and V. Cunnard	Whitehall	30.5.35/ 15.6.35	19
Love of Women	Aimée and Philip Stuart	Phoenix	2.6.35	1/3
The Partnership	Bertha N. Graham	Fortune	18.6.35	1
Green of the Spring	Muriel Sheehan-Dare	Arts	28.7.35	1
Pirate Mallory	Mary Pakington	Arts	6.10.35/ 13.10.35	3
The Pleasure Garden	Beatrice Mayor	Grafton	7.10.35/ 19.10.35	14
Two Share a Dwelling	Alice Campbell	St James'	8.10.35/ 26.10.35	22
Cul De Sac	Elsa Malik	Arts	18.10.35/ 22.10.35	3
Call It A Day	Dodie Smith	Globe	30.10.35/ 9.1.37	509
Legend Yesterday	Ruth Howe	Aldwych	3.11.35	1
Our Own Lives	Gertrude Jennings	Ambassadors	27.11.35/ 25.1.36	67
Grand Hotel	Vicki Baum	Vaudeville	1.12.35	1
Alice Through the Looking Glass	Nancy Price	Little	23.12.35/ 18.1.36	23 mat.
Buckie's Bears	'Erica Fay' (Marie Stopes)	Garrick	26.12.35/ 11.1.36	30 mat.
Bitter Harvest	Catherine Turvey	Arts	29.1.36/ 30.3.36	10
			12.5.36/ 6.6.36	30
Bright Star	Dorothy Hewlitt	Arts	16.2.36/ 17.2.36	3
The Mask	F. Tennyson-Jesse and H. Harwood	Vaudeville	23.2.36	1

Play	Author	Theatre	Dates	No. of perfs
1936				
Pride and Prejudice	Helen Jerome	St James'	27.2.35/ 21.11.36	317
Cold Comfort Farm	Mabel Constanduros	Arts	1.3.36/ 9.3.36	3
Children, To Bless You	G. Sheila Donisthorpe	Ambassadors	3.3.36/ 21.3.36	109
		Duke of York's	23.3.36/ 6.6.36	
Sonata	Evelyn Millard	Ambassadors	7.3.36	1 mat.
		Cambridge	23.5.36/ 30.5.36	13
Her Last Adventure	Mrs Belloc Lowndes	Ambassadors	30.3.36/ 4.4.36	7
The Happy Hypocrite	Clemence Dane	His Majesty's	8.4.35/ 6.6.36	68
The Greeks Had a Word For It	Zoë Akins	Victoria Palace	11.4.36/ 18.4.36	12
Indian Summer (The Unquiet Heart)	Aimée and Philip Stuart	Arts	19.4.36/ 26.4.36	3
Belmont Revisited	Nora Nicholson	Palace	26.4.36	1
Boy Meets Girl	Bella and Sam Spewack	Shaftesbury	27.5.36/ 15.8.36	92
The King's Leisure	Edith Savile and John Carlton	Dalys	29.5.36/ 4.7.36	44
The Emperor of Make Believe	Madge Pemberton and Maureen Morley	Westminster	3.6.36/ 20.6.36	21
When the Bough Breaks	Henrietta Leslie and Laurier Lister	Arts	7.6.36/ 11.6.36	3
Heroes Don't Care	Margot Neville	St Martin's	10.6.36/ 17.10.36	149
Rain Before Seven	Joyce Dennys	Arts	14.6.36/ 16.6.36	2
Lucretia	Ernita Lascelles	Arts	21.6.36/ 22.6.36	2
The Insect Play (adpt. Kapek)	Nancy Price	Little	23.6.36/ 22.8.36	127
The Lady of La Paz	Edith Ellis	Criterion	2.7.36/ 31.10.36	139
The Two Bouquets	Eleanor and H. Farjeon	Ambassadors	13.8.36/ 30.1.37	300
		Garrick	2.2.37/ 1.5.37	
The Ante-Room	Kate O'Brien	Queen's	14.8.36/ 22.8.36	10

Play	Author	Theatre	Dates	No. of perfs
1936–1937				
What Really Happened	Mrs Belloc Lowndes	Duke of York's	13.9.36	1
Mademoiselle	Audrey and Wavenby Carten	Wyndham's	15.9.36/ 14.1.37	147
Girl Unknown	Margaret Webster	New	16.9.36/ 26.9.36	12
Do You Remember	Edith Savile and John Carlton	Vaudeville	22.9.36/ 5.12.36	86
Follow Your Saint	Leslie Storm	Queen's	24.9.36/ 3.10.36	11
Jane Eyre	Helen Jerome	Queen's	13.10.36/ 16.1.37	299
		Aldwych	19.1.37/ 26.6.37	
Parnell	Elsie Schauffler	New	4.11.36/ 6.2.37	108
Poor Man's Castle	Mandy Whitehouse and Barbara Blackburn	Arts	7.11.36/ 11.11.36	6
The Dogs of War	Marjorie R. Watson	Vaudeville	8.11.36	1
The Machine	Anna Thompson Cook	Vaudeville	8.11.36	1
Her Affairs In Order	Mada Gage Bolton	Vaudeville	8.11.36	1
Twenty Shadows	Dorothy Mande	Arts	15.11.36/ 16.1136	2
Honor Thy Father	Diana Hamilton	Arts	6.12.36/ 14.12.36	3
Busman's Holiday	D.L. Sayers	Comedy	16.12.36/ 25.9.37	431
		Victoria	27.9.37/ 11.12.39	
		Palace	15.1.39	
Crooked Cross	Sally Carson	Westminster	13.1.37/ 30.1.37	21
Because We Must	Ingaret Giffard	Wyndham's	15.2.37/ 20.2.37	18
The Cup of Trembling	Grace Carlton	Aldwych	7.2.37	1
Wuthering Heights	May Pakington and Olive Walter	Strand	7.2.37/ 1.2.37	2
Come Out To Play	John Sand and Fanny Jocelyn	Arts	9.2.37/ 14.2.37	
First Night	G. Sheila Donisthorpe	Arts	21.2.37/ 28.2.37	3
Retreat From Folly	A.K. Gould and E. Russell	Queen	24.2.37/ 10.4.37	47

Play	Author	Theatre	Dates	No. of perfs
1937				
The Heavenly Passion	Olga Racster and Jessica Grove	Arts	7.3.37/ 8.3.37	2
Bats in the Belfry	Diana Morgan and R. McDermot	Ambassadors	11.3.37/ 14.8.37	196
		Winter Garden	30.8.37/ 11.9.37	
The Case of Constance Kent	Shirley Bax	Savoy	4.4.37	1
The Good Fairy	Jane Hint	Royalty	14.5.37/ 22.5.37	10
A Ship Comes Home	Daisy Fisher	St Martin's	15.5.37/ 5.6.37	25
The Bridge	Cecile Adair	Arts	17.6.37/ 18.6.37	2
The Man Who Meant Well	Kathleen Hewitt	Arts	20.6.37/ 27.6.37	3
In the Best Families	Anita Hart and M. Bradell	Arts	30.6.37/ 2.7.37	3
But Not Your Heart	'Francis (Charlotte) Frances' (Mrs John Longden)	Arts	4.3.37/ 5.7.37	2
The Phanton Light	Evadne Price	Haymarket	7.9.37/ 12.2.38	182
Bonnet Over the Windmill	Dodie Smith	New	8.9.37/ 4.12.37	101
Rich Martha	Bertha N. Graham	Grafton	4.10.37	1–2 wks
Youth's the Season	Mary Manning	Westminster	5.10.37/ 16.10.37	15
The Dead Hand	Cicelly Fraser and E.G. Hemmerde	Whitehall	7.10.37/ 16.10.37	11
Autumn	Margaret Kennedy and G. Ratoff	St Martin's	15.10.37/ 5.3.38	161
Anything But the Truth	Christine Longford	Westminster	18.10.37/ 30.10.37	16
Madame Fears the Dark	Margaret Irwin	Playhouse	1.11.37/ 2.11.37	3
Triumph	Dorothea Flower	Little	5.11.37	1
Hands Never Lie	Olive Temple	Grafton	15.11.37	1
Flying Blind	Pamela Kellino and James Mason	Arts	21.11.37/ 22.11.37	2
Identity Unknown	Alice Wagstaffe	Duke of York's	5.12.37/ 19.12.37	3
The King's Breakfast	Rita Weiman and M. Mars	Savoy	12.12.37	1

Play	Author	Theatre	Dates	No. of perfs
1937–1938				
The End of a Fairy Tale	Violet Rutter	Fortune	13.12.37	1
Roses and Rue	Winifred Fraser	Fortune	12.12.37	1
When Knights Were Bold	('Charles Marlow')	Fortune	27.12.37/ 15.1.38	36
Beloved	Valerie Wyngate	Arts	16.1.38/ 17.1.38/	2
Gentleman's Agreement	Elsa De Szasz and Owen Rutter	Duke of York's	16.138/ 30.1.38	3
Mary Goes To See	Rosemary Casey and B.I. Payne	Haymarket	16.2.38/ 26.3.38	45
No More Music	Rosamond Lehmann	Duke of York's	27.2.38/ 1.3.38	3
Zeal of Thy House	D.L. Sayers	Westminster	2.9.38/ 30.4.38	102
		Garrick	10.5.38/ 11.6.38	
		Duke of York's	14.6.38/ ` 27.3.38	
April Clouds	Peggy Barwell and M. Malleson	Royalty	20.4.38/ 7.5.38	21
Murder Without Tears	Florence A. Kilpatrick	Arts	24.4.38/ 25.4.38	2
High Dever	Winifred Carter	Arts	1.5.38/ 2.5.38	2
Melodrama	Aimée Stuart	Aldwych	22.5.38	1
Storm	Elizabeth Goudge	Cambridge	22.5.38	1
This, My Life	Daphne Lennard and J. Plowden	Phoenix	29.5.38	1
Spring Meeting	M. J. Farrell and John Perry	Ambassadors	31.5.38/ 4.3.39	310
Trumpeter Play	Vere Sullivan	Garrick	13.6.38/ 25.6.38	16
Nanny	V. Beringer	Fortune	24.6.38	1 mat.
Little Stranger	Katherine Hillier and H.H. Caldwell (trans. N. Hunter)	Royalty	13.7.38/ 23.7.38	12
She Was Too Young	Hilda Vaughan and Laurier Lister	Wyndham's	16.8.38/ 8.10.38	110
		New	10.10.38/ 19.11.38	
Dear Octopus	Dodie Smith	Queen's	14.9.38/ 2.9.39	376
Behind the Blinds	Vivian Tidmarsh	Winter Garden	10.10.38/ 29.10.38	24

Play	Author	Theatre	Dates	No. of perfs
1938–1939				
Dearly Beloved Wife	Jeanne De Casalis	Vaudeville	30.10.38/ 31.10.38	2
Elizabeth of Austria	Katriona and Elizabeth Sprigge	Garrick	3.11.38/ 28.1.39	94
The Lady of Glamys	Margaret Snowdon	Strand	6.1.38	1
Traitors Gate	Morna Stuart	Duke of York's	17.11.38/ 14.1.39	54
Funeral Flowers for the Bride	Bev du Bose Hamer	Duchess	27.11.38	1
Hamlet Wears Homespun	Nora Ratcliff	Duchess	27.11.38	1
The Ladies of Edinburgh	Constance Smedley	Duchess	27.11.38	1
Lucy, Bless Her	Ann Stephenson	Kingsway	27.11.38/ 28.11.38	2
The Love of Ming-Y	Mary Basil Hall	Phoenix	27.11.38	1
The Crooked Circle	Ann Casson	Vaudeville	4.12.38	1
Tony Draws a Horse	Lesley Storm	Criterion	26.1.39/ 11.3.39	363
		Strand	13.3.39/ 3.6.39	
		Comedy	5.6.39/ 6.1.40	
Hundreds of Thousands	Sara B. Tapping and Leon M. Lion	Garrick	31.1.39/ 4.2.39	7
Father Christmas	Diana Morgan	Vaudeville	12.3.39	1
The Courageous Sex	Mary D. Sheriden	Globe	19.2.39/ 26.2.39	2
The Gate Review	Diana Morgan and Mr Ritchie	Ambassadors	9.3.39/ 29.8.39	450
Mrs Van Kleek	Elinor Mordaunt	Playhouse	17.3.39/ 15.4.39	31
Sons of Adam	Beatrice Thomson	Arts	26.3.39/ 27.3.39	2
Ring in the Moon	Evelyn P. Medd and R.H. Casson	Arts	19.4.39/ 25.4.39	8
The Women	Claire Booth	Lyric	20.4.39/ 2.9.39	155
Quiet Wedding	Esther McCracken	Wyndham's	8.5.38/ 29.4.39	291
		Piccadilly	8.5.39/ 1.7.39	
		Colliseum	28.8.39/ 2.9.39	12

Play	Author	Theatre	Dates	No. of perfs
1939–1942				
Uneasy Living	Florence Kilpatrick	Kingsway	18.5.39/ 17.6.39	24
The Jews of York	Nesta Pain	Duchess	4.6.39	2
Spring Meeting	M. J. Farrell	Piccadilly	3.7.39/ 5.8.39	40
		Colisseum	4.12.39/ 9.12.39	13
Cousin Muriel	Clemence Dane	Globe	7.3.40/ 11.5.40	75
Jeannie	Aimée Stuart	Wyndham's	3.4.40/ 22.6.40	100
A House in the Square	Diana Morgan	St Martin's	4.4.40/ 25.5.40	67
Rebecca	Daphne Du Maurier	Queen's	5.4.40/ 7.9.40	180
The Women	Clare Booth	Strand	23.4.40/ 4.5.40	16
Dear Octopus	Dodie Smith	Adelphi	27.7.40/ 31.8.40	42
Margin for Error	Clare Booth	Apollo	1.8.40/ 20.8.40	45
Under One Roof	Kim Peacock	St Martin's	24.4.41/ 13.5.41	24
Quiet Week End	Esther McCracken	Wyndham's	22.7.41/ 29.1.44	1059
Other People's Houses	Lynne Dexter	Ambassadors	30.10.41/ 14.3.42	172
Ducks and Drakes	M. J. Farrell	Apollo	25.11.41/ 13.12.41	23
Little Women	Marian De Forest	Westminster	22.12.41/ 7.2.42	56
Other People's Houses	Lynne Dexter	Phoenix	19.3.42/ 9.5.42	131
		Whitehall	11.5.42/ 27.6.42	
Watch on the Rhine	Lillian Hellman	Aldwych	22.4.42/ 4.12.43	672
Rebecca	Daphne Du Maurier	Strand	21.5.42/ 5.9.42	176
		Lyric	12.9.42/ 24.10.42	
		Ambassadors	26.12.42/ 9.1.43	
		Scala	26.4.42/ 22.5.42	

Play	Author	Theatre	Dates	No. of perfs
1942–1944				
Baby Mine	Margaret Mayo	Westminster	9.6.42/ 27.6.43	390
Claudia	Rose Franken	St Martin's	17.9.42/ 15.1.44	559
The Little Foxes	Lillian Hellman	Piccadilly	21.10.42/ 21.11.42	37
Mothers Are Waiting	Audrey Lucas	Adelphi	9.5.42	1 mat.
Case 27, VC	Maud Flannery and T. Browne	Comedy	2.6.43/ 26.5.43	30
Living Room	Esther McCracken	Garrick	9.6.43/ 9.10.43	142
Lottie Dundass	Enid Bagnold	Vaudeville	21.7.43/ 9.10.43	147
		Cambridge	12.10.43/ 20.11.43	
Landslide	Dorothy Albertyn and David Peel	Westminster	5.10.42/ 6.11.42	38
Alana Avenue	Mabel and Denis Constanduros	Vaudeville	14.10.42/ 15.4.44	231
Ten Little Niggers	Agatha Christie	St James'	17.11.42/ 24.2.44	261
		Cambridge	29.2.44/ 6.5.44	
		St James'	9.5.44/ 1.7.44	
Alice in Wonderland	Clemence Dane	Scala	24.12.42/ 12.2.44	86
		Palace	26.12.44/ 27.1.45	
Where The Rainbow Ends	Mrs Clifford Mills and J.R.R. Quilter	Winter Garden	27.12.43/ 29.1.44	46 mat.
Donabel Wrote a Tragedy	H. and H. Granville Barker	Arts	13.1.44/ 6.2.44	30
This Was a Woman	Joan Morgan	Comedy	15.3.44/ 30.12.44	380
Quiet Weekend	Esther McCracken	Wyndham's	25.4.44/ 2.9.44	137
The Last of Summer	Kate O'Brien	Phoenix	7.6.44/ 1.7.44	29
Three's a Family	Phoebe and Henry Ephron	Saville	21.9.44/ 12.5.45	317
		Winter Garden	15.5.45/ 23.6.45	

Play	Author	Theatre	Dates	No. of perfs
1944–1946				
No Medals	Esther McCracken	Vaudeville	4.10.44/ 20.7.46	740
Scandal at Barchester	Vera Wheatley	Lyric	5.10.44/ 9.12.44	109
		Wyndham's	12.12.44/ 6.1.45	
Daughter Janie	J. Bentham and H. Williams	Apollo	18.10.44/ 28.10.44	14
Quiet Weekend	Esther McCracken	Playhouse	9.11.44/ 3.2.45	101
The Years Between	Daphne Du Maurier	Wyndham's	10.1.45/ 22.6.46	618
Laura	Vera Caspary and George Sklar	St Martin's	14.2.45/ 7.4.45	67
Great Day	Lesley Storm	Playhouse	14.3.45/ 7.4.45	29
Yellow Sands	Eden and Adelaide Philpotts	Westminster	29.3.45/ 23.6.45	103
Appointment With Death	Agatha Christie	Piccadilly	31.3.45/ 5.5.45	42
Lady from Edinburgh	Aimée Stuart and L. Arthur Rose	Playhouse	10.4.45/ 10.8.46	560
Maid Marion	Joan Brampton	His Majesty's	15.4.45	1 mat.
Duet For Two Hands	Mary Hayley Bell	Lyric	27.6.45/ 11.5.46	364
The Shouting Dies	Ronda Keane	Lyric	5.10.45/ 3.11.45	37
Fit For Heroes	H. Brooke and Kay Bannerman	Whitehall	19.12.45/ 29.12.45	11
Stage Door	Edna Ferber and George Kaufman	Saville	21.2.46/ 30.3.46	44
And No Birds Sing	Jenny Laird and John Fernald	Comedy Aldwych	17.3.46 14.11.46/ 25.1.47	1 84
Murder on the Nile	Agatha Christie	Ambassadors	19.3.46/ 2.4.46	46
No Room at the Inn	Joan Temple	Winter Garden	3.5.46/ 24.5.47	427
The Kingmaker	Margaret Luce	St James'	14.5.46/ 20.8.46	97
Grand National Night	Dorothy and Campbell Christie	Apollo	12.6.46/ 1.2.48	268
Green Laughter	Rose Simon Kohn	Comedy	13.6.46/ 8.7.46	29

APPENDIX

Play	Author	Theatre	Dates	No. of perfs
1946–1948				
The Man from the Ministry	Madeleine Bingham	Whitehall Comedy	7.7.46 24.12.46/ 5.7.47	1 220
Love Goes to Press	Martha Gelhorn and Virginia Cowles	Duchess	22.7.46/ 24.8.46	40
Pick Up Girl	Elsa Shelley	Prince of Wales' Casino	23.7.46/ 5.10.46 14.10.46/ 14.12.46	170
Fear No More	Diana Hamilton and C. Aiken	Lyric	5.8.46/ 31.8.46	33
Soldiers Wife	Rose Franken	Duchess	27.8.46/ 19.10.46	62
Mother of Men	Ada G. Abbott	Comedy	12.9.46/ 19.10.46	49
Literally Speaking	Madeline and Cyric Campion	Aldwych	6.10.46	1
Call Home the Heart	Clemence Dane	St James	10.4.47/ 17.5.47	44
Angel	Mary Hayley Bell	Strand	6.6.47/ 14.6.47	10
The Conqueror's Gate	Dorothy Lang	Savil	5.10.47	1
Still She Wished for Company	Margaret Irwin and J. R. Monsell	Whitehall	12.10.47	1
Rebecca	Daphne Du Maurier	Theatre Royal E15	10.11.47/ 22.11.47	16
The Little Dry Thorn	Gordon Daviot	Lyric	11.11.47/ 6.12.47	30
Daddy Long Legs	Jean Webster	Comedy	23.12.47/ 17.1.48	19 mat.
Diamond Lil	Mae West	Prince of Wales'	24.1.48/ 8.5.48	180
The Lady from Edinburgh	Aimée Stuart and L. Arthur Rose	Theatre Royal E15	9.2.48/ 21.2.48	16
Family Portrait	Lenore Coffee and W. J. Cowen	Strand	17.2.48/ 20.3.48	38
Cockpit	Bridget Boland	Playhouse	19.2.48/ 10.4.48	58
Castle Anne	Elizabeth Bowen and John Perry	Lyric	24.2.49/ 20.3.48	30
Dark Eyes	Glena Miranova	Strand	24.3.48/ 29.5.48	76

Play	Author	Theatre	Dates	No. of perfs
1948–1949				
Happy with Either	Margaret Kennedy	St James	22.4.48/ 22.5.48	35
Royal Circle	Romily Cavan	Wyndham's	27.4.48/ 29.5.48	38
Top Floor	Rita Anderson	Whitehall	13.6.48	1
Someone at the Door	Dorothy and Campbell Christie	Theatre Royal E15	12.7.48/ 24.7.48	16
A Man Must Die	Felicity Douglas	St Martin's	4.8.48/ 28.8.48	29
Sixteen	Aimée and Philip Stuart	Theatre Royal E15	9.8.48/ 21.8.48	16
Valerious	Gordon Daviot	Saville	3.10.48	1
September Tide	Daphne Du Maurier	Aldwych	15.12.48/ 6.8.49	267
Where the Rainbow Ends	Mrs Cliff Mills	Cambridge	22.12.48/ 22.1.49	27 mat.
Harvey	Mary Chase	Prince of Wales' Piccadilly	5.1.49/ 11.3.50 14.3.50/ 1.7.50	610
Quaint Honour	Barbara Gregory	Wyndham's	9.1.49	1
Sweethearts and Wives	G. and M. Hackforth Jones	Wyndham's	22.2.49/ 12.3.49	23
The Foolish Gentlewoman	Margery Sharp	Duchess	23.3.49/ 30.7.49	180
Love's A Funny Thing	Jane Hinton	Ambassadors	10.3.49/ 12.3.49	4
Acacia Avenue	D. and Mabel Constanduros	Theatre Royal E15	21.3.49/ 26.3.49	8
A Woman's Place	Wendy Grimwood	Vaudeville	24.3.49/ 21.5.49	67
The Years Between	Daphne Du Maurier	Theatre Royal E15	11.4.49/ 16.4.49	7
Royal Highness	Margaret Webster	Lyric	13.4.49/ 14.5.49	35
Rebecca	Daphne Du Maurier	Scala	13.6.49/ 19.6.49	8
No Room at the Inn	Joan Temple	Theatre Royal E15	20.6.49/ 25.6.49	7
Western Wind	Charlotte Frances	Theatre Royal E15 Piccadilly	4.7.49/ 9.7.49 9.9.49/ 1.10.49	27

Play	Author	Theatre	Dates	No. of perfs
1949–1951				
Treasure Hunt	M. J. Farrell and John Perry	Apollo	14.9.49/ 10.6.50	358
		St Martin's	12.6.50/ 22.7.50	
John Keats Lived Here	Diana Raymond	Wyndham's	25.9.49	1
Love's a Funny Thing	Jane Hinton	Adelphi	30.10.49	1
Bonaventure	Charlotte Hastings	Vaudeville	6.12.49/ 15.4.50	149
Murder at the Vicarage (adpt.)	Moie Charles and Barbara Toy	Playhouse	14.12.49/ 1.4.50	126
The Silver Curlew	Eleanor Farjeon	Arts	22.12.49/ 22.1.50	40
Tomorrow's Pride	Lydia Ragosin	Lyric	12.2.50	1
The Platinum Set	Reg Denham and Mary Orr	Saville	30.3.50/ 8.4.50	11
The Man with the Umbrella	Roma June	Duchess	5.4.50/ 29.4.50	29
Cry Liberty	Esther McCracken	Vaudeville	21.4.50/ 12.5.50	26
The Gates of Brass	Sheila Hodgson	Apollo	14.5.50	1
His Excellency	Dorothy and C. Campbell	Princes	23.5.50/ 29.10.50	452
		Piccadilly	31.10.50/ 23.6.51	
If This Be Error	Rachel Grieve	Lyric	24.5.50/ 24.6.50	37
Always Afternoon (adpt.)	Dido Milroy	Garrick	25.7.50/ 26.8.50	38
The Little Hut (adpt. from A. Roussin)	Nancy Mitford	Lyric	23.8.50/ 5.9.53	1261
Spring Song	Bella and Sam Spewack	Saville	4.9.50/ 30.9.50	31
Sing Cuckoo	Judy Campbell	Whitehall	10.12.50	1
Lace on her Petticoat	Aimée Stuart	Ambassadors	14.12.50/ 26.5.51	188
The Silver Curlew	Eleanor Farjeon and Clifton Parkes	Fortune	22.12.50/ 20.1.51	50
Spring at Marino	Constance Cox	Arts	13.2.51/ 18.3.51	40
Temple Folly	Bridget Boland	Whitehall	25.2.51	1
The Seventh Veil	Muriel and Sydney Box	Princes	14.3.51/ 12.5.51	68

Play	Author	Theatre	Dates	No. of perfs
1951–1952				
The Martin's Nest	Joan Morgan	Westminster	12.4.51/ 12.5.51	35
The Hollow	Agatha Christie	Fortune	7.6.51/ 6.10.51	376
		Ambassadors	8.10.51/ 2.5.52	
Come Live With Me	Dorothy and C. Christie	Vaudeville	21.6.51/ 14.7.51	28
Poor Judas	Enid Bagnold	Arts	18.7.51/ 5.8.51	23
The Enchanted Garden	Madge Pemberton	Saville	14.10.51	1
Women of Twilight	Sylvia Rayman	Vaudeville	7.11.51/ 19.4.52	235
		Victoria Palace	18.6.52/ 1.11.52	
The Young Eliza-beth	Jeannette Dowling and F. Letton	Cambridge	9.12.51	1
The Day's Mischief	Lesley Storm	Duke of York's	11.12.51/ 2.2.52	60
Where the Rainbow Ends	Mrs Clifford Mills	Winter Garden	24.12.51/ 10.1.52	31 33
		Princes	20.12.52/ 17.1.53	38
		Stoll	26.12.53/ 16.1.54	
The Same Sky	Yvonne Mitchell	Lyric	31.1.52/ 1.3.52	80
		Duke of York's	18.3.52/ 26.10.52	
To See Ourselves	E.M. Delafield	Arts	26.2.52/ 23.3.52	32
The Young Elizabeth	Jeanette Dowling and F. Letton	New Criterion	2.4.52/ 21.6.52 30.6.52/ 20.6.53	504
The Valley and the Peak	Joan Morgan	Whitehall	6.4.42	1
Monserrat	Lillian Hellman	Lyric	8.4.52/ 10.5.52	38
Lords of Creation	Edward Percy and Lilian Denham	Vaudeville	24.4.52/ 10.5.52	4
After My Fashion	Diana Morgan	Ambassadors	8.5.52/ 9.8.52	107

Play	Author	Theatre	Dates	No. of perfs
1952–1953				
The Step Forward	Anne Trego	Strand	30.7.52/ 6.9.52	48
Two Loves I Have	Dorothy and Howard Bauer	Arts	24.9.52/ 19.10.52	31
Husbands Don't Count	Patricia Hollender	Winter Garden	1.10.52/ 29.11.52	62
Lord Arthurs Saville's Crime	Constance Cox	Court	7.10.52/ 25.10.52	21
Letter From Paris	Dodie Smith	Aldwych	10.10.52/ 1.11.52	27
Murder Mistaken	Janet Green	Ambassadors	4.11.52/ 22.11.52-	156
		Vaudeville	24.11.52/ 28.3.53	
The Blue Lamp	Ted Willis and Jan Read	Hippodrome	19.11.52/ 6.12.52	32
The Mousetrap	Agatha Christie	Ambassadors	2.11.52	15,500 +
Sweet Peril	Mary Orr and Reg Denham	St James'	3.12.52/ 10.1.53	44
The Man	Mel Dinell	Her Majesty's	30.12.52/ 7.2.53	95
		St Martin's	16.2.53/ 28.3.53	
The Gift	Mary Lumsden	St Martin's	22.1.53/ 14.2.53	28
Red-Headed Blond	Val Guest	Vaudeville	1.4.53/ 11.7.53	116
Here We Are	Dorothy Parker	Adelphi	26.4.53	1
They Owe It All to Us	John Hurst and Priscilla Malcolm	Adelphi	26.4.53	1
The Uninvited Guest	Mary Hayley Bell	St James'	27.5.53/ 13.6.53	21
The Man with Expensive Tastes	Ed Percy and Lilian Denham	Vaudeville	23.7.53/ 15.8.53	21
Carrington V C	D. and C. Campbell	Westminster	28.7.53/ 29.8.53	205
Age of Consent	Charlotte Haldane	Princes	22.8.53/ 29.8.53	9
The Secret Tent	Elizabeth Addyman	Strand	4.10.53	1
Witness For the Prosecution	Agatha Christie	Winter Garden	28.10.53/ 29.1.55	458
The Return	Bridget Boland	Duchess	9.11.53/ 16.1.54	29

Play	Author	Theatre	Dates	No. of perfs
1953–1955				
A Christmas Carol	Joan Littlewood	Theatre Royal E15	9.12.53/ 19.12.53	13
			16.12.58/ 17.1.59	45
A London Actress	Emma Litchfield	Arts	16.12.53/ 10.1.54	32
Treasure Island	Joan Littlewood	Theatre Royal E15	26.12.53/ 16.1.54	36
			26.12.56/ 12.1.57	31
Alice Through the Looking Glass	Felicity Douglas	Princes	9.2.54/ 20.3.54	37
The Fifth Season	Sylvia Reagan	Cambridge	24.2.54/ 22.5.54	107
I Capture the Castle	Dodie Smith	Aldwych	4.3.54/ 24.4.54	58
The White Countess	J. B. Priestley and Jacquetta Hawkes	Saville	24.3.54/ 28.3.54	5
The Prisoner	Bridget Boland	Globe	14.4.54/ 5.6.54	60
The Sun Room	Romill Cavan	Arts	29.4.54/ 23.5.54	30
Three Weeks Ahead	Laurie Wylie	Princes	2.5.54	1
Its Never Too Late	Felicity Douglas	Westminster	3.6.54/ 26.6.54	196
		Strand	28.6.54/ 20.11.54	
All For Mary	H. Brooks and Kay Bannerman	Duke of York's	9.9.54/ 11.6.55	312
The Cruel Daughters (Balzac: Le Père Goriot)	Joan Littlewood	Theatre Royal E15	19.10.54/ 6.11.54	19
The Immoralist	Ruth and Augustus Goetz	Arts	3.11.54/ 5.12.54	39
The Chimes (adpt.)	Joan Littlewood	Theatre Royal E15	30.11.45/ 18.12.54	23
Spider's Web	Agatha Christie	Savoy	14.12.54/ 3.1.56	774
The Prince and the Pauper	Joan Littlewood and E. MacColl	Theatre Royal E15	27.12.54/ 15.1.55	32
The Yellow Curtains	Joyce Dennys	Adelphi	9.1.55	1
Its Different for Men	M. Pertwee and Brenda and Monica Danischesky	Duchess	11.4.55/ 14.5.55	40

Play	Author	Theatre	Dates	No. of perfs
1955–1956				
The Lovers	Marcelle Maurette	Winter Garden	6.5.55/ 21.5.55	19
The Mimosa Man	Elizabeth Milne	Strand	9.5.55	1
My Three Angels adpt.	Sam and Bella Spewack	Lyric	12.5.55/ 26.11.55	228
The Lost Generation	Patricia Hollender	Garrick	1.6.55/ 2.7.55	32
Home and Away	Heather McIntyre	Garrick	19.7.55/ 13.8.55	30
The Bandit's Hat	Eve Morganti	Strand	9.10.55	1
The Famous Five	Enid Blyton	Princes	23.12.55/ 21.1.56	26
		Hippodrome	20.12.56/ 19.1.57	36 mat.
Darkling Child	W. S. Merwin and Dido Milroy	Arts	21.7.56/ 19.2.56	29
Doctor Jo	Joan Morgan	Aldwych	15.2.56/ 17.3.56	37
Tabitha	Arnold Ridley and Mary Cathcart	Duchess	8.3.56/ 14.4.56	43
Tolka Row	Maura Laverty	Wyndham's	8.4.56	1
The Chalk Garden	Enid Bagnold	Haymarket	11.4.56/ 9.11.57	658
Day After Tomorrow	Anne Walters	Strand	6.5.65	1
Gigi	Anita Loos	New	23.3.56/ 1.9.56	117
Love Affair	Dulcie Gray	Lyric	1.6.56/ 16.6.56	19
The Long Echo	Leslie Storm	St James'	1.8.56/ 1.9.56	37
The Young and The Beautiful (adp)	Sally Benson	Arts	15.8.56/ 30.11.57	39
Towards Zero	Agatha Christie	St James'	4.9.56/ 2.3.57	205
The Children's Hour	Lillian Hellman	Arts	19.9.56/ 28.10.56	47
Plaintiff in a Pretty Hat	Hugh and Margaret Williams	Duchess	12.10.56/ 15.12.56	311
		St Martin's	18.12.56/ 13.7.57	
Mr Parker – From Paris	Tanya Teronova	Whitehall	21.10.56	1
Cold Water Flat	Nancy Hamilton	Adelphi	28.10.56	1

Play	Author	Theatre	Dates	No. of perfs
1956–1958				
The Touch of Fear	Dorothy and C. Christie	Aldwych	5.12.56/ 16.2.57	84
Never Say Die	Diana Marr Johnson	Strand	13.1.57	1
Light Falling	Teresa Deevey	Lyric	14.1.57/ 16.2.57	40
The Member of the Wedding	Carson McCullers	Court	5.2.57/ 9.3.57	38
Dom Kobiet (The House of Women)	Zofia Nalkowska	Scala	7.6.57	1
Time to Speak	Sylvia Rayman	Arts	11.6.57/ 23.6.57	16
The Waiting of Lester Abbs	Kathleen Sully	Court	30.6.57	1
Roar Like a Dove	Lesley Storm	Phoenix	26.9.57/ 5.3.60	1007
The Queen and the Welshman	Rosemary Anne Sisson	Lyric	7.11.57/ 23.11.59	20
Paddle Your Own Canoe	Lucienne Hill	Criterion	4.12.57/ 29.3.58	132
Be My Guest	Mary Jukes	Winter Garden	11.12.51/ 4.1.58	28
The Happy Man	Hugh and Margaret Williams	Westminster	13.12.57/ 1.2.58	55
Love From Margaret	Evelyn Ford	Court	16.2.58	1
The Sport of My Mad Mother	Ann Jellicoe	Court	25.2.58/ 8.3.58	14
Each His Own Wilderness	Doris Lessing	Court	23.3.58	1
The Quiet Room	Jean Dalrymple	Wyndham's	30.3.58	1
Verdict	Agatha Christie	Strand	22.5.58/ 21.6.58	35
A Taste of Honey	Shelagh Delaney	Theatre Royal E15	27.5.58/ 28.6.58	27
			21.1.59/ 7.2.59	368
		Wyndham's	10.2.59/ 6.6.59	
		Criterion	8.6.59/ 12.12.59	
The Party	Jane Arden	New	28.5.58/ 22.11.58	205
Speaking of Murder	Audrey and William Roos	St Martin's	4.6.58/ 1.11.58	173
Noon Has No Shadows	Patricia Joudry	Arts	18.7.58/ 17.8.58	37

Play	Author	Theatre	Dates	No. of perfs
1958–1959				
Dear Augustine	Alison MacLeod	Court	28.7.58/ 2.8.58	8
The Unexpected Guest	Agatha Christie	Duchess	12.8.58/ 30.1.60	612
The Grass Is Greener	Hugh and Margaret Williams	St Martin's	2.12.58/ 6.2.60	492
Eighty in the shade	Clemence Dane	Globe	8.1.59/ 13.6.59	179
The Hidden River (adpt. from Storm Jameson)	Ruth and Augustus Goetz	Cambridge	13.4.59/ 25.4.59	16
Dark Halo	Sylvia Leigh	Arts	14.4.59/ 10.5.59	32
The Pleasure of his Company	S. Taylor and Cornelia O. Skinner	Haymarket	24.4.59/ 9.4.60	403
Natural Causes	Vera Colebrook	Arts	12.5.59/ 17.5.59	8
Ulysses In Nightown (adpt.)	Marjorie Barkenton	Arts	21.5.59/ 5.7.59	54
Beware of Angels	Audrey E. Lyndor and D. Leslie	Westminster	26.5.59/ 6.7.59	6
Detour After Dark (adpt.)	Lucia Victor	Fortune	8.6.59/ 13.6.59	8
A Raisin In the Sun	Lorraine Hansberry	Adelphi	4.8.59/ 10.10.59	78
Rollo	Felicity Douglas	Strand	27.10.59/ 30.1.60	133
		Duchess	1.2.60/ 20.2.60	
Wear a Green Willow	Casha Hunter	Strand	13.12.59	1

NOTES

1 INTRODUCTION

1 J. Osborne, *Look Back in Anger* (London: Faber, 1957). Jimmy Porter is seen by many to have been the first 'angry young man' and as such heralded a breed of angry young male characters in the late 1950s and early 1960s in British theatre. The play may represent a different class as protagonist, the content is 'new', but the form adheres to that of the well-made play, toward which the author shows little subversive intention.

2 One such publication is A. K. Boyd, *The Interchange of Plays between London and New York, 1910–1939: A Study in Audience Response* (New York: Kings Crown Press, Columbia University, 1948). Boyd's figures do not always correlate with Wearing's for London runs.

3 It is very difficult to gain access to accounts of production costs, lists of backers, profit margins, etc. once theatres become owned by businesses and productions are put on with financial aid from backers for whom the whole process is, it would seem, a gamble. The Theatre Managers Association were unable to provide financial figures for the period under examination.

4 W. A. Darlington, *Daily Telegraph*, 12 August 1971 (from the Obituary of Esther McCracken). Although this quote is taken from a fairly recent article, it was written by a critic who was working at the time when Esther McCracken's plays were taking the West End by storm. The framing of her career as being home based as opposed to professional is typical in terms of the way in which women playwrights of her era were often critically constructed as amateur professionals.

5 Margot Neville, *Heroes Don't Care* (London: French's Acting Edition, 1936). The play was produced at the St Martin's theatre in June 1936, where it ran for 149 performances.

2 WOMEN IN SOCIETY 1918–1962

1 D. Beddoe, *Back to Home and Duty: Women between the Wars, 1918–1939* (London: Pandora Press, 1989), pp. 8–21. The bias of magazines such as *Good Housekeeping* (1922), *Woman and Home* (1926), *Woman's Own* (1932) and *Woman* (1937) was toward informing middle-class women how to manage

their housekeeping efficiently without the aid of domestic help. Beddoe also points out that the glamorous world of female film stars was juxtaposed to magazine articles showing their domestically blissful home lives. Thus the fantasy which fed their imaginations of how life *could* be, was presented in co-ordination with the reality of how life *should* be.

2 E. Showalter, *The Female Malady* (London: Virago, 1987), pp. 167–194. Showalter points to the fact that the phenomenon named as 'shell shock' caused great changes in the direction of psychiatry in Britain because of the symptomatic similarities with hysteria which had hitherto been understood to be a female-specific illness.

3 THE LONDON STAGE 1918–1962

1 The cartel was created in the following manner. The Prince Littler Consolidated Trust Ltd took over the Stoll Theatres Corporation in 1942, and as managing director of Stoll Theatres Corporation, Littler then took over the controlling interest in Associated Theatre Properties (London) Ltd in 1943. In 1945, Moss Empires Ltd appointed Prince Littler and Stewart Cruickshank (already working with Littler) onto their board of directors, at which point the announcement was made that Stoll Theatres Corporation had acquired substantial shares in Moss Empires Ltd. Then, in 1947, Moss Empires announced that it intended to buy eight of the General Theatre Corporation Ltd's theatres. Stewart Cruickshank also had a working relationship with Howard and Wyndham Ltd, as well as a 'substantial interest in the old-established Daniel Mayer Co.' (Sandison 1953: 22). H. M. Tennent and Hugh (Binkie) Beaumont became joint managers in 1933 of a newly formed touring productions company, Moss Empires and Howard & Wyndham. Tennent and Beaumont, who in 1936 formed H. M. Tennent Ltd were, alongside the Group (which consisted of the above-named companies), the main operating forces in terms of production and ownership of the West End theatres.

2 Arthur Miller's *All My Sons* was produced in 1948, transferring to the Globe theatre in the same year and Lillian Hellman's *Montserrat* was produced in 1952. For a full list of the Company of Four productions and those of H. M. Tennent Ltd between 1936 and 1973 see K. Black, *Upper Circle* (London: Methuen, 1984), pp. 231–243.

3 From the 1950 grant of £643,994 only £119,000 was put aside for theatre which, as Findlater points out, was half the amount received by France's drama section, the Comédie Française, and far less than the total grant awarded to Covent Garden. R. Findlater, *The Unholy Trade* (London: Victor Gollancz, 1952), p. 68.

4 This quote is a collation, derived from the first and the fifth annual reports of the society. The second half, according to Dymkowski (1992), reflects the society's interest in producing foreign plays and the work of dramatists 'not engaged with contemporary issues'. However, Craig was as much a theatre producer as a feminist, and I would argue that the difference reflects, more, a shift away from focus on suffrage issues, the fight for which was virtually halted by the war.

NOTES

5 The Three Hundred Club was founded, financed and directed by Mrs Geoffrey Whitworth in 1923 and due to lack of funds amalgamated with the Stage Society in 1926. Marshall's chapter on the Sunday Theatres gives a concise description of a number of these play producing societies. N. Marshall, *The Other Theatre* (London: Lehmann, 1948), pp. 72–85.

6 The AFL was largely a middle- and upper-class organisation, but when Sylvia Pankhurst spread the work of the WSPU into the East End just before the war, the AFL was a useful tool for gathering support. See C. Dymkowski, 'Entertaining ideas', in V. Gardner and S. Rutherford (eds) *The New Woman and Her Sisters* (London: Harvester Wheatsheaf, 1992), pp. 221–233; V. Gardner, *Sketches from the Actresses Franchise League* (Nottingham: University of Nottingham, 1985); C. Hirschfield, 'The Actresses Franchise League and the campaign for women's suffrage', *Theatre Research International* 10 (2) (1985), pp. 129–153; and J. Holledge, *Innocent Flowers* (London: Virago, 1981).

7 There is often a similar approach to the work of the female playwrights of the Restoration, generally seen to represent the first 'flourish' of women and on occasion feminist playwrights, in a history of dramatic texts written by women. Their work has at times been framed as existing on the margins yet, in context, they were in the minority in terms of gender but in terms of theatre they were part of the mainstream, producing plays for the two patented theatres of the day.

8 For example, the *Literary Digest*, carried an article entitled, 'Men fading out of the play', in which the author proposed that the number of plays written by women in production might suggest that the theatre was becoming feminised. *Literary Digest*, 24 December 1932, pp. 114–115.

4 TO WORK OR NOT TO WORK

1 *The Matriarch* was produced in 1929 at the Royalty theatre and ran for 229 performances. The most vehement criticism of the *Man Who Pays the Piper* was that the play contained far too much conversation, and the implication is that the subject matter held less interest for the reviewer in question than the physical attributes of the leading actress:

> She had built a dressmaker's business. Then she got married, and after a lot more yap, ventured to remark that the war had ruined women's careers as well as those of men.... This idea should have made a good play.... After the first act, however, I lost complete interest – that is until Diana Wynyard came on and looked beautiful.
>
> (*Daily Express*, 11 February 1931)

2 Spark continues to use Leonora as a device whereby the audience is asked to accept the reality of their own position as *audience*. Leonora makes reference to being watched, and to feeling that she has an audience. At one point the characters are placed in chairs directly in front of the audience, relating to them directly, through the 'invisible fourth wall', thus breaking the traditional realist/naturalist convention of actor/audience relationship. Spark also has Charlie Brown, an outsider to the family unit, moving stage scenery and adjusting working pulleys, during the action of Act Two, Scene One, thus

breaking away from a tradition of realism, subverting the 'invisibility' of the mechanics of staging.

3   *Our Ostriches*, originally ran at the Court theatre for ninety-one performances, and *Buckie's Bear*, a play for children which she wrote under the name of Erica Fay, ran in 1932, 1935 and 1936, during the Christmas season; each run was of between twenty-four and thirty-eight performances. *Vectia*, a play about marital relationships and sexual desires, was banned in 1926 and so, although published, was not performed in front of a public audience.

4   Unpublished letter from Martha Gellhorn to the author, April 1994. The play was originally produced at the Embassy in June 1946, and later transferred to the Duchess where it ran for forty performances.

5   *Her Shop* ran at the Criterion for ninety-nine performances in 1929. The two businessmen are reversed comic stereotypes of 'good' businessmen, Mr Jacob is a 'Lowland Scot', and Mr McDonald 'A Jew'.

6   Letter from Constance Smedley, Lyceum Club W., to the editor of the *Sunday Times*, 2 March 1930.

7   Both Jane Lewis and Deidre Beddoe stress that although the Central Committee for Women's Employment was set up during the First World War, with the aim of providing re-training grants for various types of low-grade work, by 1921 most of its funds were tied up in domestic service re-training projects. 'Domestic service' was the only job for which a re-training scheme was offered to unemployed women during the inter-war period. (See D. Beddoe, *Back to Home and Duty: Women Between the Wars, 1918-1939* (London: Pandora Press, 1989), and J. Lewis, *Women in England 1870-1950*, (London: Wheatsheaf Books, 1984).)

5 MOTHERHOOD AND THE FAMILY

1   See E. A. Kaplan, *Motherhood and Representation* (London: Routledge, 1993), and Marianne Hirsch, *The Mother/Daughter Plot* (Bloomington and Indianapolis: Indiana University Press, 1989). Both authors give precise information about and analysis of the social and psychoanalytic theories which affected the practice or at least the prescribed practice of mothering in America and Britain over the past 150 years. In terms of cultural / artistic output, the novel and the film are used to show narrative parallels and subversions of the new prescriptions for the role of 'mother'.

2   J. Lewis, *Women in England 1870-1950* (London: Wheatsheaf Books, 1984). Lewis points out that acts such as the Anomalies Act (1931) aligned marriage with 'retirement' from the public workforce, as it assumed that the male partner would support the wife after marriage, therefore there was no 'need' (defined in economic terms only) for the woman to work.

3   Working-class women were also encouraged and, in some cases, given no choice but to give up their work as part of the 'public' workforce and return into domestic service, i.e. into the private service industries. This was particularly the case after the First World War and to an extent the Second World War. (See D. Beddoe, *Back to Home and Duty* (London: Pandora Press, 1989), and E. Wilson, *Only Half Way to Paradise* (London: Tavistock, 1980).)

4 Before this point melodrama had been seen as a form somewhere between comedy and tragedy characterised by its supposed innate appeal to a female audience. As such it was scorned because of its popularity and seen as a largely inferior category of dramatic textual form.

5 Kaplan gives a very clear, more contemporary analysis and comparison of theories on motherhood. She cites Parveen Adams as pointing out the fault in essentialist theories such as those of Chodorow, as being caused by a confusing of the social and the psychic. Her main criticism of Chodorow is that the image of the 'good' mother is too close to the essentially patriarchal image proposed by D. W. Winnicott. See M. Hirsch, 'Review: mothers and daughters', *Signs: Journal of Women and Culture* 7 (1) (1981), pp. 200-222 (p. 207); N. Chodorow, *The Reproduction of Mothering: Psychoanalysis and the Sociology of Gender* (California: University of California Press, 1978); and D. Dinnerstein, *The Mermaid and the Minotaur: Sexual Arrangements and the Human Malaise* (New York: Harper & Row, 1976), used by Hirsch as an example of work on mother–daughter relationships and on the woman as 'other'.

6 Deutsch had been in analysis with one of Freud's former colleagues and founders of the Viennese Psychoanalytic Society, Karl Abraham. (See H. Deutsch, 'Motherhood and sexuality', in P. Lee and R. Stewart (eds) *Sex Differences: Cultural and Developmental Dimensions* (New York: Urizen Books, 1976), pp. 91-104 (p. 92).

7 Stern was on the payroll of Metro Goldwyn Mayer British Pictures, London, along with Evelyn Waugh, Graham Greene and Richard Dimbleby, for a short time from the early 1940s until 1946.

8 G. Jennings, *Family Affairs*, in *Famous Plays of 1934* (London: Gollancz, 1934). The play opened at the Ambassadors theatre in August 1934, and ran for a total of 331 performances D. Smith, *Dear Octopus*, in *Plays of the Thirties, Vol. 1* (London: Pan, 1966). The play opened at the Queen's theatre in September 1938 and ran for 376 performances. Co-produced by Glen Byam Shaw and Dodie Smith, the production starred Marie Tempest as Dora Randolph and John Gielgud as her son Nicholas.

9 E. Lamont Stewart, *Men Should Weep* (Scotland: 7:84 Publications, 1983). The play was written for Glasgow Unity in 1947 and centres on Maggie Morrison's life as mother of an extended family living in Glasgow during the depression of the 1930s.

6 DRAMATISING HISTORY

1 See J. C. Trewin, *The Turbulent Thirties* (London: Macdonald, 1960). Trewin points out that of the playwrights who had established themselves by the mid-1920s 'only Shaw, Coward and Clemence Dane' kept going through the 1930s' (p. 19).

2 F. Morgan (ed.) *The Years Between: Plays by Women on the London Stage 1900-1950* (London: Virago, 1994). Morgan suggests one of the possible factors which kept audiences away, and therefore why the play had only a ten-week run, was because the opening coincided with the famous influenza epidemic which swept Europe after the First World War. (Other sources cite the epidemic as having effect more immediately after the war, in 1919.) It seems

appropriate to note here that the play was expensive to produce and as audience figures were slow to build, the production was losing money each time it was performed. In fact the audience figures built and the production, which was initially rumoured to be closing after only a week or so, was continued. Low attendance may have had much to do with the fact that reviews were very mixed and as the play was written in verse it would not have attracted the same audiences which made her play *Bill of Divorcement* such a success earlier in the same year.

3 *The Laughing Woman* opened at the New theatre in April 1934 and ran for forty-one performances. The plot borrows very heavily from H. S. Ede, *Savage Messiah* (London: Abacus, 1972).

4 *Alison's House* was produced at the Little theatre in October 1932 and ran for twenty-three performances. Few of her plays had long West End runs and even though a number of critics rated her work alongside that of Eugene O'Neill, in terms of merit, the fact that she was often considered 'highbrow' worked against her in terms of the commercial theatre. She was, however, popular with smaller arts theatres and semi-professional groups, being seen as an experimental writer who could 'say in one act what a lesser playwright could not say in three' (*Daily Express*, 30 June 1932).

5 Produced at the Ambassadors theatre in July 1931, the play ran for only four performances. Critics were unanimous in their animosity toward the fact that the play was an adaptation of an already successful novel, and therefore did not make 'good theatre'.

6 M. Box, *Angels of War*, in *Five New Full Length Plays for All-Women Casts* (London: Lovat Dickson & Thompson, 1935). I have been unable to find any records of a professional performance of this play in the West End although this does not necessarily mean that it was not performed by a professional or semi-professional company.

7 R. Gilder, 'Rainbow over Broadway,' *Theatre Arts*, March 1947, p. 18. Quote taken from editorial afterword of M. Gellhorn and V. Cowles, *Love Goes to Press*, ed. by S. Spanier (Lincoln and London: University of Nebraska Press, 1995). In London, the play opened at the Embassy in June 1946 with a West End run at the Duchess for forty performances from July 1946.

8 Ibid., p. 157. Sandra Spanier, in her editorial postscript, also likens the play to a prototype for *Thelma and Louise*, as a kind of wartime ' "new women's" road/ buddy play'.

7 SPINSTERS AND WIDOWS

1 E. Baker, *Miss Robinson* (London: Sidgwick & Jackson, 1920). The play was first produced at the Birmingham Repertory theatre in November 1918. Dorothy Massingham played the role of Angela Robinson.

2 This is certainly the case in an earlier play by Elizabeth Baker, *Chains*, in *Plays of To-Day: Vol. 1* (London, Sidgwick & Jackson, 1911), first performed at the Court theatre in London, in 1909. Here Maggie refuses to marry a man she doesn't love. For Maggie, the financial security of marriage is no substitute for the search for 'a better life', outside the claustrophobic environment of a middle-class marriage.

3 L. Hellman, *The Children's Hour*, in *The Collected Plays* (London: Macmillan, 1971). The play was banned by the Lord Chamberlain on the grounds of the way in which a child's imaginings around lesbianism were portrayed. The play was, however, performed to great acclaim at the Gate, under the direction of Norman Marshall in 1936.

4 The play was given three performances at the Phoenix, by the London Repertory Players. After the first performance cuts and changes had to be made in the text because of the censorship imposed by the Lord Chamberlain's office.

5 E. Bagnold, *Lottie Dundass* (London: French, 1944). The play was directed by Irene Hentschel and produced in London, at the Vaudeville, in July 1942, transferring to the Cambridge in October of the same year. *Lottie Dundass* ran for 147 performances; Mrs Dundass was played by Sybil Thorndike, and Ann Todd played Lottie.

6 A. Stuart, *Jeannie* (London: Hamilton, 1940). Originally produced under George Cooper and directed by Irene Hentschel at the Torch theatre in February 1940, the play transferred to the Wyndham's theatre in April where it ran for 100 performances.

BIBLIOGRAPHY

Agate, J. (1926) *A Short View of the English Stage*, London: Jenkins.
Albanesi, Mrs (1924) *Meggie Albanesi by her Mother*, London: Hodder & Stoughton.
Alberti, J. (1989) *Beyond Suffrage*, London: Macmillan.
Andrews, J. and Trilling, O. (eds) (1958) *Dobson's Theatre Yearbook 1948/9*, London: Dobson.
Anthony, M. (1990) *The Valkyries: The Women Around Jung*, London: Element Books.
Appignanesi, L. and Forrester, J. (1993) *Freud's Women*, London: Virago.
Arden, J. (1958) *The Party*, London: French.
Aston, E. (1995) *An Introduction to Feminism and Theatre*, London: Routledge.
Austin, G. (1990) *Feminist Theories for Dramatic Criticism*, Ann Arbor: University of Michigan Press.
Bagnold, E. (1970) *Four Plays*, London: Heinemann.
—— (1956) *The Chalk Garden*, London: Heinemann.
—— (1946) *National Velvet*, London: Sampson Low & Marston.
—— (1944) *Lottie Dundass*, London: French.
Baker, E. (1927) *Edith*, London: Sidgwick & Jackson.
—— (1921) *Partnership*, London: Samuel French.
—— (1920) *Miss Robinson*, London: Sidgwick & Jackson.
—— (1913) *The Price of Thomas Scott*, London: Sidgwick & Jackson.
—— (1911a) *Chains* in *Plays of Today: First Volume*, London: Sidgwick & Jackson.
—— (1911b) *Miss Tassey*, London: Sidgwick & Jackson.
Barlow, J. (ed) (1994) *Plays by American Women 1930–1960*, New York: Applause Books.
—— (1985) *Plays by American Women 1900–1930*, New York: Applause Books.
Barrie, J. (1925) *Mary Rose*, London: Hodder & Stoughton.
Bassnett, S. (1989) 'Struggling with the past: women's theatre in search of a history', *New Theatre Quarterly* V: 107–112.
Bassnett-McGuire, S. (1984) 'Towards a theory of women's theatre', in H. Schmidt and A. Van Kesteren (eds) *Semiotics of Drama and Theatre*, Amsterdam: Benjamins Co.
Battersby, C. (1989) *Gender and Genius: Towards a Feminist Aesthetics*, London: The Women's Press.
Baxter, B. (1949) *First Nights and Noises Off*, London: Hutchinson.

BIBLIOGRAPHY

Beauman, N. (1983) *A Very Great Profession: The Woman's Novel 1914–1939*, London: Virago.

Beauvoir, S. de (1969) *The Second Sex*, London: Cape.

Beddoe, D. (1989) *Back to Home and Duty: Women between the Wars, 1918–1939*, London: Pandora Press.

Bell, M. H. (1947) *Duet for Two Hands*, London: French.

—— (1943) *Men in Shadow*, London: French.

Ben-Zvi, L. (ed.) (1995) *Susan Glaspell: Essays on her Theater and Fiction*, Ann Arbor: University of Michigan Press.

Bessier, R. (1931) *The Barretts of Wimpole Street*, London: Gollancz.

Black, K. (1984) *Upper Circle*, London: Methuen.

Bloch, I. (1938) *Sexual Life in England Past and Present*, London: Aldor.

Boland, B. (1954a) *The Prisoner*, London, Elek.

—— (1954b) *The Return*, London: French.

—— (1949) *The Cockpit*, in *Plays of the Year 1948–1949*, London: Elek.

Boothe-Luce, C. (1940) *Margin for Error*, London: Hamish Hamilton.

—— (1937) *The Women*, in *Famous Plays of 1937*, London: Gollancz.

Box, M. (1935) *Angels of War*, in *Five New Full Length Plays for All-Women Casts*, London: Lovat Dickson & Thompson.

Boyd, A. K. (1948) *The Interchange of Plays between London and New York, 1910–1939: A Study in Audience Response*, New York: Kings Crown Press, Columbia University.

Braithwaite, B. and Walsh, N. (1992) *Home Sweet Home: The Best of Good Housekeeping: 1922–1939*, London: Ebury Press.

Branson, N. (1975) *Britain in the Nineteen Twenties*, London: Weidenfeld & Nicolson.

Branson, N. and Heinemann, M. (1971) *Britain in the Nineteen Thirties*, London: Weidenfeld & Nicolson.

Brater, E. (ed.) (1989) *Feminine Focus*, New York and Oxford: Oxford University Press.

Brittain, V. (1953) *Lady into Woman*, London: Dakers.

—— (1940) *Testament of Friendship*, London: Macmillan.

Brock, A. (1990) 'This Very Old Fair Lady: The Last Years of Mrs Patrick Campbell', *New Theatre Quarterly* 6 (21): 57–63.

Broe, M. (1981) 'Bohemia bumps into Calvin: the deception of passivity in Lillian Hellman's drama', *Southern Quarterly* 19: 24–41.

Brooks, P. (1976) *The Melodramatic Imagination*, New Haven: Yale University Press.

Carey, J. (1992) *The Intellectuals and the Masses*, London: Faber & Faber.

Case, S. E. (1988) *Feminism and Theatre*, London: Macmillan.

—— (ed.) (1990) *Performing Feminisms*, Baltimore and London: Johns Hopkins University Press.

—— (1991) 'The power of sex: English plays by women 1958–1988', *New Theatre Quarterly* 8 (27): 238–245.

Chambers, C. (1989) *The Story of Unity Theatre*, London: Lawrence & Wishart.

Chinoy, H. K. (1983) 'The poetics of politics: some notes on style and craft in the theatre of the thirties', *Theatre Journal* December: 475–498.

Chinoy, H. K. and Jenkins, L. W. (eds) (1981) *Women in American Theatre*, New York: Theatre Communications Group.

Chodorow, N. (1978) *The Reproduction of Mothering: Psychoanalysis and the Sociology of Gender*, California: University of California Press.

Christie, A. (1934) *Black Coffee*, London: French.

246

Christie, D. and Campbell, C. (1936) *Someone at the Door*, London: French.

Clark, J. Heinemann, M. et al. (1970) *Culture and Crisis in Britain in the 1930s*, London: Lawrence & Wishart.

Cochran, C. B. (1946) *The Showman Looks On*, London: Dent.

Coffee, L. (1940) *Family Portrait*, New York: French.

Colenbrander, J. (1984) *A Portrait of Fryn: A Biography of Fryn Tennyson-Jesse*, London: Deutsch.

Collier, C. (1929) *Harlequinade*, London: Allen Lane & The Bodley Head.

Compton, J. (ed.) (1927) *The Curtain Rises*, London: Methuen.

Cotes, P. (1949) *No Star Nonsense*, London: The Burleigh Press.

Coward, N. (1986) *Autobiography*, London: Methuen.

—— (1940) *Present Indicative*, London: Heinemann.

Coward, R. (1981) *Female Desire*, London: Paladin.

Curb, R. (1985) 'Re/cognition, Re/presentation, Re/creation in woman-conscious drama: the Seer, the Seen, the Scene, the Obscene', *Theatre Journal* 37 (3): 302–316.

Dane, C. (1961a) *Approaches to Drama*, London: The English Association Presidential Address.

—— (1961b) *Bill of Divorcement*, in *The Collected Plays of Clemence Dane*, London: Heinemann.

—— (1961c) *Wild Decembers*, in *The Collected Plays of Clemence Dane*, London: Heinemann.

—— (1961d) *Will Shakespeare*, in *Recapture: A Clemence Dane Omnibus*, London: Heinemann.

—— (1959) *Eighty in the Shade*, London: French.

—— (1947) *Call Home the Heart*, London: Heinemann.

—— (1940) *Cousin Muriel*, London: Heinemann.

—— (1938) *Come of Age*, London: Heinemann.

—— (1934) *Moonlight is Silver*, London: Heinemann.

—— (1932) *Granite*, in *Recapture: A Clemence Dane Omnibus*, London: Heinemann.

—— (1928) *Adams Opera*, London: Heinemann.

—— (1926) *The Women's Side*, London: Jenkins.

Davies, A. (1987) *Other Theatres*, London: Macmillan.

Davis, T. C. (1989) 'Questions for a feminist methodology in theatre history', in T. Postlewait and B. McConachie (eds) *Interpreting the Theatrical Past*, Iowa: University of Iowa Press: 55–81.

Daviot, G. (1966) *Richard of Bordeaux*, in *Plays of the Thirties*, London: Pan.

—— (1935) *The Laughing Woman*, in *Famous Plays of 1934–1935*, London: Gollancz.

—— (1934) *Queen of Scots*, in *Famous Plays of 1934*, London: Gollancz.

Dean, B. (1956) *The Theatre at War*, London: Harrap.

Delafield, E. M. (1933) *The Glass Wall*, London: Gollancz.

—— (1930) *To See Ourselves*, London: Gollancz.

Delaney, S. (1989) *A Taste of Honey*, London: Methuen.

—— (1977) *The Lion in Love*, London: Methuen.

Dellar, P. (1989) *Plays Without Theatres*, London: Highgate Publications Beverly Ltd.

Deutsch, H. (1976) 'Motherhood and sexuality', in P. Lee and R. Stewart (eds) *Sex Differences: Cultural and Developmental Dimensions*, New York: Urizen Books: 91–104.

Dickinson, T. (1917) *The Contemporary Drama of England*, Boston: Little Brown.

Diner, S. J. (1978) 'George Herbert Mead's ideas on women and career: a letter to his daughter-in-law, 1920', *Signs: Journal of Women and Culture and Society* 4 (21).

Dinnerstein, D. (1976) *The Mermaid and The Minotaur: Sexual Arrangements and the Human Malaise*, New York: Harper & Row.

Donkin, E. (1995) *Getting into the Act: Women Playwrights in London 1776–1829*, London: Routledge.

Drinkwater, J. (1922) *Abraham Lincoln*, London: Sidgwick & Jackson.

Duff, C. (1995) *The Lost Summer: The Heyday of the West End Theatre*, London: Nick Hern Books.

Duffy, M. (1988) *Change*, London: Methuen.

Du Maurier, D. (1994) *The Years Between*, in F. Morgan (ed.) *The Years Between: Plays by Women on the London Stage 1900–1950*, London: Virago.

Dymkowski, C. (1992) *Entertaining Ideas*, in V. Gardner and S. Rutherford (eds) *The New Woman and her Sisters*, London: Harvester Wheatsheaf: 221–233.

Ede, H. S. (1972) *Savage Messiah*, London: Abacus.

Ehrenreich, B. and English, D. (1988) *For Her Own Good*, London: Pluto Press.

Ellis, H. (1932) *Views and Reviews*, London: Harmsworth.

Elsom, J. (1976) *Post-War British Theatre*, London: Routledge & Kegan Paul.

—— (1971) *Theatre Outside London*, London: Macmillan.

Ervine, St J. (1924) *The Organised Theatre*, London: Unwin Bros.

Evreinoff, N. (1927) *The Theatre in Life*, New York: Brentano's.

Farrell, M. J. (1951) *Treasure Hunt*, London: French.

—— (1938) *Spring Meeting*, London: Collins.

Féral, J. (1984) 'Writing and displacement: women in theatre', *Modern Drama* 27: 549–563.

Ferber, E. (1939) *A Peculiar Treasure*, London: Heinemann.

Ferber, E. and Kaufman, G. (1937) *Stage Door*, London: Heinemann.

—— (1936) *Theatre Royal*, London: French.

Ferris, L. (1990) *Acting Women*, London: Macmillan.

Findlater, R. (1967) *Banned*, London: MacGibbon & Kee.

—— (1952) *The Unholy Trade*, London: Gollancz.

Francke, L. (1994) *Script Girls: Women Screenwriters in Hollywood*, London: British Film Institute.

Franken, R. (1948) *The Hallams*, New York: French.

—— (1945) *Claudia*, New York: French.

—— (1943) *Outrageous Fortune*, New York: French.

—— (1933) *Another Language*, London: Rich & Cowan.

Freud, S. (1977) *On Sexuality: Three Essays on the Theory of Sexuality and Other Works*, London: The Penguin Freud Library.

—— (1937) 'The psychology of women', in E. Jones (ed.) *New Introductory Lectures on Psychoanalysis*, London: Hogarth Press.

Friedlander, J. (1986) *Women in Culture and Politics*, Indiana: Indiana University Press.

Frosh, S. (1987) *The Politics of Psychoanalysis*, London: Macmillan.

Fulford, R. (1958) *Votes for Women: The Story of a Struggle*, London: Faber.

Gainor, J. E. (1989) 'A stage of her own: Susan Glaspell's *The Verge* and women's dramaturgy', *Journal of American Drama and Theatre* Spring: 79–99.

BIBLIOGRAPHY

Gale, M. (1995) 'Women playwrights on the London Stage 1918–1968', in E. Woodrough (ed.) *Women in European Theatre*, England: Intellect.

—— (1994) 'A need for reappraisal: women playwrights on the London stage 1918–1958', *Women: A Cultural Review* 5 (2), Oxford: Oxford University Press: 175–184.

Gale, M. and Bassnett, S. (eds) (1994) *Women and Theatre Occasional Papers 2*, Birmingham: University of Birmingham.

Gardner, V. (1985) *Sketches from the Actresses Franchise League*, Nottingham: University of Nottingham.

Garrison, D. (1981) 'Karen Horney and feminism', *Signs: Journal of Women and Culture* 6 (4): 627–691.

Gellhorn, M. and Cowles, V. (1995) *Love Goes to Press*, ed. by S. Spanier, Lincoln, USA and London: University of Nebraska Press.

Glaspell, S. (1987) *The Verge*, in C. W. E. Bigsby (ed.) *Plays By Susan Glaspell*, Cambridge: Cambridge University Press.

—— (1930) *Alison's House*, in *Six Plays*, London: Gollancz.

—— (1924) *Bernice*, London: Benn.

Gledhill, C. (ed.) (1987) *Home is where the Heart is*, London: BFI Publishing

Glucksman, M. (1986) 'In a class of their own? Women workers in the new industries in inter-war Britain', *Feminist Review* 24: 7–37.

Godfrey, P. (1933) *Back Stage*, London: Harrap.

Goldberg, I. (1926) *Havelock Ellis: A Biographical and Critical Survey*, London: Constable.

—— (1922) *The Drama of Transition: Native and Exotic Playcraft*, Cincinatti: Stewart Kidd.

Gooddie, S. (1990) *Annie Horniman: A Pioneer in the Theatre*, London: Methuen.

Goodlad, J. S. R. (1971) *A Sociology of Popular Drama*, London: Heinemann.

Goodman, L. (1993) *Contemporary Feminist Theatres*, London: Routledge.

Gould, A. and Russell, E. (1937) *Retreat from Folly*, London: Deane & Sons.

Gregory, A. (1972) *Our Irish Theatre: A Chapter of Autobiography by Lady Gregory*, London: Colin Smythe.

Griffin, G. and Aston, E. (eds) (1991) *Herstory: Vol. 1*, Sheffield: Sheffield Academic Press.

Griffiths, T. R. and Llewellyn-Jones, M. (eds) (1993) *British and Irish Women Dramatists since 1958*, London: Open University Press.

Grimwood, W. (1950) *A Woman's Place*, London: French.

Grosskirth, P. (1980) *Havelock Ellis*, London: Allen Lane.

Grove, V. (1996) *Dear Dodie: The Life of Dodie Smith*, London: Chatto & Windus.

Guthrie, T. (1987) *A Life in the Theatre*, London: Columbus Books.

Gysegham, A. Van (1970) *British Theatre in the Thirties: An Autobiographical Record*, ed. by J. Clark et al., London: Lawrence & Wishart.

Hall, S. (1981) 'Beyond naturalism pure', in C. Marowitz et al. (eds) *New Theatre Voices of the Fifties and Sixties*, London: Methuen: 212–220.

Hamilton, C. (1926) *The Old Vic*, London: Cape.

—— (1925) *Diana of Dobsons*, London: French.

Hanscombe, G. and Smyers, V. (1987) *Writing for their Lives*, London: The Women's Press.

Hart, L. (ed.) (1989) *Making a Spectacle*, Ann Arbor: University of Michigan Press.

Hartley, J. (ed.) (1995) *Hearts Undefeated: Women's Writing of the Second World War,* London: Virago.

Haskell, M. (1987) *From Reverence to Rape,* Chicago: University of Chicago Press.

Hastings, C. (1955) *Uncertain Joy,* London: French.

Hellman, L. (1974) *Pentimento,* London: Macmillan.

—— (1971) *The Children's Hour,* in *The Collected Plays,* London: Macmillan.

—— (1961) *Toys in the Attic,* New York: French.

—— (1939) *The Little Foxes,* London: Hamilton.

Hirsch, M. (1989) *The Mother/Daughter Plot,* Indiana: Indiana University Press.

—— (1981) 'Review: mothers and daughters', *Signs: Journal of Women and Culture* 7 (1): 200–222.

Hirschfield, C. (1985) 'The Actresses Franchise League and the campaign for women's suffrage', *Theatre Research International* 10 (2): 129–153.

Holledge, J. (1981) *Innocent Flowers,* London: Virago.

Holtby, W. (1934) *Women in a Changing Civilisation,* London: Allen Lane & The Bodley Head.

Honey, M. (1976) 'Images of women in the *Saturday Evening Post*: 1931- 1936', *Journal of Popular Culture* 3: 352–358.

Horney, K. (1967a) 'Maternal conflicts', in H. Kelman (ed.) *Feminine Psychology,* London and New York: Norton.

—— (1967b) 'On the genesis of the castration complex in women', in H. Kelman (ed.) *Feminine Psychology,* London and New York: Norton.

—— (1967c) 'The flight from womanhood', in H. Kelman (ed.) *Feminine Psychology,* London and New York: Norton.

Howard, R. (1985) ' "The dramatic sense of life": theatre and historical simulation', *New Theatre Quarterly* 1 (3).

Hudson, L. (1946) *The Twentieth Century Drama,* London: Harrap.

Hughs, C. (1941) 'Women playmakers', *New York Times Magazine,* 4 May.

Humphries, S. and Gordon, P. (1994) *Forbidden Britain: Our Secret Past 1900–1960,* London: BBC Books.

Hutchison, R. (1982) *The Politics of the Arts Council,* London: Sinclair Browne.

Ingram, D. H. (ed) (1991) *Karen Horney: Final Lectures,* New York and London: Norton.

Jacobus, M. (1979) *Women Writing and Writing about Women,* New York and London: Harper & Row.

Jameson, S. (1928) *Full Circle,* Oxford: Blackwell.

—— (1920) *Modern Drama in Europe,* London: Collins.

Janssen-Jurret, M. (1982) *Sexism, the Male Monopoly on History and Thought,* London: Pluto Press.

Jeffreys, S. (1985) *The Spinster and her Enemies: Feminism and Sexuality 1880–1930,* London: Pandora Press.

Jellicoe, A. (1985) *The Knack and The Sport of my Mad Mother,* London: Faber.

—— (1973) *The Rising Generation,* London: Hutchinson.

—— (1967) *Some Unconscious Influences in the Theatre,* Cambridge: Cambridge University Press.

Jenkins, L. W. (1984) 'Locating the language of gender', *Women and Performance Journal* 2 (1): 5–20.

Jennings, G. (1985) 'A woman's influence', in D. Spender and C. Hayman (eds) *How the Vote was Won,* London: Methuen.

—— (1934) *Family Affairs*, in *Famous Plays of 1934*, London: Gollancz.

—— 1930) *These Pretty Things*, London: French.

—— (1921) *Me and my Diary*, London: French.

Jerome, H. (1937) *Charlotte Corday*, in *Five Plays of 1937*, London: Hamish Hamilton.

Joannu, M. (1995) *'Ladies Please Don't Smash These Windows'*, Oxford: Berg.

John, G. (1923) *The Prince*, London: British Drama League.

—— (1925) *Luck of War*, London: Benn.

Jung, C. G. (1989) *Aspects of the Feminine*, London: Ark.

Kaplan, E. A. (1992) *Motherhood and Representation: The Mother in Popular Culture and Melodrama*, London: Routledge.

Kennedy, M. (1934) *Escape Me Never*, London: Heinemann.

—— (1930) *The Constant Nymph*, London: French.

Kennedy, M. and Ratoff, G. (1939) *Autumn*, in S. Box (ed.) *Five Plays of our Time*, London: Thomas Nelson.

Keown, E. (1955) *Peggy Ashcroft*, London and New York: Rockliff.

Keyssar, H. (1984) *Feminist Theatre*, London: Macmillan.

Klein, V. (1983) *The Feminine Character*, London: Routledge.

Komarovsky, M. (1946) 'Cultural contradictions and sex roles', *American Journal of Sociology* November: 184–189.

Komisarjevsky, T. (1935) *The Theatre*, London: Allen Lane & The Bodley Head.

Kristeva, J. (1982) *Powers of Horror: An Essay in Abjection*, Columbia: Columbia University Press.

Kruger, L. (1990) 'The dis-play's the thing: gender and public sphere in contemporary British theatre', *Theatre Journal* 42: 27–47.

Lacey, S. (1995) *British Realist Theatre: The New Wave in its Context 1956–1965*, London: Routledge.

Lamont Stewart, E. (1983) *Men Should Weep*, Scotland: 7:84 Publications.

Laye, E. (1958) *Boo to my Friends*, London: Hirst & Blackett.

Lehmann, R. (1939) *No More Music*, London: Collins.

Lessing, D. (1962a) *The Golden Notebook*, London: Michael Joseph.

—— (1962b) *Play with a Tiger*, London: Michael Joseph.

—— (1959) *Each his own Wilderness*, in *New English Dramatists*, London: Penguin Plays.

Lewis, J. (1984) *Women in England 1870–1950*, London: Wheatsheaf Books.

Light, A. (1991) *Forever England: Femininity, Literature and Conservatism Between the Wars*, London: Routledge.

Llewellyn-Jones, M. (1994) 'A third wave? Women's writing into the 1990s', *New Playwrights Trust Newsletter*, London: New Playwrights Trust: 3–7.

London Feminist History Group (1982) *The Sexual Dynamics of History*, London: Pluto Press.

McConachie, B. (1985) 'Towards a post-positivist theatre history', *Theatre Journal* 37 (1): 455–486.

McCracken, E. (1947) *No Medals*, London: French.

—— (1945) *Quiet Weekend*, London: French.

—— (1938) *Quiet Wedding*, London: Hamilton.

Mais, S. P. B. (1933) *Some Modern Authors*, London: Grant & Richards.

Mander, R. and Mitchenson, J. (1962) *The Theatres of London*, London: New English Library.

BIBLIOGRAPHY

Marks, E. and Courtivron, I. de (eds) (1981) *New French Feminisms*, Brighton: Harvester.

Marowitz, C. et al. (eds) (1981) *New Theatre Voices of the Fifties and Sixties*, London: Methuen.

Marshall, N. (1948) *The Other Theatre*, London: Lehmann.

Massingham, D. (1933) *The Lake*, London: Rich & Cowan.

Mead, M. (1962) *Male and Female*, London: Pelican.

Melville, J. (1987) *Ellen and Edy*, London: Pandora Press.

Merkin, R. (1992) 'Mrs Smith of Wigan: women and the ILP Art's Guild', in M. Gale and S. Bassnett (eds) *Women and Theatre Occasional Papers 1: Practitioners Past and Present*, Warwick: University of Warwick: 119–126.

Miles, B. (1958) *The British Theatre*, London: Collins.

Miller, J. (1974) *Psychoanalysis and Women*, London: Pelican.

Millet, F. (1935) *Contemporary British Literature*, London: Harrap.

Mitchell, J. (1983) *Psychoanalysis and Feminism*, London: Pelican.

Mitchell, Y. (1951) *The Same Sky*, in J. C. Trewin (ed.) *Plays of the Year Vol 6*, London: Elek.

Mitchison, N. (1934) *The Home, and a Changing Civilisation*, London: Allen Lane & The Bodley Head.

Modleski, T. (1990) *Loving with a Vengeance*, London: Routledge.

Morgan, C. (1938) *The Flashing Stream*, London: Macmillan.

Morgan, D. (1979) *My Cousin Rachel*, London: French.

—— (1940) *A House in the Square*, London: French.

Morgan, F. (ed) (1994) *The Years Between: Plays by Women on the London Stage 1900–1950*, London: Virago.

Morgan, J. (1960) *Square Dance*, London: French.

—— (1946) *This was a Woman*, London: Fortune Press.

Mowat, C. L. (1984) *Britain Between the Wars*, London: Methuen.

Myrdal, A. and Klein, V. (1956) *Women's Two Roles: Home and Work*, London: Routledge & Kegan Paul.

Nathan, G. (1941) 'Playwrights in petticoats', *American Mercury*, 52: 750–755.

Neville, M. (1936) *Heroes Don't Care*, London: French.

Nicholson, M. (1995) *What Did You Do in The War, Mummy?*, London: Chatto & Windus.

Nochlin, L. (1994) *Women, Art, and Power and Other Essays*, London: Thames & Hudson.

O'Brien, K. (1926) *Distinguished Villa*, London: Benn.

O'Casey, S. (1971) *The Flying Wasp*, New York: Blom.

Olauson, J. (1981) *The American Woman Playwright: A View of Criticism and Characterisation*, Troy, New York: Whitson Publishing Company.

Osborne, J. (1957) *Look Back in Anger*, London: Faber.

Ouditt, S. (1994) *Fighting Forces, Writing Women: Identity and Ideology in the First World War*, London: Routledge.

Paglia, C. (1992) *Sexual Personae: Art and Decadence from Nefertiti to Emily Dickinson*, London: Penguin.

Pasquier, M. C. (1986) 'Women in the theatre of men: what price freedom?', in J. Friedlander (ed.) *Women in Culture and Politics*, Indiana: Indiana University Press: 194–206.

Pellizzi, C. (1935) *English Drama; The Last Great Phase*, London: Macmillan.

BIBLIOGRAPHY

Pick, J. (1983) *West End Management and Snobbery*, London: Offord Publications.

Pick, J. (ed) (1980) *The State and the Arts*, London: Offord Publications.

Pogson, R. (1952) *Miss Horniman and the Gaiety Theatre Manchester*, London: Rockliff.

Postlewait, T. (1988) 'The criteria for periodisation in theatre history', *Theatre Journal* 40 (3): 299–320.

Postlewait, T. and McConachie, B. (eds) (1989) *Interpreting the Theatrical Past*, Iowa: University of Iowa Press.

Powell, V. (1983) *The Constant Novelist: A Study of Margaret Kennedy 1896–1967*, London: Heinemann.

Priestley, J. B. (1947) *Theatre Outlook*, London: Nicholson & Watson.

Ramelson, M. (1976) *The Petticoat Rebellion*, London: Lawrence & Wishart.

Rayman, S. (1951) *Women of Twilight*, London: Evans.

Redmond, J. (ed.) (1989) *Themes in Drama 11: Women in Theatre*, Cambridge: Cambridge University Press.

Reich, W. (1951) *Sexual Revolution*, London: Vision Press.

Richards, S. (1993) *The Rise of the English Actress*, London: Macmillan.

Ridler, A. (1961) *The Shadow Factory*, London: Faber.

Rose, J. (1993) *Marie Stopes and the Sexual Revolution*, London: Faber.

Rose, N. (1985) *The Psychological Complex: Psychology, Politics and Society in England 1869–1939*, London: Routledge & Kegan Paul.

Rowbotham, S. (1977) *A New World for Women: Stella Browne, Socialist Feminist*, London: Pluto Press.

Royde-Smith, N. (1931) *Mrs Siddons*, London: Gollancz.

—— (1927) *A Balcony*, London: Benn.

Rubins, J. L. (1979) *Karen Horney: Gentle Rebel of Psychoanalysis*, New York and London: Weidenfeld & Nicolson.

Russ, J. (1984) *How to Suppress Women's Writing*, London: The Women's Press.

Samuel, R., McColl, E. et al. (eds) (1985) *Theatres of the Left*, London: Routledge & Kegan Paul.

Sandison, G. (1953) *Theatre Ownership in Britain*, London: Federation of Theatre Unions.

Sayers, D. (1971) *Are Women Human?*, Michigan: Eerdmans.

Schlueter, J. (ed.) (1990) *Modern American Drama: The Female Canon*, London and Toronto: Farleigh Dickinson Press.

Sebba, A. (1986) *Enid Bagnold: A Biography*, London: Weidenfeld & Nicolson.

Shauffler, E. (1936) *Parnell*, in *Famous Plays of 1936*, London: Gollancz.

Sherriff, R. C. (1929) *Journey's End*, London: Gollancz.

Short, E. (1951) *Sixty Years of Theatre*, London: Eyre & Spottiswoode.

—— (1942) *Theatrical Cavalcade*, London: Eyre & Spottiswoode.

Smith, D. (C. L. Anthony) (1979) *Look Back with Astonishment*, London: Allen.

—— (1978) *Look Back with Mixed Feelings*, London: Allen.

—— (1967) *Autumn Crocus*, in *Plays of the Thirties, Vol. 2*, London: Pan.

—— (1966) *Dear Octopus*, in *Plays of the Thirties, Vol. 1*, London: Pan.

—— (1936) *Call it a Day*, in *Famous Plays of 1935–1936*, London: Gollancz.

—— (1934) *Touchwood*, London: Gollancz.

—— (1933) *Service*, in *Famous Plays of 1932–1933*, London: Gollancz.

Smithers, D. (1988) *Therefore Imagine: The Works of Clemence Dane*, Tonbridge: The Dragonfly Press.

Spark, M. (1962) *Doctors of Philosophy*, London: Macmillan.

BIBLIOGRAPHY

Spender, D. (1984) *Time and Tide Wait For No Man*, London: Pandora Press.

—— (1983) *There's Always Been a Women's Movement This Century*, London: Pandora Press.

Spock, B. (1955) *Problems of Parents*, New York: Crest/Fawcett Publications.

Sprigge, E. (1971) *Sybil Thordike Casson*, London: Gollancz.

Stern, G. B. (1931a) *The Matriarch*, London: French.

—— (1931b) *The Man Who Pays the Piper*, London: French.

Stewart, E. L. (1983) *Men Should Weep*, Scotland: 7: 84 Publications.

Stopes, M. (1926) *A Banned Play (Vectia) and A Preface on Censorship*, London: Bale, Sons and Daniellson.

—— (1923) *Our Ostriches*, London: Putnam.

—— (1918) *Married Love*, London: A. C. Fifield.

Storm, L. (1994) *Black Chiffon*, in F. Morgan (ed.) *The Years Between*, London: Virago.

Stowell, S. (1992) *A Stage of Their Own: Feminist Playwrights of the Suffrage Era*, Manchester: Manchester University Press.

Stuart, A. (1951) *Lace on Her Petticoat*, London: French.

—— (1940) *Jeannie*, London: Hamilton.

Stuart, A. and Stuart, P. (1934) *Sixteen*, in *Famous Plays of 1933–1934*, London: Gollancz.

—— (1930) *Nine Till Six*, London: French.

—— (1929a) *Her Shop*, London: Benn.

—— (1929b) *Clara Gibbings*, London: Benn.

—— (1929c) *Life Line*, London: Benn.

Stuart, M. (1939) *Traitor's Gate*, London: Collins.

Sutherland, C. (1978) 'American women playwrights as mediators of the "Woman Problem" ', *Modern Drama* 21: 319–336.

Taylor, G. (1976) *The Amateur Theatre*, New York: Venton.

Taylor, J. R. (1978) *Anger and After*, London: Methuen.

—— (1967) *The Rise and Fall of the Well Made Play*, London: Methuen.

Taylor, L. (1993) 'Early stages: women dramatists 1958–68', in T. R. Griffiths and M. Llewellyn-Jones (eds) *British and Irish Women Dramatists since 1958*, London: Open University Press.

Temple, J. (1948) *Deliver My Darling*, London: Sampson Low Marston.

—— (1946) *No Room at the Inn*, London: Embassy Successes.

—— (1930) *Charles and Mary*, London: Allen & Unwin.

—— (1926) *The Widow's Cruise*, London: Benn.

Tennyson-Jesse, F. (1925) *Anyhouse*, London: Heinemann.

—— (1918) *The Sword of Deborah: First Hand Impressions of the British Women's Army in France*, London: Clay & Sons.

Tennyson-Jesse, F. and Harwood, H. (1930) *How To Be Healthy Though Married*, London: Heinemann.

—— (1926) *The Pelican*, London: Benn.

—— (1918) *Billeted*, London: Benn.

Thordike, R. (1950) *Sybil Thorndike*, London: Rockliff.

Todd, S. (1984) *Women and Theatre*, London: Faber.

Trewin, J. C. (1976) *The Edwardian Theatre*, Oxford: Blackwell.

—— (1960) *The Turbulent Thirties*, London: Macdonald.

—— (1958) *The Gay Twenties*, London: Macdonald.

—— (1954) *Edith Evans*, London: Rockliff.

—— (1953) *Dramatists of Today,* London: Staples Press.

—— (1952) *A Play Tonight,* London: Elek Books.

Trewin, J. C. and Trewin, W. (1986) *The Arts Theatre London, 1927–1981,* London: The Society for Theatre Research.

Tuckett, A. (1979) *The People's Theatre Movement in Bristol 1930–45,* History Group of the Communist Party of Great Britain, 'Our Pamphlets', no. 72.

Tynan, K. (1958) *The Observer Plays,* London: Faber.

Van de Velde, T. (1961) *Ideal Marriage,* London: Heinemann.

Vernon, F. (1924) *The Twentieth Century Theatre,* London: Harrap.

Vinson, V. (ed.) (1982) *Contemporary Dramatists,* London: Macmillan.

Wandor, M. (1987) *Look Back in Gender: Sexuality and Gender in Post War British Drama,* London: Methuen.

—— (1984) 'The impact of feminism on theatre', *Feminist Review* 18: 76–92.

—— (1981) *Understudies: Theatre and Sexual Politics,* London: Methuen.

Weales, G. (1959) 'The madrigal in the garden', *Tulane Drama Review* 3 (1958–1959): 42–50.

Wearing, J. P. (1993) *The London Stage: 1950–1959,* Metuchen, N.J.: Scarecrow Press.

—— (1992) *The London Stage: 1940–1949,* Metuchen, N.J.: Scarecrow Press.

—— (1990) *The London Stage: 1930–1939,* Metuchen, N.J.: Scarecrow Press.

—— (1990) *The London Stage: 1920–1929,* Metuchen, N.J.: Scarecrow Press.

—— (1982) *The London Stage: 1910–1919,* Metuchen, N.J.: Scarecrow Press.

Webster, M. (1969) *The Same Only Different,* London: Gollancz.

—— (1972) *Don't Put Your Daughter on the Stage,* New York: Knopf.

Weeks, J. and Rowbotham, S. (1977) *Socialism and the New Life,* London: Pluto Press.

Wehr, D. (1988) *Jung and Feminism,* London: Routledge & Kegan Paul.

Weskott, M. (1986) *The Feminist Legacy of Karen Horney,* New Haven: Yale University Press.

Whitelaw, L. (1990) *The Rebellious Times of Cicely Hamilton,* London: The Women's Press.

Williamson, A. (1956) *Contemporary Theatre 1953–1956,* London and New York: Rockliff.

Willis, T. (1991) *Evening All: Fifty Years Over a Hot Typewriter,* London: Macmillan.

Wilson, E. (1980) *Only Half Way to Paradise: Women in Postwar Britain: 1945–1968,* London: Tavistock Publications.

Wilson, R. (1927) *The Social Climbers,* London: Benn.

Winnicott, D. W. (1957) *Mother and Child: A Primer of First Relationships,* New York: Basic Books.

Winslow, C. (1933) *Maids in Uniform,* in *Famous Plays of 1932–1933,* London: Gollancz.

Wright, N. (1988) *Mrs Klein,* London: Nick Hern Books.

Wood, G. and Thompson, P. (1993) *The Nineties,* London: BBC Books.

Woolf, V. (1983) *A Room of One's Own,* London: Granada.

—— (1982) *Three Guineas,* London: Penguin.

Wyndham-Goldie, G. (1935) *The Liverpool Repertory Theatre 1911–1934,* London: Hodder & Stoughton.

INDEX

256

INDEX